THE SPECIAL INFANT

THE SPECIAL INFANT

An Interdisciplinary Approach to the
Optimal Development of Infants

Editor

Jack M. Stack, M.D.

Family Health Research,
Education and Service Institute
Alma, Michigan

HUMAN SCIENCES PRESS, INC.
72 FIFTH AVENUE,
NEW YORK, N.Y. 10011

Copyright © 1982 by Human Sciences Press, Inc.
72 Fifth Avenue, New York, New York 10011

Printed in the United States of America
23456789   987654321

Library of Congress Cataloging in Publication Data
Main entry under title:

The Special Infant.

Papers presented at the 3rd annual conference of the
Michigan Association for Infant Mental Health, held Apr.
4–6, 1979, in Ann Arbor.
  Bibliography
  Includes index.
  1. Child development deviations—Congresses.   2. In-
fants—Growth—Congresses.   3. Infants—Diseases—Con-
gresses.   4. Infant psychology—Congresses.   I. Stack,
Jack M.   [DNLM: 1. Child development—Congresses.
2. Child development deviations—Congresses.   3. Child
Psychology—Congresses.   4. Handicapped—Child, Excep-
tional—Psychology—Congresses.   WS 105.5.H2 S741 1979]
RJ135.S65   362.7'95   LC   81–4478
ISBN 0–89885–028–2   AACR2

CONTENTS

5

PREFACE

Editor's Introduction

The field of infant mental health is a new and exciting interdisciplinary field. There are professionals from many backgrounds of training and experience making observations and interventions in prenatal, newborn, and early developmental stages in the lives of infants and families. Individuals and agencies are facing the challenges, opportunities, and responsibilities of prevention, early detection, and early intervention to promote the optimal development of emotional, social, physical, and cognitive health of infants, children, and their families.

The Michigan Association for Infant Mental Health was created in 1976 to bring together people from the many and varied professions as well as lay persons who had an interest in infant mental health. Often these people were not aware of the work that others were doing. It is difficult for each of us to read and attend meetings sufficiently in our own disciplines and even more difficult to keep abreast of the developments in allied professions.

The Michigan Association for Infant Mental Health has sponsored three annual conferences to bring together people from many different disciplines.

The third annual conference of the Michigan Association for Infant Mental Health brought together 1,200 participants from three countries, England, Canada, and the United States, to share experiences and concerns for the problem of special infants and children, their families, and the professionals working with them. The three-day conference, held on April 4–6, 1979 in Ann Arbor, Michigan, covered a wide range of topics. This book is an edited compilation of papers, workshops, and seminars from the third annual conference—"An Interdisciplinary Approach to the Optimal Development of Infants: The Special Infant."

The conference was an opportunity for us to learn together from our friends and colleagues from different training backgrounds and from different points of observation and service, but all with the same concern and commitment to the optimal growth and development of children and their families.

For many of us it was a unique opportunity to learn about special problems such as blind or deaf babies from pioneers in those fields. For others it was an opportunity to renew friendships and encouragement from long-known but seldom-seen colleagues.

For everyone it was an opportunity to renew our love for our art, our fellow caregivers, ourselves, and most of all for those whose care has been entrusted to us.

We wish to share with you, the reader, the proceedings of our conference and our commitment to nurturing in the future our most precious endowment and trust—our children.

Jack M. Stack, M.D.
Editor

ACKNOWLEDGMENTS

We would like to acknowledge the dedicated work of a number of people. The third annual conference committee of the Michigan Association for Infant Mental Health deserves special recognition for their conception of the format for the conference and for their attention to all of the details which went into making such a successful conference.

Conference Chair: Alice Marie Carter, R.N., M.P.H., Director, Infant Mental Health Services, Washtenaw County Community Mental Health Center, and Assistant Professor, School of Nursing, The University of Michigan, Ann Arbor

Conference Coordinator: Barbara Banet, M. Ed. in Human Development, Author/Consultant on Early Education and Parenthood, Ann Arbor

Assistant Conference Coordinator: Nancy Tilford, Infant Mental Health Specialist, Huron Valley Child Guidance Clinic, Ypsilanti

Assistant Conference Coordinator: Ann Saffer, M.Ed. in Early Childhood, Special Education Consultant, Ann Arbor

Linda Kreger, Ph.D. Instructor, Department of Psychology, Henry Ford Community College, Dearborn; Antal E. Solyom, M.D., Ph.D., Clinical Assistant Professor of Psychiatry, Director, Infant Study Program, Child Analytic Study Program, Children's Psychiatric Hospital, The University of Michigan Medical Center, Ann Arbor; Laurel Torgoff, Ph.D., Clinical Psychologist, Flint; Margaret Gainer, R.N., M.S., Instructor, Parent-Child Nursing Program, School of Nursing, The University of Michigan, Ann Arbor; Emma Dunstan, Secretary.

I would like to thank personally the creative and tenacious work of special assistant to the editor, Kathy Kolb, without whose competent help this book would not have been born. In addition we are grateful to our typist, Sara Williams, for her able assistance in preparing the final manuscript.

Jack M. Stack, M.D.
Editor

PRESIDENT'S REMARKS

The papers offered in this volume were presented at the third annual conference of the Michigan Association for Infant Mental Health (MAIMH) in April, 1979. It was a special meeting for us, with nearly 1,200 guests and presentors coming to Ann Arbor from all over the United States, Canada, and England.

The organizational caucus for an international infant mental health group occurred during off hours at the conference and stimulated the incorporation of the International Association for Infant Mental Health (IAIMH) a few months later. A board of directors for the IAIMH has been developed, representing 12 states in the U.S., two Canadian provinces, and seven other nations.

The publication of this edited volume, *The Special Infant,* coincides with the commencement of publication of the *Infant Mental Health Journal,* sponsored by the Michigan Association for Infant Mental Health and published by Human Sciences Press. Subscriptions to this new quarterly are offered in conjunction with membership in either the state or international association, or may be procured alone by writing to the editor, Jack Stack, M.D., 510 Prospect, Alma, Michigan 48801. Papers, film reviews, book reviews, and suggestions for topical issues may also be addressed to the editor for consideration.

We in the MAIMH are pleased with our progress in meeting our stated purposes: increasing the sophistication of our members' responses to the needs of infants and their families, and encouraging the realization that infancy is a critical period in the psychosocial development of individuals. Our association developed out of the determination of a few infant mental health specialists (trained in a special program by the University of Michigan Child Development Project, then directed by Selma Fraiberg) to meet each other's considerable needs for support and to "spread the word" about the significance of infancy. We invite your interest in the exacting and strenuous task of promoting (in whatever you deem to be your life's work) the optimal development of infants and their families. We would be pleased to have you join us in membership, to participate in our annual conference, to write or review for our journal, to ask us for guidance or support in your work. The monumental dimensions of our task in caring for babies and their families, after all, require that we tackle this thing together.

> Michael David Trout, Chairman
> Board of Trustees
> Michigan Association for Infant Mental Health

Part I

DEVELOPMENT AND ASSESSMENT

This section deals with the special characteristics and problems of the child with a physical or emotional handicap from prematurity, addiction at birth, through psychosis. The specific problems discussed are not a complete or exhaustive list of problems encountered with infants and young children, but the principles and approaches to these problems can give guideposts to professionals for dealing with similar problems.

Chapter 1

PRECOCIOUS SEXUAL DEVELOPMENT IN GIRLS DURING THE FIRST THREE YEARS OF LIFE

Antal E. Solyom, M.D., Ph.D.
Carol C. Austad, M.D.
George E. Bacon, M.D.

INTRODUCTION

The usual progression of sexual maturation in normal girls consists of breast budding, pubic and axillary hair, and menstruation. By definition, any portion of this sequence occurring prior to the age of eight years is considered precocious.[1] The precocity syndromes are classified as: (1) precocious thelarche (breast development only), (2) precocious adrenarche (pubic hair only), and (3) precocious puberty (two of the following: breast development, pubic hair, vaginal bleeding).

Breast development is the most common initial sign of early sexual maturation. If this occurs during early childhood, the majority of cases will be diagnosed as precocious thelarche, a benign condition with normal hormone levels and without progression of the breast enlargement. If the onset is later, the likelihood that the breast development is the first sign of precocious puberty increases with the chronologic age. Thus, in the first few years of life precocious puberty is fairly rare, but precocious thelarche is not uncommon. The general practitioner, pediatrician, and even the gynecologist[2] may see several cases of precocious thelarche a year. At the Pediatric Endocrinology Clinic of The University of Michigan Medical Center in Ann Arbor, at least 10 cases of precocious thelarche are seen per year.

MEDICAL EVALUATION AND TREATMENT

Precocious thelarche usually develops during the first two years of life. The possibility of exogenous estrogen administration must be ruled out. Further evaluation consists of assessment of growth rate, bimanual abdominal-rectal examination, inspection of the vaginal mucosa (maturational index is probably not necessary nor entirely reliable), and determination of skeletal age. If these are normal, periodic follow-up visits are sufficient. The breast tissue may or may not regress, but the remaining pubertal changes should occur at the usual time.

An advanced bone age is evidence that the early breast development actually represents the onset of precocious puberty. In this case, or if pubic hair or vaginal discharge occurs, further investigation is mandatory. This should include abdominal-rectal or pelvic examination under sedation or anesthesia, possibly pelvic ultra-sonography,[3] skull roentgenograms, and visual field examination in older children. Precocious puberty may be caused by an organic lesion of the ovary (e.g., cyst, granulosa cell tumor) or central nervous system (CNS) (e.g., tumors, congential anomalies). A number of less frequent etiologies must be considered, but about 90% of cases in girls are diagnosed as idiopathic. This implies a functional hypothalmic-pituitary disorder without demonstrable organic pathology, although an increased incidence of electroencephalographic abnormalities has been described. Random serum gonadotropin measurements are of limited value, but recently we have been determining the gonadotropin response to gonadotropin releasing hormone (GnRH test) in these patients.[4] An exaggerated response is consistent with precocious puberty of central origin. A suppressed response is indicative of ovarian pathology, either tumor or cyst. In the latter case, spontaneous resolution, temporary or permanent, may occur.

Early appearance of pubic hair in the absence of breast tissue or vaginal bleeding (precocious adrenarche), is usually a benign condition, but occasionally is followed by true precocious puberty. Evaluation consists of assessment of skeletal maturation and urinary (or serum) androgens, both of which may be normal or slightly increased. Marked advancement of bone age or elevation of androgens is more consistent with adrenal tumor, a rare cause of precocious adrenarche.

Precocious thelarche and adrenarche carry a good prognosis and require no medical treatment. Children with idiopathic precocious puberty may be treated with progesterone in an effort to suppress the secretion of gonadotropins. Therapy will inhibit the onset of menses and possibly retard further breast development, but probably has little or no effect on skeletal maturation. Therefore, these patients, while frequently tall as children, may become short adults because of early fusion of the epiphyses.

Psychological Correlates

In the literature, there is no report at all on the emotional impact of early breast development on the girl. In a review article on precocious thelarche, the only reference to an emotional reaction was that "the condition is often first noticed by the mother, who usually reacts with great distress and rushes to the doctor."[2] Surprisingly, the psychological aspects of breast development of the normal female adolescent have not been paid much attention to either. It is suggested, however, that many adolescent girls are more interested in their breast development than in menstruation.[5]

In a recent study, we have compared the results of the psychiatric evaluation of three groups of girls with the diagnosis of precocious thelarche, precocious adrenarche, or precocious puberty.[6] We found that in cases where breast development occurred (precocious thelarche and puberty), the parents' initial worry was that the girl might have cancer. Otherwise, they felt embarrassed about the girl's breast development. Girls with precocious thelarche tended to think of themselves as defective and have a negative self-image. Girls who had precocious puberty tended to be embarrassed, self-conscious, and excessively shy, but only a few of them had a negative self-image. It seemed that the embarrassment of the girl with precocious puberty was not due to reaction to true sexual maturation, but was mainly the result of early breast development.

During the past two decades, several authors have addressed the question of the psychological aspects of idiopathic precocious puberty in girls.[7-12] The overall impression has been that the cognitive and psychological development of the girl does not parallel the acceleration of biological development in precocious puberty. There are definite emotional reactions, like feeling and appearing different, shy, and embarrassed, but these emotional problems have usually been considered mild, requiring only minor preventive or supportive therapeutic and educative interventions.[11,12] There are only very few cases reported in the literature where the onset of precocious puberty occurred in the first three years and the emotional development of the girl was assessed at a later age. In cases where the precocious puberty was diagnosed at birth or before one year of age, there appeared to be no significant emotional consequences later in development.[8,10,11] However in one case the major initial emotional impact of the illness was associated with a traumatic diagnostic hospitalization around one and one-half years of age, followed by significant psychological symptoms which required long-term intensive treatment.[9] Yet, in those cases where the onset was between two and one-half and three years of age, there again was no outstanding psychological problem noted upon follow-up visits.[8,11]

CASE REPORTS

In this chapter, we report on a girl whose precocious puberty appeared to have started between one and one-half and two years of age, and who had developed unusually severe psychopathology. She was referred to us at eight years of age for inpatient psychiatric treatment from another locality where her medical treatment had been terminated. We compare her with another girl whose precocious puberty had an onset around two and one-half years of age with significantly milder emotional consequences. In addition, we report on three cases of precocious thelarche, in which the onset was before one year of age. The latter four girls were all seen in an outpatient psychiatric evaluation as volunteer participants in a research project.[6] This consisted of a detailed parent interview, psychiatric evaluation of the girl in a playroom setting, and psychological testing. These cases are used as illustrations of the importance of the chronologic age and of the stage of psychological development at the time of the appearance of sexual precocity. Retrospectively, they offer some understanding as to what the bodily change, which signals early sexual maturation, may mean for a one-, two-, or three-year-old girl and her parents.

Case 1

A is the second of three children: her sister is 15 months older, her brother four years younger. The pregnancy was unplanned. Once accepted, the parents wished for a boy. At birth, A weighed more than either sibling: 9 lb., 4 ½ oz. She was breast-fed on a 4-hour schedule until 13 months of age; she was a good eater. She smiled when she was five weeks old. At seven weeks, the mother started to take birth control pills. At three months, she was weaned from the breast to the bottle and was able to turn over. At four and one-half months, she was separated from her parents for one week when they left for a vacation. By this time, she slept through the night. At six months she sat alone; at seven and one-half she was able to crawl. Between 8 and 20 months of age, she was frequently left with baby sitters for a few hours at a time while the rest of the family went to visit with the father's mother who was hospitalized with cancer. At 11 months she stood alone. At 12 months she was weaned from the bottle; finger feeding started at 13 months, and she used utensils by 17 months.

She said single words at 13 months. The parents do not remember when she started to speak in sentences, but it is clear that her language development was delayed and her speech was never clearly articulated. A did not walk until 15 months because her ankles buckled inwards, requiring corrective shoes. She was toilet trained between 15 and 18 months in a somewhat rigorous and impatient manner by her mother.

The period between 18 and 30 months of age was very critical in her development. At 18 months, she already was as tall as her 33-month-old sister. She started to withdraw from people: she became frightened, anxious, and clung to mother in the company of unfamiliar people. However, when she was within the immediate family, signs of developing emotional problems were not yet evident. During this time, the parents had their own anxieties: when A was 19 months old, her mother's psychological father died, and at 20 months, her paternal grandmother died of cancer after a year of illness. At 21 months, A's father was briefly taken to the hospital with what appears to have been an anxiety attack. By two years of age, A was taller than her sister. At the same time she started to point to her breasts indicating that they hurt. She also masturbated by rubbing herself against objects, but due to the mother's prohibition apparently stopped. At two years, four months, she was taken to a pediatric endocrinologist for the first of many medical/genital examinations.

By age three, the diagnosis of *idiopathic precocious puberty* was established, and treatment with Depo-Provera injections began. The treatment was considered successful and terminated at eight years of age. (At this time her bone age was 12 years, her height 58 inches.) The medical/genital checkups, X-rays, blood tests, and injections were fearful experiences for A, and she attempted to fight them. She had difficulty separating from her mother on these occasions.

Separation anxiety was also intense when left with baby-sitters, although it gradually improved between the ages of two and five. A did not go to nursery school. In the family, she was seen as assertive, verbal, playful, and affectionate. She was four years old when her younger brother was born, and she seemed affectionate toward him. Yet, in family photos and movies, a tight-lipped and unhappy facial expression is increasingly evident after three years of age. At age five and one-half, she resisted going to kindergarten and would not talk at all to other children or to her teacher. These symptoms intensified in the first and second grades. Major school-phobic episodes (tantrums, screaming, and kicking) required that the father come home from work and take her to school. Academically she did well. Peer relations were extremely poor.

There is no evidence of A having had a transitional object early in her development or an imaginary companion somewhat later. However, she developed a special interest in animals and had very many stuffed animals by two years of age. Later she also developed a strong liking for live animals, especially for horses.

At age six and one-half her speech defect was diagnosed, but speech therapy was discontinued because it seemed too stressful. She gradually became very indecisive and stubborn, even at home. At age seven and one-half individual psychotherapy was tried for six months with a female social worker, but

A would not talk. This led to the first psychiatric consultation on the case which resulted in residential treatment.

When she was admitted to the hospital at eight years of age, she had the following identifiable symptoms and behavioral characteristics: elective and selective mutism; school-phobic behavior and separation anxiety; poor peer relations; indecisive, isolating, sterotyped, inhibited, passive-aggressive behavior, including temper tantrums; low self-esteem with depressive affect; poor gross motor coordination with somewhat clumsy movements; increased physical growth and sexual development which corresponded to a prepubertal girl of 12 to 13 years of age; speech defect (her voice was somewhat hoarse and deeper than normal, and her articulation was poor). During hospitalization, mild scoliosis was also diagnosed. It also became apparent that A had significantly greater difficulty relating to adult males than females. Psychological testing suggested that she viewed men as dangerous and experienced herself as living in an extremely frightening world to which she reacted by grossly limiting her interaction with it. Although she appeared to have at least average intelligence and intact abilities in all areas, including abstract thought, the test results demonstrated that in her thinking she disallowed herself any active role and perceived things outside of herself as the sources of influence and power. In response to stress, her thought and perception became constricted, and she grew more concrete in her thinking. A rather passive view of the world sometimes gave her thoughts an infantile quality. The testing also revealed serious problems with self-esteem and depression. A was extremely vulnerable to feelings that she had failed and was inadequate.

The development of an unusually severe psychopathology is probably best understood on the basis of the following considerations: the concommitant influence of several types of developmental interferences[13] and the particular developmental stage at which this illness had its onset and its major emotional impact. One can identify several early and ongoing developmental interferences: (1) rapid bone growth with the related body-image problems and lags in gross motor coordination, including difficulty in walking; (2) physical pain in the breasts, change in voice, increased sensations in the genitals, stressful medical/genital examinations and treatment; (3) parental conflicts, anxieties, and somewhat intolerant attitudes. An additional possibility is that the sex hormones also intensified her libidinal strivings. Although some of these interferences were already present prior to 18 months of age, it seemed that for all practical purposes there were no major problems with her development until that age. A probably experienced the major impact of the several types of interferences between 18 and 30 months of age, i.e., during the anal phase of psychosexual development and the rapprochement phase of separation-individuation.[14] This is a very crucial and vulnerable period in human personality development with significant emphasis on such areas as the aggressive drive, the active-passive conflict, intense ambivalence in object relations, crystalization of the body image and of the sense of self. Neurophysiological maturation leads to effective control over the sphincters and the mechanisms involved in speech; rapidly expanding repertoire of new motor skills offers narcissistic pleasure in motility and mastery; intensive linguistic experimentation in the process of language acquisition and, by age two, the intensive use of language in the exploration of the child's relationship with others and with the external world (while the symbolic meaning of it is still egocentric and concrete) signals new dimensions of functioning.

The psychopathology that emerged offers good support to the formulation that A's development was markedly interfered with in the above areas of personality functioning. This means that many normal developmental conflicts were intensified and/or could not reach successful resolution (conflicts over the aggressive drive, ambivalence, conflicts of the separation-individuation process, etc.), or that the mastery of some tasks and the acquisition of some functions (motor and language development, body image, and sense of self, etc.) was hampered. It is important to emphasize that there seemed to be no problems with the establishment of libidinal object constancy and gender identity, both of which are usually established by 18 months of age.

Therefore, A's psychopathology is consistent with a massive impact of developmental interferences between 18 and 30 months of age, with a continued interference by several of these factors later on. As a result, fixation occurred at the anal phase of psychosexual development, which served as the basis for a neurosis with obsessive-compulsive and depressive features. Her psychosexual development appeared to have been arrested in the phallic-oedipal phase, as she was not able to make the move from the parent-centered object relationships into the latency period. She easily regressed to the major fixation points at the anal level. A's concept of self appears to have had bad connotations. The active-passive conflict was decided in favor of passivity, and the Eriksonian dilemma of "autonomy vs. shame and doubt" in the favor of shame and doubt.[17] The symptom of elective mutism, when it is severe, may specifically be related to emotional problems experienced during the second and third years irrespective of the nature of the condition.[15,16]

Two years of multi-dimensional inpatient psychiatric treatment followed by one year of outpatient psychotherapy and concommitant conjoint parent therapy through all three years was needed to gradually improve A's social-emotional functioning and to sufficiently free her developmental potential from internalized conflicts and from ongoing developmental interferences to give her a reasonable chance at mastering the tasks of adolescent development. The elective mutism started to diminish only after one and one-half years of treatment.

Case 2

B is a three-year-, seven-month-old white girl, the youngest and only daughter among the four natural children of her parents. There is an adopted sister, a fifth child, in the family who was adopted after B's birth and who is actually older than her. Early developmental milestones were unremarkable. B spoke in sentences before two years of age. However, she was hard to toilet train. The mother started toilet training at eight months of age, because at that time she toilet trained the later-adopted older girl, who was approximately two years of age. B was strapped onto the potty seat, was very angry, and never liked the potty afterwards. After a few weeks the mother stopped this practice and resumed toilet training at two years of age. Toilet training was completed at the age of two and one-half. The mother had experienced her as a fairly difficult toddler who was a "pistol," very dominating and aggressive in her peer relationships. In the family she could be, at times, extremely loving and lovable but at other times very nasty and stubborn. The mother denied any sexual curiosity, sexual play, or masturbation.

When B was two years, six months old, the mother noticed that her left breast seemed to be "puffed up." Two months later, the right breast started to show also. At three years and two months of age she was hospitalized for the purposes of an endocrinologic workup that resulted in the diagnosis of *idiopathic precocious puberty*. She was placed on oral Provera medication. Five months later when she was three years, seven months of age, she was seen in a psychiatric evaluation as a volunteer participant in a research project. After the hospitalization and the start of medication, there was no progression in her sexual development. Nevertheless she was taller than her five-year-old sister and almost as tall as her seven-year-old brother. Her left breast was still obviously enlarged, about 2 inches in diameter, but it was not too noticeable because of her chubby appearance.

The mother's initial reaction to the breast enlargement was alarm associated with the fantasy that the girl had cancer. The father was also worried. The parents were relieved when the diagnosis of precocious puberty instead of cancer was made. The mother's main concern was how B would be accepted by peers. So far, B had not appeared embarrassed or shy about the breast enlargement and actually showed it "like a new tooth" to some relatives and seemed to like the fact that she was big because that way she was more powerful. However, the hospitalization was a traumatic experience for her, particularly the taking of blood, genital examinations, and being tied down to the bed for urine collections. The immediate impact of the hospital experience on B seemed to be the following: (1) a partial regression manifested in bed-wetting and her need to have her baby blanket with her every night; (2) intense fear of doctors that showed in a very negative reaction in the dentist's office later. However, B did not object to coming to the psychiatric evaluation once she was assured that no physical examination and taking of blood would be involved.

At the psychiatric evaluation she was initially reluctant to separate from her mother to be with the female child psychiatrist alone, but then she got involved in play with the doll family, coyly toileting each doll by shutting them in the bathroom one at a time. However, when the male child psychologist joined them later for the psychological testing, B became completely silent, sucked her finger, and was so resistant to cooperative work in the testing that part of it had to be administered by the female child psychiatrist. Even with her, she was generally timid, anxious, and somewhat controlling. She talked little and often communicated nonverbally. She would not spontaneously express herself in drawing either, but she did direct the examiner, with a coy giggle, to draw "boobies" on the stick figure that the child psychiatrist drew according to B's specifications. Later when she drew two figures herself, she drew the faces but scribbled the bodies. (The poor execution of her drawings may be consistent with her young age.) On the Rorschach test there was no indication of disturbances of her body image. However, the material was suggestive of oral (biting) fixation. It was also suggestive of a possible anxious excitement around males and hence of possible oedipal involvement (which is age-appropriate). Her estimated IQ was 108 suggesting an average intelligence.

The data suggest that B had moved to the age-appropriate, phallic-oedipal phase of psychosexual development but partially regressed to oral and anal fixations after the traumatic hospital experience. The precocious puberty probably contributed to her self-consciousness, shyness, and elective mutism. She was rendered more vulnerable to the precocious puberty and to the hospital experience by her earlier experience with harsh toilet training.

The mother often felt overwhelmed by her many children and appeared vulnerable in terms of this mother-child relationship. While B had a special significance for her, she experienced her as a very difficult toddler. Furthermore, the onset of B's precocious puberty was close to the age at which the mother had lost her own father. Nevertheless, both mother and child seemed to cope well enough. The continued emotional development of the girl did not appear significantly interfered with. Therefore, we did not recommend any intervention at the time.

Case 3

C is a five-year-, eight-month-old white girl, the youngest of three daughters. C was born with unilateral breast enlargement; the left nipple looked swollen. This condition has remained unchanged ever since: the left nipple can be seen through a tight T-shirt. The pregnancy, delivery, and early development was unremarkable. The parents did experience some disappointment inasmuch as they expected a boy. When at three and one-half years of age the mother returned to full-time work and C stayed at home with a baby sitter, she showed significant separation anxiety which made the mother cut back to part-time work. The parents have been separated for most of the past three years with occasional periods of staying together. C is much more sensitively affected by the separation than the other two girls. After the father leaves, she cries, has sleep disturbances, and asks for him. She was also noticed to draw sad faces in school, and she herself had a sad affect during such periods.

The unilateral breast enlargement did not concern the parents initially because the two older daughters were also born with the same condition, which disappeared by six months of age. At approximately three years of age C started to notice her breast and asked the parents about her breast enlargement. The mother reassured her that she was born that way and that it did not mean that anything was wrong with her at all. Nevertheless, between three and four years of age C became more "modest" in that she dressed privately and did not want to be seen bare-chested or naked. C did not talk to other people about her condition but did not avoid wearing T-shirts either, which might show her breast enlargement a little bit.

When C started to be concerned about her breasts, the parents started to worry about it, too. Both of them fantasized and worried that it might be a tumor. The pediatrician thought of possible precocious puberty and made the referral to pediatric endocrinology where she was seen at four years of age. She showed little apprehension, although she was definitely tense during the genital examination. With the establishment of the diagnosis of *precocious thelarche* the parents finally accepted the benign nature of the condition and repeatedly tried to reassure C when the issue of her breast enlargement came up. When more than a year and a half later they came for the psychiatric evaluation, C wanted to make sure that she was not going to get any shots and that there would be no physical examination. Once she was assured of that, she had no objections to coming.

C is an attractive, small, delicately built, blond-haired girl. At first she was very shy upon meeting the female child psychiatrist but separated easily from the parents, and after a few minutes she went to the dollhouse and started to elaborate family themes. With a sad affect she spontaneously revealed that the father did not live at home. Even when she talked about happier things, like friends and school, she remained soft-spoken. She remained very guarded about her fantasy life. When the question of her past visit to the pediatric clinic came up, she seemed anxious and only nodded that she remembered the examination. She admitted that she was a little scared of doctors. When the difference in this visit was reassuringly explained, she seemed to relax. Nevertheless, when the male child psychologist was introduced to her, she immediately became more shy but with apparent coyness: apprehension was mixed with pleasure, and she gradually warmed up and moved closer to the psychologist.

Her estimated IQ was 102. In the Draw-A-Picture Test, (DAP) C chose to draw a boy, age five, first. This was very primitively done, consisting of a circle, two eyes, a nose, a mouth, and two stick-like legs projecting directly from the circle, but *no torso* and *no arms*. She said that the boy was playing in his bedroom. Then she drew a picture of a girl, similarly very tiny, age five, but there were more details in that she included arms drawn directly from her head and she added long hair. There was still *no torso*, however. The girl was said to be "dancing." (Later when she was again alone with the female child psychiatrist, she drew a picture of a girl whom she named C, and this picture was about 6 inches tall and the girl was in a bell-shaped, ankle-length dress, implying a very thin, shapeless upper body to which short arms with spider-like hands with long fingers were attached. In this picture the nose was missing from the face. It may be of interest that earlier in the Rorschach testing, when she was asked about whether some human percepts were "ladies or men," after some hesitation she thought she saw a lady there because ladies' "noses point out," while men's noses look different). C's performance on the Rorschach was erratic. She was visibly upset and her function was impaired when exposed to blots with colors. An immature quality was reflected in the complete absence of any human percepts, while there were several animal movement responses. To card II she said that it looked like "blood inside of a body," and on card III she saw "mice" instead of the popular percept of "people." When asked whether she could see people, she acknowledged this, and when her attention was drawn to the red detail adjacent to the chest area of the "people," she said that "something is in their bodies," and gave an expression of disgust.

C is seen as a moderately anxious, shy, inhibited, and depressed girl. She is in the age-appropriate, phallic-oedipal phase of psychosexual development with triangular object relations and without proper fixations. While she has a feminine identity, she is unconsciously conflicted about it. She seems to feel that there is something disgusting about it. She seems to feel that there is something disgusting about herself, something to be hidden about her body. She may feel damaged and have a somewhat disturbed body image and self-image.

Besides the thelarche, there are other developmental interferences that have to be considered. The conscious awareness of the breast enlargement very closely coincided chronologically with the parental separation. These two events might have had a mutually intensifying effect on the impact of each on her (e.g., maybe she imagined that the father left her because something was physically wrong with her or because it was wrong to become like mother?). In addition, one has to keep in mind the mother's feeling of being rejected, her own depression and anxiety related to the ongoing marital separation and uncertainty. One has the clear impression that the precocious thelarche had an emotional impact on C and probably rendered her more vulnerable to the parents' separation. Due to her ego strengths there appears to be no need for individual psychotherapy at this time. However, marital counseling is indicated for the parents.

Case 4

D is a four year-, ten-month-old black girl, the second daughter of her parents. Her bilateral breast enlargement started at nine months of age and reached the size of about 1 inch in diameter at one year of age. It has not changed since that time. She was seen at pediatric endocrinology at one year of age: the diagnosis of *precocious thelarche* was established. The mother was not much alarmed about the breast development because her older daughter (now eight years old) was born with bilateral breast development which did not subside until four years of age. Nevertheless she did fantasize and worried that D might start developing too early. The mother recalled no negative reaction on D's part to the endocrine visit, and D does not remember it. However, when D was one year old her vagina was itching, and she scratched herself and stuffed things into the genital area. Now she is very curious about sexual matters, often trying to look into the bathroom when somebody is there. A year ago she used to put an apple or an orange into the bra that she would put on but she does not do this now. At times she attacks and hits the mother's breasts. At other times she puts on a bra and says, "I got some titties."

D was very sickly until five months of age and "cried all the time." She was "born without white blood cells" and was seen regularly at the hematology clinic. She became healthier later on, and the mother now considers her a "spoiled child" who has crying spells at times when she is not held. D was breast-fed until three months, when the mother went back to work, and the caretaking was transferred to the grandmother. Bottle-feeding lasted until 18 months of age. D walked at nine months, was toilet trained by one and one-half years, and talked in sentences between two and one-half and three years of age. At approximately three years of age she was stuttering, seemed anxious, and she had problems with her daredevil behavior in the nursery school. No separation anxiety was noticed, and D was said to be friendly "with anybody." D loves physical contact with both parents and wants them to hug and kiss her. D apparently loves school, watches TV at home, or helps the grandmother wash dishes, and does other household chores.

D is a small, attractive girl, who was very shy and reserved, cold and distant, and probably feeling confusion and dislike about the interview, both with the female child psychiatrist and the male psychologist. She did not volunteer anything spontaneously. Initially there was no noticeable difference in her behavior toward the two interviewers, but when she was alone with the female child psychiatrist she became pleasingly animated.

Her estimated IQ was 75, which appeared an underestimation of her real intellectual potential. In the DAP she drew female figures first, actually three of them. They had *no arms* but had long hair. She then drew two male figures, each had something on the chin, which she could not explain, but it looked as if they were beards. They had *no arms*, but the male drawings were larger than the female ones and they had larger feet. On several points in her Rorschach responses there were clear references to aggressive tensions in her. In addition, on card III she saw a "monster," instead of "people." When further questioned, she thought that these "monster-people" were women because of the chest area. On cards II and X she identified "blood," which upset her.

D appears to have entered the age-appropriate, phallic-oedipal phase of psychosexual development but evidences pre-oedipal (mainly anal) fixation and increased aggressivity. She has established female identity but has some negative feelings about it. It is likely that her experience with thelarche makes her think of females as monsters. Her object relations are impaired, characterized by some hostility and by her potential for "promiscuity." While she has a conscious pride in being black, she appears depressed and may at times be excessively shy and withholding.

There are several additional, parental interferences which may have significantly contributed to this psychological profile. There is a positive history of mental illness in the mother's family, and the mother had episodes of emotional problems in the past. She was depressed and made a suicide attempt during the first trimester of this pregnancy and seemed to have a somewhat inconsistent and distant involvement in her relationship with D. She sees D as a "weird child." The mother's difficulty in positively cathecting this girl was likely enhanced by the fact that she had to deal with a sickly and crying baby early on, and with the thelarche later, in the first year. The mother herself developed breasts earlier than average and has bad memories and feelings about that. All this contributed to a difficult early period in the mother-daughter relationship, which had the obvious potential to undermine D's self-esteem and to make it in her mind connected possibly with the thelarche, a visible disorder of her body. Nevertheless, despite some significant early difficulties D's emotional development is not halted. The progressive forces clearly have the upper hand in her personality development. There is no need for direct individual intervention at this time. However, parent guidance for the mother is recommended.

Case 5

E is a four-year-, seven-month-old white girl, the older of two daughters of her parents.

Sometime during the first year the mother noticed unilateral breast enlargement in E: the right breast was the size of a tea bag. It worried her as she fantasized that it might be a tumor. The father did not have such worries because he had "complete confidence" in the pediatrician who finally, in order to reassure the mother, made the referral to pediatric endocrinology, where E was seen at the age of two years, ten months. The diagnosis of *precocious thelarche* was established. Later during the fourth year the swelling of the breast diminished and by now there is practically no breast enlargement noticeable. The parents did not see any change in E's behavior in relationship to the breast enlargement or to the visits to the doctors. Even the genital examination caused her little apprehension. The parents felt that at pediatric endocrinology everything was well explained to E to minimize her apprehension. Soon after this, however, E was found to have a vaginal infection. During this time E frequently scratched herself in the genital area, which the parents did not consider masturbation. Since about that time she often put one finger in her mouth: not sucking, just keeping her fingertip between her lips. In addition, E sometimes used baby talk and a whiny voice when she wanted to get more attention. However, these behaviors have diminished recently. E was "always shy and timid" until she started nursery school at three and one-half years of age. That resulted in a marked positive change in her overall behavior, and now she takes great pride in what she learns and does. Her developmental history is otherwise unremarkable. From two and one-half years of age E has had imaginary playmates, and recently she has involved her sister in her plays. She is always in charge, very active and imaginative.

E is an attractive, tiny, brown-haired, fragile, and shy-appearing girl, neatly and femininely dressed. She separated easily from her parents, presented a mixture of appropriate childishness with a pseudomature quality of competency and efficiency. She did have her finger in her mouth on several occasions. She was soft-spoken but cooperatively engaged in conversation and volunteered information. She seemed to want to be sure that the female child psychiatrist was still there during the psychological testing, and after the male psychologist left she continued her creative play and rich productions in which she talked a lot about her nursery school friends and a cousin, all of whom were boys, and then talked about many aspects of her identifications with her mother. She put emphasis on separating daddy from the females of the family, although she put the mother and daddy dolls in the double bed and made them rub together excitedly while "dressing."

Her estimated IQ was 113, which appeared an underestimation of her intelligence. Her drawings were quite small in size and on the bottom of the page, in keeping with her timid presentation of herself. She drew the girl figure first, who was playing "golf," and then the boy, who was playing tennis. Both were very primitive drawings, particularly in light of her intelligence. The top half of the *torso* of the girl was *missing*, the arms were coming out of the head with sun-like hands, and under the head a space was left; then she drew a circle, calling it the "stomach," with lines (legs) extending down from this. Even after questioning she steadfastly held onto the accuracy of her drawing and did not add the chest area. In the boy's figure the *body* was *omitted* entirely; she drew the legs as projections directly from the head. Her Rorschach responses gave the impression of a very intelligent, potentially creative child, but one probably limited by conflicts in freely expressing her feelings and thoughts. On card III she saw two "ghosts," instead of "people" otherwise she seemed very aware of "stomachs," and she made two references to "food," suggesting some oral concerns. She may be anxious around and about males, as she identified two people as men but said that they were "nurses."

E appears to be a very intelligent and well-endowed girl who has reached dominance in the age-appropriate, phallic-oedipal phase of psychosexual development (with possible but not significant oral fixation). She has firmly established a feminine identity. However, the impact of the precocious thelarche seemed evident in her disturbed body image.

It is important to note that at the time of the psychiatric evaluation there was no longer any physical evidence of breast enlargement. The mother's anxiety about the thelarche, about E's scratching in the genital area and her fingering in the mouth represented no significant interference. At this point there seem to be no obstacles to E's continued healthy emotional development.

DISCUSSION

The case vignettes presented here and the reports published in the literature clearly suggest that the signs of early sexual maturation, including the hormonal changes in precocious puberty, do *not* necessarily result in severe emotional problems. The nature and severity of the emotional and developmental impact does not depend simply on the appearance of sexual characteristics, particularly in early childhood. In order to understand and predict the possible psychological sequelae of such a condition at least five factors have to be considered: (1) the girl's reaction to the change in her body; (2) the parents' reaction to the change in the girl's body; (3) the girl's experience with the medical/genital examinations and treatment; (4) previous history of physical and emotional development of the girl and of the parent-child and marital relationships; and (5) the time (age) at which the above factors exert the major emotional impact.

The five precocious thelarche cases reported here indicate that early breast development alone in the first year does have an emotional impact on the girl which is recognizable a few years later, such as a negative self-image and the feeling of being defective. These girls also tend to show a lack of spontaneity in behavior and emotional expression. When drawing a person, these girls all omitted limbs or torso, and from some of their Rorschach responses one could further infer a somewhat disturbed body image. These latter findings, regarding body-image problems, characterize all the thelarche cases reported here. However, in other girls whose precocious thelarche had an onset after three years of age this was not evident al all, even though the ages at which the psychiatric evaluation was done were comparable.[6] Most likely, cognitive limitations of the girl during the first year of life make it difficult to integrate the experience of the breast development into her developing body image. These observations may also suggest that the infant's reaction, and possibly also the recording of parental responses, to their bodies may be exquisitely sensitive. How this may translate into possible longer term effects on the narcissistic line of personality development will need and deserve further study. What appears clear is that early breast development itself would not interfere with appropriate progression in psychosexual development; all the girls with precocious thelarche were in the age-appropriate, phallic-oedipal phase of development and oral fixation has not been a necessary concomitant of breast development in the first year.

Precocious puberty itself is not expected to cause severe emotional problems either, as some reports in the literature[7,8,10–12] and the second case vignette of this paper suggest. However, in all these cases the onset and/or the major emotional impact was either before 12 months or after 30 months of age. These are contrasted with the psychopathology observed in A's case, the first vignette, where the onset and major emotional impact occurred between 18 and 30 months of age. It seems that A's case represents the most severe emotional sequelae associated with precocious puberty thus far published in the literature. The case published by Thomas et al.,[9] comes closest to A regarding the age at which the illness' major impact was experienced during the diagnostic medical/genital workup at 19 months of age. The initial symptomatology also showed some similarities, particularly regarding the intense separation anxiety, stranger anxiety, withdrawal from people, and elective mutism. As it was pointed out in connection with A's case history, it is not surprising that the anal phase of psychosexual development and the rapprochment subphase of separation-individuation would appear to be a particularly vulnerable period in emotional development. The budding autonomy and the consolidation of the body image and of the sense of self may be very sensitive to the type of changes, reactions, and medical interventions that precocious sexual maturation brings about. Thus, in addition to some problems with body image and a negative self-image seen in the thelarche cases, the distressing affects of shame, doubt, helplessness, and anger may make it very difficult for a girl of this age to cope effectively. Shame is not a striking feature in the reactions of the girls who developed thelarche in the first year of life. On the other hand, a negative self-image and problems with body image are not typical findings in precocious puberty when the onset is after three years of age; these girls tend to be "only" self-conscious, embarrassed, and shy.[6] Regarding possibly increased sexual interests and activities, the follow-up studies of Money and Walker[11] suggest that precocious puberty does not necessarily lead to increased masturbation, to sexual relations at an early age, or to promiscuity. Although few of their cases had an onset before three years of age, there is now indication that those cases would represent a separate group in terms of sexual behaviors.

The sexual nature of the bodily change in early childhood probably has a more particular and loaded meaning for the parents than for the girl. It is useful to ask the parents about what is imagined to be wrong prior to the endocrine diagnosis and to encourage them to voice any sexual concerns about the child and to help them to compare these with the facts presented after the diagnosis is established. Most parents are embarrassed by the girl's condition and wish to deny that she is developing sexually. It is striking that when breast development is the first sign of sexual precocity, the most typical initial fantasy of the parents is that the girl has cancer.[6] This may be an indication of the marked parental alarm and anxiety, whether manifest or not. The parental guilt and the nature of the "premorbid" parent-child and marital relationships are very important determinants of how the parents and the girl are going to be able to cope. For example, A's mother felt guilty for having taken birth control pills while breast-feeding A since she thought that caused the precocious puberty. Yet her obvious concern about contraception seemed just another manifestation of her ambivalent feelings about the pregnancy (and hence about A and the husband), which conflicts were further complicated by the fact that A was not born a boy, but physically resembled the father. In the case of E, who had precocious thelarche, the mother felt guilty about the possibility of having caused the problem and the fantasied tumor by taking the fertility drug, Clomid. In some cases, of which C is an example, the parental interferences may occur and have an impact on the girl at a significantly later time than the onset of the sexual precocity.

The medical/genital examinations and interventions may at times be clearly traumatic for the girl. This is more likely to be true in cases of precocious puberty where the medical/genital examinations and intervention tends to be more extensive and intensive (including hospitalization). In addition, the particular vulnerability of the one and one-half to two and one-half-year-old child, as well as the previous experience with (or the status of) toilet training have to be considered, as seen in the cases of A and B. A particular feature of the impact of a genital examination on a girl of less than three years of age may be an increased scratching in the genital area or intense fingering in the mouth for a period of time afterwards, as it is suggested in the cases of D and E. It would certainly seem advisable to pay attention to preparing a two- or three-year-old girl for the medical/genital examinations. Direct, sympathetic comments regarding her need to be sure that all is well with her body and to know what is going to be done, as well as educative comments to the parents on the emotional development and reactions at the girl's age would be helpful. The mother's presence and availability should, of course, be assured.

The consideration of the above factors in the clinical approach to the girl and her parents is expected to minimize possible interferences with the child's healthy emotional development. It has to be emphasized, however, that the reviews, observations, clinical vignettes, and thoughts presented in this chapter are based on retrospective information. Anterospective and preventive work with such cases could contribute significantly to the practical and theoretical aspects of the infant mental health field. It is important to recognize that a medically benign condition (thelarche) or the girl's very young age may represent special psychological and developmental risks for the girl, her parents, and the parent-child relationship.

SUMMARY

Breast development is the most common initial sign of early sexual maturation. In the first three years of life, precocious puberty is fairly rare, but precocious thelarche (breast development only) is not uncommon. There is no report in the literature on the emotional impact of early breast development on the girl and her parents. In this chapter five case vignettes illustrate that both precocious thelarche and precocious puberty have an emotional impact on the girl and her parents and in some cases may constitute a developmental interference. However, signs of early sexual maturation do not necessarily result in severe emotional problems. The possible psychological sequelae depend on the contribution of at least five factors: (1) the girl's reaction to the change in her body; (2) the parents' reaction to the change in the girl's body; (3) the girl's experience with the medical/genital examinations and treatment; (4) previous history of physical and emotional development of the girl and of the parent-child and marital relationships; and (5) the time (age and developmental stage) at which the above factors exert the major emotional impact. Attention is called to the fact that a medically benign condition (thelarche) or the girl's very young age may represent special psychological and developmental hazards for the girl, her parents, and the parent-child relationship. Some practical issues regarding the clinical approach to the girl and her parents are discussed.

REFERENCES

1. Bacon, GE, Spencer, ML, & Kelch, RP: *A practical approach to pediatric endocrinology.* Chicago: Year Book Medical Publishers, 1975.

2. Altchek, A: Premature thelarche. *Pediatr. Clin. of No. Am., 19:* 543–545, 1972.

3. Lippe, BM, & Sample, WF: Pelvic ultrasonography in pediatric and adolescent endocrine disorders. *J. Pediatr., 92:* 897–902, 1978.

4. Zipf, WB, Kelch, RP, Hopwood, NJ, Spencer, ML, Bacon, GE: Unresponsiveness to Gonadotropin-releasing hormone (GnRH) in girls with unsustained isosexual precocity. *J. Pediatr.* (in press).

5. Benedek, EP, Poznanski, E, & Mason, S: A note on the female adolescent's psychological reactions to breast development. *J. Am. Acad. Child Psychiatry* (in press).

6. Solyom, AE, Austad, CC, Sherick, I, & Bacon, GE: Precocious sexual development in girls: A study of its possible emotional and developmental impact. Presented at 25th Anniversary Meeting of the American Academy of Child Psychiatry, San Diego, California, October 25–29, 1978.

7. Hampson, JG, & Money, J: Idiopathic sexual precocity in the female. *Psychosom. Med., 17:* 16–35, 1955.

8. Stadeli, H: Eine Psychopathologische Querschmittuntersuchung bei 9 Patienten mit idiopathischer Pubertas Praecos. *Helv. Paediat. Acta, 5/6:* 711–722, 1961.

9. Thomas, R, Folkart, L, & Model, E: The search for a sexual identity in a case of constitutional sexual precocity. *The Psychoanal. Study of the Child, 18:* 636–662, 1963.

10. Connor, DV, & McGeorge, M: Psychological aspects of accelerated pubertal development. *J. Child Psych. Psychiatr., 6*: 161–177, 1965.

11. Money, J, & Walker, PA: Psychosexual development, maternalism, nonpromiscuity, and body image in 15 females with precocious puberty. *Arch. Sexual Behavior, 1:* 45–60, 1971.

12. Erhardt, AA, & Meyer-Bahlburg, HFL: Psychological correlates of abnormal pubertal development. *Clin. Endocrinol. Metab., 4:* 207–222, 1975.

13. Nagera, H: *Early childhood disturbances, the infantile neurosis, and the adulthood disturbances.* New York: International Universities Press, Inc., 1966.

14. Mahler, MS, Pine, F, & Bergman, A: *The psychological birth of the human infant.* New York: Basic Books, 1975.

15. Chethik, M: Amy: The intensive treatment of an elective mute. *J. Am. Acad. Child Psychiatry, 12:* 482–498, 1973.

16. Busch, F: The silent patient: Issues of separation-individuation and its relationship to speech development. *Int. Rev. of Psycho-analysis, 5:* 491–500, 1978.

17. Erickson, EH, *Childhood And Society.* Second Edition W. W. Norton & Co., New York, 1963.

Chapter 2

THE SILENT CRY

Development of Young Children with Long-term Tracheostomies

Carolyn R. Aradine, R.N., Ph.D.

INTRODUCTION

Robbie was born very prematurely, weighing only 2¼ lb. He is hospitalized in a busy intensive care nursery surrounded by a vast amount of complex medical equipment, bright lights, and the constant movement of staff members caring for many very sick infants. His mother sits in a chair beside his isolette, sadly watching the baby whom she cannot hold. Robbie is encumbered with tubes and equipment. Fluids and nourishment are administered through a nasogastric tube and an intravenous tube. His eyes are closed to avoid the bright lights. His respirations are assisted by an endotracheal tube through his mouth which pulsates with the regular rhythm of the respirator. Monitor leads are connected to his chest to record his temperature, respiration, and heart rate. How difficult it is in the midst of so much equipment for mother and father to see the "real baby." This is not the child they anticipated having. Mother wonders aloud about herself and her baby. Let me paraphrase her words: "How close do I dare let myself get to the baby? There have been so many ups and downs. He may not live. He cannot cry aloud. He may need a tracheostomy to help him breathe. If so, he will not be able to vocalize or cry. He may need to stay in the hospital. How can I take care of a baby at home who can't cry, who might need me in the middle of the night and whom I would not be able to hear?"[1]

Elizabeth is a pretty baby with blond hair and blue eyes. She lies quietly in her crib in the hospital nursery. She is now three months old but she has not yet been home from the hospital. She too was born prematurely and needed the respirator to assist her breathing for the first few days of life. Now she needs a tracheostomy to help her breathe. She must stay in the hospital until her parents learn her special care. They come faithfully to the hospital twice a day and participate in her care. For many weeks their visits were disappointing; Elizabeth was asleep. Now she is often awake and active when they come. She is beginning to reach for the toys they offer and to smile toward them. They are pleased to receive her smiles, but they are sad when she cries. Her cry is a silent one, accompanied by facial expressions of distress and tears but no sound.

Roger is eight months old. He began to snore at night. Then his breathing became more noisy and difficult. His parents rushed him to the hospital. His respiratory distress increased. The doctors advised that a tracheostomy must be done immediately. His mother and father knew this was necessary, but they felt devastated. What was happening to their baby? In the intensive care area after the surgery they were reunited with Roger. Roger, however, refused to look at either mother or father. He turned to the nurse. He was angry; he looked scared. He tried to cry but there was no sound. This seemed to frighten Roger even more. His parents were greatly distraught. They did not want this to happen and now Roger seemed to be angrily blaming them for letting it happen. They learned that he would need the tracheostomy for a long, indefinite amount of time. They felt that they must quickly learn to care for him so that they could take him home. They gathered themselves together and plunged into the tasks of learning his care.

Each of these children has an obstructive airway problem. The trachea is severely narrowed by scar tissue. They will need the tracheostomy until the trachea is large enough that they can breathe by themselves. No one knows how long this will take. The scar tissue will grow more slowly than the normal trachea. There are not yet any easy ways to correct the defect by surgery. The risks from infection, respiratory obstruction, or inadvertent removal of the trach tube are high; there is as much as a 25% risk of mortality. Staff members are reluctant to have such small children with tracheostomies cared for at home. Parents are uncertain and worried but deeply wish to have the children at home. They have many questions. How will we understand what the baby needs if he cannot cry? Will his development be delayed? Will she ever be able to talk? How will this long hospitalization affect the baby's relationship with us? No one seemed to have definitive answers to the parents' questions. Staff members could find no research or literature to which they could turn for help in answering the parents' questions.

Clinical experience with infants with long-term tracheostomies and their parents stimulated me to study a small group of young children who needed long-term tracheostomies to relieve their airway obstruction. This chapter focuses on some of the findings of that study.

PURPOSE OF THE STUDY

Description was the essential first research step. Before interventions could be designed to help these infants and their parents, I needed to know what the children experienced. Did the children experience developmental difficulties because sound production was impeded by the tracheostomy? What concerns did their parents have? I began with a detailed look at a few of these children and their families. The study[2] had two purposes: (1) to describe the development of children who had long-term tracheostomies, and (2) to describe the experiences and needs of their parents. Only the first purpose, however, is addressed in this chapter.

METHODOLOGY

The possible subjects were identified—children who were between 12 and 24 months of age and had had a tracheostomy since infancy. The parents were contacted by letter and telephone. Five (of seven) families agreed to participate in the study. The children were all being cared for at home by their parents in intact families. Three children had received their tracheostomies in early infancy to relieve subglottic stenosis (i.e. severe narrowing of the trachea below the larynx). They had been premature infants who had suffered severe respiratory distress and had been treated with endotracheal-assisted ventilation for extended periods of time. Two other children, born at term, had developed respiratory distress at home later in infancy. One child had subglottic stenosis; respiratory distress had occurred suddenly with a bout of croup. The other child had glottic stenosis (i.e., narrowing at the level of the vocal cords) and had gradually developed increasing respiratory distress over a period of weeks. When the distress became severe, tracheostomy had been essential.

I visited the children and their parents at home. Five visits were made to each family at about 1-week intervals. During the home visits the children were observed with their parents and I interviewed the parents using open-ended questions. The development of each child was assessed using the *Bayley scales*.[3] The children were filmed at play with their mothers to gain more information about their developmental abilities and communication skills. The children's home environment was assessed using an observation and interview tool developed by Caldwell, the *Home Inventory* (Home Observation for Measurement of the Environment).[4] Medical records were obtained and reviewed for detail about the children's respiratory difficulties and other health problems. All visits were process recorded in detail, and the conversation on the videotape was transcribed. All these data were then reviewed using both selected statistical techniques and detailed content analysis.

DATA ANALYSIS

The development of the children was a central issue addressed in the study. I wondered whether or not the children's development would be delayed by the tracheostomy. If so, in what ways did the tracheostomy interfere? What difficulties did the children experience? How did the children communicate when the tracheostomy impeded sound production? How was their attachment to their parents affected by their silence and their long hospitalizations?

Two approaches were used to address developmental questions. The children's developmental abilities were formally assessed using the *Bayley Scales of Infant Development.* Both the mental and motor scales were administered. Scores were calculated and corrected for gestational age. The children's development was observed on each home visit. Process recordings of each visit included detailed descriptions of the children's abilities and behavior. The videotapes provided additional information about the children's development and communication.

The developmental information was then compiled into a clinical, descriptive report about each child. The reports were reviewed by a group of experts in child development who rated each child on several developmental dimensions. Ratings were made using a 6-point categorical scale which extended from "adequate" to "critically impaired."[5]

FINDINGS

Analysis of the developmental information suggested that children need *not* necessarily be delayed in their development by the presence of the tracheostomy. In general, three children fell within the normal range while two children were delayed, in some or all areas of performance. The details are described in the subsequent sections.

Bayley Mental Developmental Index

The children's scores for the Bayley Mental Developmental Index (MDI) ranged from 55 to 118; three fell within the normal range and two were seriously delayed. (Bayley mean = 100; normal range = 84 to 116).

The mental scale of the Bayley is a composite of items which assess the child's cognitive ability. It includes items which assess fine motor skills, object constancy, language production, receptive language, adaptive abilities, and social interactions. Detailed analyses of these data showed that the two children who scored below the normal range were delayed in multiple areas: language, adaptive hand behaviors, fine motor skills, and object constancy. Failures were *not* limited to the language area.

In contrast, three children, including one premature, scored within the normal range. Two children excelled in selected areas of development. One of these children passed language production items three months above age level. The other child excelled in problem-solving skills, passing advanced puzzle items eight months above age level. I wondered if any relationships might exist between the children's early experiences and these developmental findings. Analyses of the data revealed that the two children who suffered delays in development had been the most ill prematures in the group and had suffered other medical difficulties which might have affected their performance (e.g., possible CNS bleed, possible anoxia). The two children who excelled in given areas were noted to have been term births and to have received their tracheostomies in later infancy. One premature infant did fall within the normal range. Statistical analyses, conducted using correlational and regression techniques, suggested three factors to be significantly associated (p = .05 better) with the children's performance on the Bayley Mental Scale: (1) those children who had more interactions with their mothers had higher developmental scores; (2) those children who were older when the tracheostomy was done tended to have higher scores; and (3) those children who experienced fewer serious illnesses had higher scores.

Bayley Motor Scale

The children's motor development, assessed using the *Bayley motor scale,* showed similar patterns to that found for their cognitive development. Only four children were fully assessed for their motor skills. Two children, including one premature, performed within the normal range. One child was incompletely tested but appeared on observation to be within the normal range. Two children were seriously delayed in motor skills. They were noted to be the same children who showed delays in their mental skills. Their delays occurred in both fine and gross motor behavior. There were no children who showed motor skills advanced for their ages.

Statistical analyses of these motor data suggested that two factors were significantly associated (*p* = .05 or better) with motor performance: (1) children who experienced less illness had higher motor scores; and (2) children who had more interactions with their mothers also had higher motor scores. It was interesting to note that prematurity and length of hospitalization were *not* associated with motor skills (as one might have hypothesized would have been found).

Subgroups

Analyses of the children's scores on the Bayley mental and motor scales also suggested that all children with long-term tracheostomies do not fall into one homogeneous group. Three potential subgroupings of children were identified: (1) critically ill premature infants with a tracheostomy; (2) healthy prematures with a tracheostomy; and (3) term infants who are healthy and then develop respiratory distress in later infancy and require a tracheostomy. The children in these subgroups showed differing developmental patterns.

Affective-Social Development

Several subcategories of development were reviewed and rated by the expert judges. One of these categories was affective-social development. The clinical ratings of the children's affective-social abilities included consideration of the children's means of expressing feelings, their moods, the means they used to initiate and respond to interactions, their attachment to their parents, and their ways of relating with other people. Four children were rated as adequate; one child was rated moderately impaired.

All of the children were found to express a full range of affect and demonstrated smooth transitions between various moods or states. They used multiple modes by which to express their feelings and gain social contacts. For example, they used gestures which were accompanied by a wide and impressive range of distinct facial expressions. Their eyes were particularly expressive. I noted, however, that they rarely used vocal behaviors to express their feelings or gain social contacts. (One would expect this of toddlers.)

Four of the children were predominantly happy, contented, and active youngsters. They readily became invested in play activities. They sought and responded enthusiastically to social interactions with family members. In contrast, one child was often subdued and seemed lonely. This child was less easily engaged in social interactions, approached others less frequently, and had fewer daily opportunities to interact in play.

All of the children responded warmly to their parents and showed differential responses to strangers and strange situations. They used their parents as a safe base from which to explore. Two children, however, had pronounced reactions to strangers and strange environments. They watched strangers with an intent, silent gaze. They were markedly subdued and their play constricted in such situations (even when accompanied and reassured by their parents). Analyses of the data showed that these two children had had the longest newborn hospitalizations (averaging 6 months). One may wonder if this pronounced reaction to strangers is a reflection of the long periods of hospitalization and multiple caretakers which these children endured. However, in the light of the many separations and hospitalizations all these children experienced in infancy, it was indeed remarkable that the children were not found to be experiencing serious difficulties in attachment.

Adaptive Modes

The second category rated by the experts is one we have called *adaptive modes*. This category addresses the children's many ways of using their inherent and developing abilities, their coordination of sensory and motor skills, and their growing ego development. Three children were rated as adequate in this category while two children were moderately impaired.

All of the children used multiple schemata to explore their worlds and were progressing in their coordination of these skills. However not all had achieved age-appropriate hand-eye coordination. Only two were able to vocalize enough to begin to coordinate vocalizations with their other abilities. This coordination would be expected for children of their ages, but was one aspect of development which was impeded by the tracheostomy.

All of the children used multiple approaches to their play with objects. They varied, however, in their inventiveness, curiosity, inquisitiveness, and assertiveness. One child was notably passive. The older toddlers had all begun to enjoy imitative play. All of the children enjoyed and sought interactive play experiences. Two, however, had fewer opportunities for interactions; their play was primarily solitary.

The children displayed developing autonomy. They protested in ways which were age-appropriate. They kicked, hit, threw things, moved away, and cried. Their crying was rarely accompanied by any sound. All sought help when needed, using primarily motoric gestures such as tugging, patting, or pointing, and their facial expressions. Sounds were occasionally used —tongue clicks, noisy toys, purposive coughing. One child learned to signal by turning the wall switch which operated the suction machine. Three children were active participants in self-feeding; the reasons for their delays were not fully explained. The children were learning about their body parts and did express some curiosity about their tracheostomies by feeling their tracheostomy tubes, mist masks, and other equipment. They looked curiously at the necks of other children and adults. It was, however, extremely difficult to assess their level of interest and knowledge about this area of their bodies. Although the parents were helping them learn body parts, they rarely named the tracheostomy. The parents discouraged the children's attention to the tracheostomy, fearing that the children would be more likely to pull the tube out if they named or talked about it.

Language-Communication

The third area of special interest is that of communication and language development. Before describing the findings of the study for this small group of children, let me describe the contrasting abilities of two of the children as toddlers.

Robbie is now a handsome toddler. He walks and plays actively, but in silence. He still needs a tracheostomy to facilitate respiration. He does not yet talk. He cries with tears and sad facial expressions, but without sound. He is learning to point to things he wants and tugs at his parents when he wants their attention. Sometimes, however, his requests are very hard for his parents to understand. They cited a common example. Robbie goes to the refrigerator, pointing insistently. "Is he hungry?" his parents ask. He points again at the door. His parents wonder what he might want. They ask him if he wants milk. No, he shakes his head. They could ask him a series of questions to discover what he wants, but they are not sure whether he would nod his head to indicate yes. Instead they open the refrigerator door and ask him to point to what he wants. This is easier. Robbie points to the cheese. Yes, he seems to want cheese. Mother obliges and gives it to him. Robbie eats it with delight and wanders back to his play. Mother comments on the experience, "Sometimes it is so hard to know what he wants. It is easier to let him show me than to ask him a long list of things I think he might want. I'm not sure if he would tell me 'yes.' " She acknowledges her own frustration that he cannot yet tell her what he wants in words and her tendency to respond to him in actions unaccompanied by words.

Roger, now a toddler, also still needs his tracheostomy. He, however, has a less severe narrowing of his airway and has begun to talk. His vocalizations and words are short and soft. His mother demonstrates how she encourages him to use language as she plays with him. They are playing with a telephone, a little bus, and some people figures. "Look, Roger, you can put these little people in the bus." Mother gestures as she speaks. "Then you can give them a ride." Roger pushes the bus. Mother continues, "Put more people in. Put this one in." She hands him a toy figure. Roger puts them in and vocalizes "Ah" twice as he does so. "Can you take them for a ride?" Mother asks. Roger pushes the bus across the table.

Mother introduces the telephone after they have played with the bus a few more minutes. "How about the telephone? Can you call Daddy up? Where's the telephone?" Roger looks around the table and points to the telephone. Mother moves it into reach. "Does it look funny to you? You don't have a push button phone." Roger vocalizes and begins to play with the phone. For the next several minutes he plays silently with the phone, pushing the buttons while his mother carries on a continuous monologue of comments and directions about his play. "Push the button. That's right. Do it again. . . ."

Roger turns to reach for the bus again. Mother comments, "Oh, you'd like this again. Okay, here." Roger continues to push the bus and vocalize eagerly several times. "Around and around. Around and around," comments Mother as she watches him pushing the bus in circles. "Around and around. Can you say around?" Roger says, "Round. Round. Round. Round," and then vocalizes.

Mother offers some interlocking blocks. "Can you take this apart?" Roger pulls the blocks with glee. "That's right. Pull them apart. Is it hard to do?" "Hard," says Roger. Mother repeats it. "Yes, it's hard." "Do," says Roger, handing the blocks to Mother who then helps him pull the pieces apart.

These examples are brief glimpses of two of the children and their mothers. They are typical of the children studied. Silence and gestures predominate the children's communications. Only occasionally do they use language. At the time of the study, three of the children were able to vocalize occasionally and, like Roger, had begun to talk. Two children, like Robbie, had very narrow airways and were barely able or unable to vocalize.

During the first year of life (after the tracheostomy), the children in the study had been described as markedly delayed in vocalization and language development. Some did not vocalize at all, and all were delayed in language during the first year. The language findings for these children in the second year of life were, therefore, exciting. In spite of the impediments imposed by the tracheostomy and airway defects, three of the children had age-appropriate language production skills on the Bayley assessment. In fact, one of these children showed advanced skills! Two other children, however, had few vocal capacities and showed marked delays in language, as they did in other areas of development.

Language use, however, continued to show the effects of the tracheostomy. All the children used their language abilities markedly less frequently than the average toddler. The three children who could talk did so rarely. For brief periods they would vocalize and talk eagerly but with effort; at most other times they were still notably silent. Despite their abilities, silence predominated. They relied upon gestures and facial expressions as their predominant modes of communication and developed wide repertoires of specific nonverbal communications.

Receptive language was more difficult to assess. The children were observed to be developing comprehension of spoken language as demonstrated by their ability to follow directions. It was difficult, however, to differentiate their understanding of the spoken words from their understanding of the concurrent tone of voice and gestures which accompanied these spoken communications.

The statistical analyses of the language data showed three factors to be highly associated ($p = .10$ or better) with the children's language production abilities: (1) airway size; (2) the language environment provided by their mothers; and (3) early experiences with severe illness and hospitalizations. The measurements used to determine the language relationship were less precise than desirable. However, the factors represented suggest important areas for further consideration.

Airway size appeared to be the critical variable in determining when the children were able to produce vocal sounds. The smaller the children's airways, the less sound they were able to produce and the less they used vocal communication. The data suggested that children with airways narrowed to 1 millimeter found vocalization impossible or extremely difficult. The tracheostomy tube itself posed an additional impediment. During infancy it was difficult or impossible to push any air around the tube; it nearly filled the diameter of the trachea. As the airway grew, it became possible to push air around the tracheostomy tube and easier to push it through the narrowed area of the trachea above the tube. When this became possible (during the latter part of the first year), the children seemed to try spontaneously to vocalize. However, vocalizing was difficult and required effort by the children and encouragement by the parents.

The language environment available to the children was also highly associated with language production. Some of the children were the recipients of frequent conversations provided by their mothers and other family members. Other children received little direct conversation; their daily care was often provided in silence. The data suggested that the children whose activities were accompanied by conversation were more advanced in language production and had begun to use language in interaction with family members.

The third variable associated with the children's language production was early illness and hospitalization. The study did not, however, clarify how these factors were related. The effect of early illness on language may reflect a profound impact on the children, *or* on their parents, *or* both. The data showed that the children who experienced the most serious illnesses and longest hospitalizations used little or no language at the time of the study. These children also had the smallest airways. This may account for the association observed. The likelihood of the children experiencing fewer conversations during long hospitalizations is also a viable explanation to consider. A third possibility to be entertained is the effect of the child's serious illness and hospitalization upon the parents. The parents did not perceive themselves talking less to their children with tracheostomies than to other children. However, my observations and comparison of the number of language interactions between the mothers and children with those recorded for normal infants in another study suggested that a significantly lower number of language interactions occurred between mothers and children with tracheostomies. In addition, one mother worked conscientiously to compensate; she tried to talk often to the child. Another mother noted her own tendency to talk to the child without pausing to allow the child time to respond. The mothers of these children may have found it very difficult to sustain conversations with their infants. This may reflect the lack of vocal feedback the parents receive. It may also reflect the impact of the children's long hospitalizations on their parents.

Although these language data are suggestive rather than definitive, they raise important considerations for professionals who work with these infants and their parents. This study indicates that it is very important for parents to talk with infants and children with tracheostomies, whether or not the children can yet respond vocally. Such parents may need encouragement, support, and guidance to do so. They may need help to identify the facial expressions, gestures, and other responses their children make to conversations. They may also need guidance to help them recognize the child's beginning vocal abilities and to enable them to encourage the children to use this language rather than to rely on their gestures.

Discussion

It is important to remember that these developmental findings are all based on a very small sample. This limited number of subjects does not let us draw firm conclusions. However, the finding that three of the children, including one premature infant, were functioning within the normal range of development in multiple areas including language does allow us to conclude that normal developmental achievements *are* possible when a tracheostomy is present from early infancy. Further analyses of data collected from larger populations of children with tracheostomies will be necessary before other definitive conclusions about their development can be drawn and interventions evaluated.

Summary

The child whose airway defect necessitates a tracheostomy for a long period of time poses many challenges to parents and health care professionals. This chapter has reviewed some of the findings of a descriptive study of the development of five children (aged 12–24 months) with long-term tracheostomies. The children varied in their developmental abilities. Three were within the normal range for their cognitive and motor development; two were seriously delayed. One premature functioned within the normal range. All the children had been reported to have shown delayed language production during the first year of life. During the second year, three children had age-appropriate language production skills whereas two were seriously delayed and not yet able to vocalize. Despite the presence of language production abilities, however, all the children used language very rarely and were predominantly silent. The study also suggested that the children's development was significantly associated with their early experiences of serious illness and their interaction with their parents (especially mothers).

The study is based on a small sample of children; findings cannot be generalized. However, the critical observation is made that some children with long-term tracheostomies *can* and *do* develop normally; a child's development need *not* necessarily be delayed by a tracheostomy.

REFERENCES

1. Aradine, C, Uman, H, & Shapiro, V: Collaborative treatment of a sick premature and his parents. *Issues in Comprehensive Pediatric Nursing, 3:* 29–41, July 1978.

2. Paper adapted from Aradine C: Development of toddlers with long-term tracheostomies. Doctoral dissertation, University of Michigan, 1978.

3. Bayley, N: *Bayley Scales of Infant Development.* New York: Psychological Corporation, 1969.

4. Caldwell, B: *Instruction manual: Inventory for infants (home observation for measurement of the environment).* Unpublished manuscript, n.d. Available from Center for Center Development and Education, 814 Sherman, Little Rock, Arkansas 72202.

5. Fraiberg, S., et al.: *Provisional rating scale for clinical judgments.* University of Michigan, Child Development Project. Used with permission.

Chapter 3

METHADONE-ADDICTED INFANTS

Four Years Later

Joan Lessen-Firestone, Ph.D.
Milton E. Strauss, Ph.D.
Cleofe J. Chavez, M.D.
Joan C. Stryker, M.D.

In 1972, a methadone treatment center for pregnant drug abusers was established at Hutzel Hospital, a large, urban facility in the Detroit Medical Center. Since that time, a series of longitudinal investigations focusing on the children of these women has been in progress. These studies differ slightly in terms of methodology and scope. Many characteristics of the program and of the investigations, however, have remained constant.

The Hutzel Hospital program is a low-dose, methadone maintenance program wherein women receive only enough methadone to prevent their experiencing symptoms of withdrawal. Their dosages are systematically lowered during their pregnancies, and it is unusual for women to receive an average daily dose of 20 or more milligrams of methadone for the 8 weeks prior to delivery. This treatment program contrasts with the blockade plan utilized in other programs. In this plan, women receive sufficient methadone to blunt the effect of any additional street drug they might ingest. It is not unusual for women on the blockade program to receive average daily doses of 80 or more milligrams of methadone in the last trimester of pregnancy.[4] Not unexpectedly, some clients maintained on a low-dose program do occasionally ingest drugs other than methadone. Routine urine tests have revealed illicit use of morphine, quinine, and other substances among program clients.

All pregnant drug addicts in the Detroit area are encouraged to participate in the Hutzel program. Many clients are referred by the neighborhood methadone clinics they had been attending at the time of conception. Others are referred by the Hutzel Hospital Obstetric-Gynecology Clinic. Such referrals are routinely made for all prenatal patients suspected of drug abuse. Finally, many neighborhood women are familiar with the clinic's reputation and seek admittance to the program upon discovering that they are pregnant.

After admittance, all women are placed on appropriate methadone dosages and they are all enrolled in the Hutzel Hospital Obstetric-Gynecology Clinic for routine prenatal care. Women generally remain in the program until 6 weeks postpartum. At that time, they are referred back to neighborhood methadone programs.

The personalities and life styles of the clients have made the study of their children more complex than studies of other children. The prenatal course of the children's development, for example, could be affected by the mothers' poor general health and nutrition as well as by their drug usage. Also, maternal self-reports are utilized to obtain information regarding aspects of drug history and the child's home behavior. The veracity of these reports may be influenced by the mother's concern for legal and/or protective services intervention. The high rate of mobility among drug addicts often makes it difficult to locate mothers when their children are due for follow-up examinations. Whenever possible, procedures to minimize such potential sources of difficulty are incorporated into study methodology.

Approximately 500 women and their infants have participated in the follow-up program since its inception. Criteria for inclusion in the programs have varied slightly across studies. Generally, however, women over 18 years of age, bearing healthy, normal infants weighing more than 2,500 kilograms and showing no distress related to addiction have been included. The majority of these women are black residents of Detroit's inner city. Women are enlisted in the program within 24 hours of delivery. The rates of program participation were universally high.

The first longitudinal study, begun in 1973, focused on the psychological and psychomotor development of addicted children during their first year of life. One hundred and thirteen infants, 60 of whom were progeny of methadone-treated, drug-dependent women, were enrolled in this study. An additional 53 infants, born to nondrug-dependent women, were matched with the addicted infants on the basis of birth weight, gestational age, maternal age, parity, (SES) Social Economic Status, prenatal care, and potency of obstetrical medication. All children were assessed with the Brazelton Neonatal Assessment Scale[3] at two and three days of age and the Bayley scale[1] at three, six, and twelve months of age.

The Brazelton scale assesses neurological and behavioral characteristics of neonates. It consists of 26 explicitly defined behavioral ratings that are based on the observation of the infant's response to a standardized series of interactive maneuvers. Four behavioral domains seem to be assessed by the examination.[7] They are: (1) orientation to auditory and visual stimulation during alert states; (2) cessation of responses to auditory or photic stimulation during sleep or drowsy states; (3) irritability-tension dimension; and (4) state regulation. A number of reflexes are also elicited during the examination, but these data are not reported.

During the period from 24 to 48 hours of age, the Brazelton indicated a rather consistent pattern of behavioral change that was found in both the addicted and the nonaddicted infants. In this day-long span, infants became irritable more often during the course of assessment and, consequently, were alert for more brief periods of time. They cried more intensely and frequently required the efforts of a caregiver to reduce excitability. The more intense activity during episodes of crying was paralleled in the nonirritable states in which motor activity was also more intense and extensive. These changes were suggestive of recovery from the depressing effects of obstetrical medications.[6]

Differences between addicted and nonaddicted infants were also observed. They were greatest for items similiar to those employed in the clinical assessment of neonatal abstinence and were reminiscent of the withdrawal syndrome in adults. The addicted infants showed increased irritability, tremulousness, and jerkiness of motor movement and hand-mouth movements. They are less cuddly than other infants, particularly at 24 hours of age. The examination assessed the infants' ability to inhibit responses to photic (flashlight beam), auditory (bell, rattle), and tactile (pin-prick) stimuli presented a number of times during sleep. Aversion to light is a common symptom of narcotics abstinence among adults, and significantly, it is only in response to a light stimulus that addicted infants show a deficit in habituation or response decrement.

The difficulty of these infants in dealing with visual stimuli is seen in attempts to elicit alertness and orienting responses as well. It was much more difficult to elicit alertness among the addicted infants and many orientation items could not even be completed. When orientation responses were obtained, addicted infants were slightly less competent than nonaddicted infants. This was particularly true when the stimuli were visual.

Hyperirritability is a common feature of the abstinence syndrome, and as would be expected, the addicted infants cried more often in response to stimulation than did the nonaddicted infants. When these infants became irritable in response to stimulation, however, they were as easily consoled as the nonaddicted babies.

These observed differences between addicted and nonaddicted neonates could affect the drug-dependent mothers' perceptions of their newborns. These women were very familiar with signs of drug withdrawal and could easily recognize them in their infants. Many women verbally expressed feelings of responsibility and guilt for the withdrawal their infants were experiencing. Some of the drug-dependent women also seemed to be aware of their infants' resistance to cuddling and failure to alert and orient. The mothers, however, were not likely to recognize these signs as being related to withdrawal; rather, they would seem to accept these as signs that their babies did not like them. Addicted mothers occasionally reported noticing and feeling hurt that their infants did not respond to their cuddling and attempts to get their attention. Such maternal feelings of being rejected by their babies could certainly have important implications for the developing mother-child relationship.

Although many addicted infants were affected by withdrawal, pharmacologic intervention was necessary for only the most seriously affected infants. Drug detoxification programs utilizing progressively smaller dosages of drug ingestion were not widely used, particularly as they require longer than normal hospitalization for the baby. Supportive therapy, including swaddling and frequent feedings, was utilized whenever necessary to minimize the infants' discomforts. The majority of the addicted infants were able to leave the hospital 3 to 5 days after birth.

The addicted and nonaddicted infants returned to the methadone clinic three times during their first year of life for follow-up examinations. Slightly less than half of each group of children returned for all three of the follow-up sessions. A greater number of children returned for only one or two visits. Those children who did return for all assessments are representative of their respective groups. Most children returning at one year of age were in the care of their mothers, although a few were being raised by grandparents or foster parents.

At each of the follow-up examinations, the Bayley Scales of Development were administered. This well-standardized examination provides both mental and psychomotor development indices. The mean mental and psychomotor scores of both the addicted and nonaddicted infants were at or above normal at each examination. The pattern of scores in the two groups, however, was different.

During the course of the year, both groups showed some decline in psychomotor performance. The drop in the Psychomotor Development Index (PDI) was small for the nonaddict sample, but large among the addicts' infants. Item analyses of the testing protocols in the longitudinal study indicated that the addicts' babies were less likely to be walking unaided at 12 months than were the offspring of nonaddicted women. This was the only assessed mental or motor behavior which differentiated between addicted and nonaddicted infants in the first year of life.

In addition to providing relevant research material, the Bayley assessment session was an optimal setting for increasing the mothers' awareness of their children's development. The examination was given to the infants while seated on their mothers' laps. The mothers witnessed the examination and observed the performance of their children. As many of the same materials (e.g., blocks) were utilized in examining children of different ages, the mothers were able to see development and maturation in the responses of their children to these materials. Mothers also saw types of toys and stimulation that were appropriate for their growing children. They were then able to use similar toys and play in their interactions with their children. Although these features of the Bayley examination were incidental to the main goals of the study, spontaneous comments of the mothers indicated that they found the assessment itself an interesting and valuable experience.

These children were not seen again for several years. This past year, when the children were four and five years of age, they returned to the clinic for a preschool evaluation. In the interim period, a more comprehensive, longer term follow-up program was initiated. This program also focused on the development of children of methadone-addicted women. It was concerned, however, with the physical as well as the psychological growth and development of these children. Children in this second study received all routine pediatric care as well as psychological evaluations at follow-up visits. In addition, a staff of social workers was available to work with the participating families.

The timing of our follow-up visits was also modified in this study. Infants returned to the clinic at two and four weeks of age for Brazelton and pediatric assessments in this first study. Newborn differences between addicted and nonaddicted infants disappeared by three months of age. These interim examinations were included to evaluate the course of withdrawal between three days and three months of age. Also, the follow-up examinations of these children continued twice yearly during their toddler and preschool years.

As the children grew, the scope of the psychological investigation was broadened in order to obtain more types of information. Beginning at three years of age, children were assessed with the McCarthy Scales of Children's Abilities.[5] This standardized assessment was selected because it provides separate indices of motor, verbal, memory, perceptual, quantitative, and general cognitive abilities. An area of specific performance deficit would be more easily revealed by this type of test than by a test providing one overall ability score.

By the time the children reached preschool age, however, a difference in McCarthy test performance between addicted and nonaddicted children might not necessarily have been caused by differences in prenatal drug exposure. By four years of age, differences in home environment and/or mother-child interaction patterns would certainly have had ample opportunity to impact upon the children, affecting their development. As a result, additional assessments were added to the test battery. First, we videotaped 15 minutes of mother and child interaction in the clinic waiting room prior to the beginning of the more structured assessments. Videotapes were coded for various types of verbal, initiating, and interactive behaviors exhibited by the mother and child. Second, the home of each child was evaluated with the HOME Observation for Measurement of the Environment (HOME) Inventory.[2] This is a measure of not only the physical size and condition of the environment, but also contains factors tapping the psychological effect and level of stimulation present in the home. Finally, a social history, including information concerning parenting practices, developmental knowledge, and background characteristics was given to the mothers in an interview setting.

Thus, when the preschoolers returned to the clinic for follow-up examinations, they were (1) videotaped interacting with their mothers; (2) assessed with the McCarthy; and (3) given a physical examination. At the same time, the mothers (4) completed a social history interview; and (5) made an appointment for a HOME visit.

This comprehensive assessment was also given to each of the mother-child pairs in the original study who returned to the clinic for a follow-up examination when the children reached four years of age.

Attempts were made to find 86 members of this original group as the children approached five years of age. Twenty-seven cases were ignored for a number of reasons, including earlier refusal to continue participation, removal from the state, earlier loss of contact, and in one instance, sudden infant death syndrome. Forty-six children of drug-dependent women were sought. Thirty-eight were found, and of these, 33 were seen for evaluation. Of the 40 comparison cases sought, 34 were contacted and data collected from 30 of them. These groups did not differ from cases that were lost to follow up for the maternal, delivery, or developmental variables examined or controlled for in earlier reports.

Preliminary results from the four-year follow up of these children are discussed below.

When tested at four years of age, both the addicted and the nonaddicted groups of children performed below the mean on the McCarthy scale most closely comparable to a globel intelligence measure. The scores on all other scales were also below standardized means. These results are consistent with those generally observed among disadvantaged populations. There is no difference, however, in the performance of the two groups of children on any of the ability scales. The performance of the prenatally addicted children was comparable to that of the nonaddicted group.

During the course of the testing, examiners routinely recorded their clinical impressions of the children. In most instances, the examiners were unaware of the original drug status of the parent, although it was not possible to assure control of this potentially biasing information at all times. A modified version of the Behavior Record of the Bayley Scales of Infant Development was used for this purpose: 15 of the original 27 scales were retained, some with modification of definitions. In addition, examiners were free to record any other observations made.

The children of drug-dependent women were seen as more active and energetic than the other children. The groups did not differ on gross motor coordination, but the fine motor coordination seemed to be better in the control cases. The children with a history of drug exposure were seen as immature substantially more frequently. Although these are nonindependent tests, the pattern suggests that in a structured, demanding situation, drug-exposed children display more task-irrelevant activity.

It appears that this activity pattern is found only in structured settings, for there are no differences in the behavior of the two groups of children, or their mothers, during the waiting room observations. The behaviors of mother and children were separately factor analyzed and five maternal and four child behaviors identified. Maternal factors are: (1) mother playing with child; (2) mother responding positively to child; (3) mother responding negatively to child; (4) mother initiating interaction with child; and (5) mother reprimanding child. The child factors are: (1) playing and talking; (2) relating to caregiver; (3) relating to other children; and (4) wandering. Groups did not differ in the amount of time they engaged in each of these mother and child behaviors. Neither did the addicted and nonaddicted pairs differ in the amount of gross motor movement engaged in during the observation.

Home environments, as assessed with Caldwell's scale, did not differentiate the two groups either. A number of the variables from the interaction and HOME scale, however, were associated with cognitive development in both groups of children. Children with higher general cognitive scores on the McCarthy scales came from homes with more stimulating toys and objects, and had mothers who were nonreprimanding and who tended to initiate interactions with their children. Children who wandered about the playroom and did not interact with the adult had lower cognitive scores. There were differences in the children, then, at four years of age. Some children seemed to be doing better—they had higher cognitive scores, more stimulating environments, and more accepting, initiating mothers. Other children appeared to be developing less well. They performed poorly on the cognitive tests, and ignoring adults, wandered aimlessly about the waiting room. These differences, however, were not associated with the prenatal drug exposure of the infant.

At this time, the children of drug-dependent women appear to be developing much as are similar children of nondrug-dependent women. Once the course of drug withdrawal has been completed, few cognitive or motor differences distinguish the addicted from the nonaddicted children. Both groups of children behave comparably with their caregivers, and there are no major differences in the psychosocial environment of the home, insofar as these characteristics have been assessed. There is a cluster of behavior differences between the groups that does warrant attention, however. This is the greater task irrelevant activity of the addicted children in the structured testing interaction. These differences may increase in importance as our "almost five-year-olds" begin school.

ACKNOWLEDGMENT

This research was supported by the Spencer Foundation and the National Institute on Drug Abuse, Grant No. 1 H 81 DA 01855.

REFERENCES

1. Bayley scales of infant development. New York: The Psychological Corporation, 1969.

2. Bradley, RH, & Caldwell, BM: Early home environment and changes in mental test performance in children from 6 to 36 months. *Develop. Psychol., 12:*93–97, 1976.

3. Brazelton, TB: Neonatal behavioral assessment scale. *Clinics in Developmental Medicine.,* No. 50. Philadelphia: Lippincott, 1973.

4. Dole, VP, Nyswander, ME, & Kreek, MJ: Methadone. *N.Y. J. Med., 66:*2011–2015, 1966.

5. McCarthy scales of children's abilities. New York: The Psychological Corporation, 1972.

6. Standley, K, Soule, AB, Copans, SA, & Duchowny, MS: Local-regional anesthesia during childbirth: Effect on newborn behaviors. *Science, 186:* 634–635, 1974.

7. Strauss, ME, & Rourke, DL: A multivariate analysis of the Brazelton Scale in several samples. In A. Samaroff (Ed.), *Organization and stability of newborn behavior: A commentary on the Brazelton neonatal behavior scale.* Monographs of the Society for Research in Child Development, 1979.

Chapter 4

PREMATURE INFANTS

Cognitive and Social Development in the First Year of Life

Gary M. Olson, Ph.D.
Michael E. Lamb, Ph.D.

According to the standard definition, a premature infant is one who is born less than 37 weeks after its mother's last menstrual period and whose birthweight is less than 2,500 grams. Neither criterion alone is adequate because of inaccuracies in estimating last menstrual period and because low birth-weight, full-term infants represent a different syndrome. About 8% of live births in the U.S. are premature by this definition.

Premature infants are biologically immature at birth and so their chances of survival are more uncertain than those of full-term infants. Modern medical technology, however, has made it possible for increasing numbers of premature infants to survive. With the aid of highly sophisticated neonatal intensive care units, it is not unusual today for infants weighing less than 1,500 grams, born less than 30 weeks after conception, to survive with few noticeable anomalies.[38] The survival of such infants further underscores the need to understand how prematurity influences development.

Premature delivery places infants at risk, and a great deal of research is focused on the characterization and amelioration of the hazards involved. The medical risks associated with prematurity are obvious. Prematurity is associated with physiological damage due to congenital factors or intrauterine environmental contamination by smoking, disease, malnutrition, and drugs. Immediately after delivery, premature infants often have serious breathing and feeding problems, illness, and other complications that warrant special care. Much of the early work on prematurity focused on the consequences of these medical hazards.

There are, however, a range of problems that are more psychosocial than medical in character. For most parents, the premature birth of their infant is a disrupting and stressful event. It is usually unexpected, so the parents are not fully prepared for their infant. When necessary, hospitalization introduces a period of parent-infant separation. Since prematurity is usually associated with other problems, parents often have legitimate or imagined worries concerning their infant's development. Premature infants are smaller and less attractive than full-terms, and because they gain weight slowly, these features are outgrown slowly. Parents often feel they are at fault for the premature birth, and a combination of guilt and recrimination can lead to marital conflict.[24] All in all, prematurity imposes stresses on parent-infant relationships, creating further developmental hazards.

For both scientific and practical reasons, it would be useful to identify the risks faced by premature infants and their causal influences. Given the complexity of the hazards associated with prematurity, this is a very difficult task. In this chapter, we will consider some of the factors that could adversely affect development before describing a conceptual model for understanding their mode of influence. Our focus is on cognitive development, although the model and research strategy we describe are applicable to other aspects of development. In addition, we will focus on the origin of individual differences in cognitive development. These differences are well documented, but there is little known about their origins. The study of individual differences provides an ideal context for examining the causal mechanisms of development.

The chapter is organized as follows. In the first section, we will briefly review evidence concerning the effects of prematurity on cognitive development. Then we will discuss some biological and environmental factors that are known to influence cognitive development. We shall emphasize that these factors have mutually interrelated effects, and we shall illustrate this in a conceptual model guiding our thinking in this area. Finally, we will show how this model can be tested empirically. Our purpose here is to describe a common-sense approach to the study of prematurity and its effects.

THE COGNITIVE DEVELOPMENT OF PREMATURE INFANTS

Despite many imperfections, intelligence tests continue to constitute a useful index of cognitive status. Virtually all studies of premature infants use intelligence tests as measures of cognitive outcomes. During the first three years, the measure chosen is often the Bayley Mental Development Index.[2] For older children, any of a number of standard intelligence tests—often the Stanford-Binet or the Weschler Intelligence Scales for Children (WISC)—is chosen. Scores on these tests reveal a clear picture. Even if one excludes infants with obvious congenital defects or organic damage, infant intelligence tests usually show preterm infants performing significantly more poorly than full-term infants,[5,35] though some researchers find no differences.[22] On the other hand, the long-term prognosis for preterms who show no obvious damage is quite good. As a group, prematures score slightly lower on intelligence tests during the school years than full-terms, [5,10,35] but the majority of preterms fall within the normal range. Often studies report a modest correlation between birth weight or age at delivery and later intelligence, but the small magnitude of the differences between pre- and full-terms is most impressive.

The socioeconomic status of the premature infant's family is an especially important consideration. As Sameroff and Chandler[35] have noted, "The data from these various longitudinal studies of prenatal and perinatal complication have yet to produce a single predictive variable more potent than the familial and socioeconomic characteristics of the caretaking environment" (p. 208). For instance, McDonald[28] and Illsley[23] found that prematurity was related to intellectual outcomes in lower class children but not in middle-class ones. Drillien[13] found intelligence deficits only in those with the lowest birth weights in the middle class, whereas infants in all weight categories suffered deficits in the lower class. Francis-Williams and Davies[15] found that social class was more predictive of later IQ than any perinatal variable. The fact that more premature births occur in lower class families underscores the need to investigate the origins of these differences in cognitive outcomes. Understanding these origins will be difficult, since there are both organic (e.g., maternal health and nutrition) as well as psychosocial risks associated with lower socioeconomic status.

Although we have focused to this point on the differences between preterm and full-term infants, it is also important to determine which preterm infants are likely to have developmental problems so that intervention can be attempted. This is difficult in part because infant intelligence tests do not predict IQ in later childhood.[26] Even broader-based efforts have been unsuccessful. In a major research program, for instance, Arthur Parmelee and his associates obtained a variety of medical, perceptual-cognitive, and social measures during infancy and tried to predict the cognitive competence of infants at two years of age.[36] Despite the use of sophisticated measures and complex multivariate analytic techniques, they were only able to predict 30% of the variability in intelligence scores at two years of age.

Even this figure is an overestimate because it represents the best fit of a stepwise multiple regression; if the same predictor variables were used with a new sample, prediction would probably be poorer. These levels of prediction are simply inadequate for predicting the outcome for any individual with any confidence. Similarly discouraging findings have been reported by other researchers.[35]

In sum, the student of cognitive development in premature infants faces a paradox. On the one hand, the premature infant faces a host of risks—both medical and psychosocial—which we will examine more systematically in the next section. On the other hand, the long-term prognosis is generally good, although there is an important association with social class. Furthermore, it is difficult to identify factors in early infancy that are clearly associated with later outcomes. Perhaps this is the case because we have been examining the wrong variables, both during infancy and later childhood. This is a real possibility, given how little we know about the structure and determinants of intelligence, and we will return to this issue when we discuss the kinds of factors that could be measured. Alternately, the problem may lie in our simple-minded approach to development rather than in our choice of measures. An increasing number of investigators believe that this has indeed been the problem, and a conceptual model and research strategy are described later in an attempt to cast the issue in a new light.

INFLUENCES ON COGNITIVE DEVELOPMENT

In the past, investigators tended to believe that the dominant influences on the development of premature infants were medical or biological.[35] A substantial minority of preterm infants have obvious physiological problems, and many preterms endure extended periods of physiological stress. Even when there were no obvious medical problems, it was assumed that later differences could be attributed to "minimal brain damage."[5,25] This led investigators to focus their search for predictor variables on medical factors. Such variables are clearly related to the likelihood of death during the perinatal period[38] and it was not illogical to assume that they were also associated with long-term outcomes. Their poor predictive value in this arena has since led investigators to shift focus. It seems reasonable to propose that cognitive development is affected by both the infant's biological integrity and the social environment provided by the parents, yet much more attention has been paid to the biological factors.[35] Fortunately, this is changing as researchers examine the interaction among biological and social factors.

Every infant is born with identifiable characteristics that are salient and meaningful to its parents. The parents in turn have beliefs about children and parenting, expectations about infants and their capacities, as well as distinctive personality styles. The infant's characteristics are important because they affect the type of treatment the baby elicits and they determine how the baby will be influenced by its experiences. The parents' characteristics, meanwhile, determine how they respond to the baby's characteristics and how they behave toward it. Thus, the infant's personality and cognitive status months or years later is a joint function of several interdependent determinants: Its characteristics, its parents' characteristics, and the nature of interaction between parents and infant. Perhaps we will be more successful in explaining why some preterm infants develop poorly if we consider not merely their biological status but also the characteristics of their rearing environment and the interaction between this environment and the baby's characteristics.

What sorts of characteristics are likely to be important? Let us consider the infant first. Four classes of factors are likely to be important: the degree of medical risk, the infant's ability to extract and use information, the infant's temperament, and its attractiveness. Some of these factors affect development directly, whereas others affect it indirectly through their effects on the parents. As far as the parents are concerned, we are interested in their attitudes and expectations, and the way these influence their interactions with the baby and the type of rearing environment they provide. All the parental factors mentioned earlier can be influenced by a premature birth and the individual characteristics of the child, and all may influence the child's development. Let us now examine some research implicating parental and infant characteristics in cognitive development.

Infant Characteristics

Despite the fact that medical risk factors are poor predictors of cognitive outcomes, an accurate assessment of the infant's physiological and neurological status must be included in any study of development in preterm infants. Many pre-, peri-, and postnatal events can produce neurological damage in premature infants, and one example will suffice. It is well-known that anoxia can cause brain damage, and this is why breathing difficulties are of great concern. We now know, however, that the use of oxygen to treat respiratory difficulties in preterm infants often leads to retrolental fibroplasia, a condition that can result in permanent blindness. Consequently, oxygen is now administered much less liberally. This situation illustrates the fragility of premature infants, and the multiple opportunities for neurological damage.

Minimal brain damage may indeed occur, but it has been difficult thus far to locate functional anomalies that have clear associations with cognitive deficits. Studies of basic state and sensory processes have produced few differences. Sleep periodicities and state organization,[32] like visual pattern preferences,[14] develop similarly in premature and full-term infants matched for gestational age. The data on early visual skills indicate "that maturation of the nervous system is the predominant determinant of visual responses in the early months of life,[32] "with little evidence of facilitation due to extra experience nor retardation due to organic problems." Similarly, measures of attention and learning reveal few and transient differences between premature and full-term infants.[32,35]

For the most part, attempts to measure infant functioning have concentrated on sensory, attentional, and memory tasks that are either quite simple or are imperfectly understood. Despite the recent popularity of research on the ability to detect, store, and use information,[3,9,19,30] theories of basic infant skills are still quite primitive.[29] Only recently have investigators begun to examine more complex skills such as categorization, concept formation, and the control of attention. As indices of these more complex skills become available, they may help identify deficits in preterm infants. A number of researchers are now investigating this possibility.

That infants differ in temperament from early in their lives has long been acknowledged by parents, but until relatively recently this fact was ignored by researchers. The concept is now returning to favor, and a number of recent studies have sought to link infant temperament with a variety of outcome measures.[34] Relationships between temperament and any measure of infant outcome could be due to either (1) an association between temperament and factors that are directly related to cognitive skills (for example, distractability is clearly related to attentiveness) or (2) different patterns of interaction between parents and infants elicited by the infants' temperament. In the latter case, the effect of temperament on infant outcome would be indirect, mediated by the parent-infant interaction. Furthermore, this indirect effect would not depend upon the infants' temperament alone—it would also depend upon the characteristics of the parents, since they would determine how the parents were affected by the infants' temperament.

Data collected in the New York Longitudinal Study[39] illustrate what we mean—the methodological deficiencies of the study notwithstanding. Thomas and his colleagues found that the mesh between infant temperament and the adaptability of the parents largely determined whether the children would later require psychotherapy, especially where children of "difficult" temperament were concerned. Further research conducted by Thomas and his colleagues[6,40] substantiated their predictions. More than any other study, this research has served to establish infant temperament as a concept worthy of investigation.

Studies like the New York Longitudinal Study suggest that it is necessary to take into account the characteristics of infants and parents and their interactions over time in order to explain differential development outcomes. We shall argue below that this is especially appropriate when studying the cognitive development of premature or low birth-weight infants. The potential importance of differences in attractiveness and term status are underscored by the findings of recent studies which demonstrate that infant characteristics affect parental behavior, and that this in turn affects cognitive development.

Parental Characteristics

The longitudinal studies of Ainsworth and Clarke-Stewart illustrate most clearly the role social experience plays in facilitating cognitive development, especially in infancy. Having conducted triweekly observations of mother-infant interaction throughout the first year of the infant's life, Ainsworth found that the best predictor of competence at one year was maternal sensitivity to infant signals.[1] Sensitivity was significant from as early as the first three months of life. Clarke-Stewart,[7] meanwhile, observed infants of 9 to 18 months interacting with their mothers. Like Ainsworth and several other researchers,[27,41-43] Clarke-Stewart found that mothers who were responsive to their infant's cries had more competent infants. In addition, she found that maternal responsiveness to positive infant signals (e.g., nondistress vocalizations) also facilitated the growth of competence. By using cross-lagged panel correlations, furthermore, Clarke-Stewart was able to show in this study as well as in a later replication sample[8] that the direction of effect was indeed from maternal responsiveness to infant competence. Stevenson and Lamb[37] discuss the effects of parental behavior on infant cognitive development in greater detail.

The Effects of Infant Characteristics on Parental Behavior

Four recent studies suggest that maternal responsiveness is at least partially determined by maternal perceptions of the infant's temperament and the mother's experience with the infant. First, Donovan[11,12] found that the mothers of difficult infants were less sensitive to infant signals than were the mothers of easy infants. Their diminished responsiveness, argued Donovan, explains why their infants later performed more poorly on an object-permanence task. Second, Sameroff[34] found that the best predictor of cognitive performance at 30 months was the difficulty of perceived temperament at four months. Again, it seems likely that the temperament of the infants affected their cognitive development through the effect of infant temperament on parental behavior. Findings consistent with this have also been reported by Campbell[4] and Ploof.[33] As far as attractiveness is concerned, the most relevant study is that reported by Parke and Sawin[31] who found that parental evaluations of their infant's attractiveness predicted the way in which the parents interacted with their infants.

Thus, there is sufficient evidence that variations in infant characteristics as well as parental attitudes, expectations, and behavior play critical interdependent roles in mediating development. We believe that preterm infants comprise a population among whom these factors are likely to be especially important for at least two reasons. First, the premature birth of a baby heightens the sensitivity of parents to its characteristics because the infant is, in a dramatic sense, atypical. In addition, the unexpectedly early arrival of preterm infants places them in the care of parents who are not psychologically prepared for parenthood.[24] This too may maximize the impact of the infant's characteristics upon the parent's interactional styles and expectations.

Some recent experimental research indicates that adults indeed respond differently to premature infants and infants they think are premature. Frodi et al. [16] showed videotaped segments of smiling and crying infants to mothers and fathers, and monitored their responses on psychophysiological and emotional report indices. Frodi et al. found that cries were perceived as more aversive when the stimulus baby was labeled "premature" than when it was called "normal," and that the "premature" infant elicited less sympathy than the "normal" infant did. This demonstrated that cognitive sets in the parents could lead them to respond differently to signals that were in fact identical. In addition, there is evidence that the cries of premature and full-term infants are perceptibly different. Frodi et al.[17] showed that the cries of premature infants were markedly more aversive than the cries of full-term infants, and that the aversiveness of the cries was maximized when the cry and appearance of the preterm infant were combined. Interesting, it seems that the mothers of preterm infants find the cries of prematures especially aversive.[18]

A MODEL OF DEVELOPMENTAL INFLUENCE

Figure 4-1 summarizes our point of view. Later individual differences in cognitive performance are viewed as the joint products of enduring infant characteristics and environmental inputs. A considerable portion of the infant's environment is under the control of the parents, whose behavior is jointly determined by their characteristics in interaction with the infant's. Thus, in order to understand infant outcomes, one needs to measure infant characteristics, parental characteristics, and parent-infant interaction repeatedly as they change and affect one another over time. Sameroff and Chandler[35] describe the

model portrayed in Figure 4-1 as transactional. They characterize this view as follows:

> According to this transactional view, successful predictions re-
> garding long-range developmental outcomes cannot be made on
> the basis of a continuum of reproductive casualty alone. An
> equally important continuum of caretaking casualty exists to
> moderate or perpetuate earlier developmental difficulties. . . .
> Transactions between the child and his caretaking environment
> serve to break or maintain the linkage between earlier trauma
> and later disorder and must, according to this view, be taken into
> account if successful predictions are to be made. (pp. 189–190)

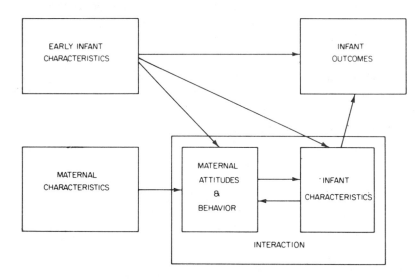

Figure 4–1   The Conceptual Model.

Research strategies embodying the transactional view have
only become popular recently for several reasons. First, despite
the apparent simplicity of Figure 4-1, the model is extremely
complex. The multiple paths of influence over time are difficult
to conceptualize and to measure. As a result, this complex
approach has only been adopted when simpler models have

been proven unsatisfactory. Second, statistical methods for handling complex longitudinal data have only become available recently. [20,21])

An Illustrative Research Design

In order to study development using a conceptual model like that depicted in Figure 4–1, a rich set of longitudinal data must be obtained from a large sample of infants. If one's goal is to account for individual differences in cognitive outcomes at some later point, one must first choose a satisfactory outcome measure. As noted earlier, this in itself is a controversial task. Then one would have to measure the following types of variables reliably:

(a) general demographic characteristics (e.g., SES, parental education, parents' family history);
(b) indicators of the infants' biological status (e.g., birthweight, gestational age, congenital problems);
(c) early events that affect the degree of risk (e.g., sickness, anoxia, length of hospitalization, feeding problems);
(d) parental attitudes and expectations about their infants, and parental perceptions of their infants' temperaments;
(e) early cognitive skills; and
(f) patterns of parent-infant interaction.

Since the model holds that each of these factors influences the others, these variables must be measured repeatedly in a longitudinal design. This is especially true of (d), (e), and (f), which are likely to change substantially.

In Figure 4–2, we have indicated how this research strategy might be translated into an actual study in which the investigator wished to predict performance on the Bayley scales at one year of age. According to the figure, the degree of medical risk at birth may affect both the baby's performance on measures of basic cognitive skills, as well as the parent's perception of the infant. These perceptions, in interaction with a variety of parental attitudes which may themselves be related to the family's socioeconomic status, affect the way baby and parent interact. As the result of these interactions, furthermore, the baby's cognitive status, as well as the parent's attitudes and perception, will be modified, so that both parent and infant will enter future interactions with altered characteristics. The arrows indicating the direction of influence among the variables measured amply illustrate the potential complexity of the interrelationships among developmental determinants.

As mentioned earlier, statistical techniques have been developed to permit one to assess patterns of influence among variables over time. Path analysis, for instance, allows one to measure the magnitude of predictive relations along hypothesized paths of influence like those shown in Figure 4–2. This makes it possible to evaluate alternative conceptual models. As in all research, of course, these analytic tools must be used carefully: they cannot rescue poorly designed research! When properly used, however, they allow one to investigate the complex causal relationships proposed by transactional models. These techniques promise to advance our understanding of development, and may help us determine why some premature infants suffer long-term consequences while others are later indistinguishable from full-term infants.

CONCLUSION

Premature infants face a variety of hazards that might affect their development. As a group they show small though reliable long-term deficits in cognitive functioning, particularly in lower class families. However, many premature infants are indistinguishable from matched full-terms by the school years, thus showing little long-term effects of the early hazards they

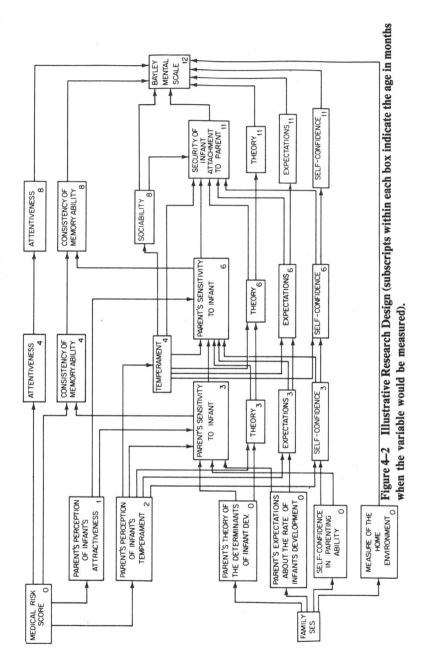

Figure 4–2 Illustrative Research Design (subscripts within each box indicate the age in months when the variable would be measured).

faced. Our understanding of the mechanisms responsible for long-term deficits as well as long-term recovery is very important. Research based on conceptual models that take into account the effects of biological and psychosocial factors will be needed to sort out these mechanisms. In this chapter we have attempted to describe some of the factors that must be taken into account, and have illustrated the kind of research plan that will be needed to analyze these factors. Several research projects currently in progress that are based on this conceptualization should, in the next few years, add to our understanding of the development of premature infants.

Acknowledgments

The preparation of this chapter was facilitated by a Research Career Development (HD 00169) Award, and a research grant (HD 10486) fron NICHD to the first author, and a research grant from the National Foundation—March of Dimes to both authors.

References

1. Ainsworth, MD, & Bell, SM: Mother-infant interaction and the development of competence. In K. J. Connolly & J. S. Bruner (Eds.), *The growth of competence.* New York: Academic Press, 1974.

2. Bayley, N: *Bayley scales of infant development.* New York: Psychological Corporation, 1969.

3. Bornstein, MH, & Kessen, W: (Eds.), *Psychological development from infancy: Image to intention.* Hillsdale, N.J.: Lawrence Erlbaum Associates, 1979.

4. Campbell, SB: Maternal and infant behavior in normal, high risk, and "difficult" infants. Paper presented at the meeting of the Society for Research in Child Development, New Orleans, April 1977.

5. Caputo, DV, & Mandell, W: Consequences of low birth weight, *Dev. Psychol. 3,* 363–383, 1970.

6. Chess, S, & Thomas, A: *Temperament and development.* New York: Brunner/Mazel, 1977.

7. Clarke-Stewart, KA: Interactions between mothers and their young children: Characteristics and consequences. *Monographs of the Society For Research in Child Development, 38,* Whole No. 153, 1973.

8. Clarke-Stewart, KA: The father's impact on mother and child. Paper presented at the meeting of the Society for Research in Child Development, New Orleans, April 1977.

9. Cohen, LB, & Salapatek, P: (Eds.), *Infant perception: From sensation to cognition* (2 vols). New York: Academic Press, 1975.

10. Davies, PA, & Stewart, AL: Low-birth weight infants: Neurological sequelae. *Brit. Med. Bull. 31,* 85–89, 1975.

11. Donovan, WL, & Leavitt, LA: Early cognitive development and its relation to maternal physiologic and behavioral responsiveness. Paper presented at the meeting of the Society for Research in Child Development, New Orleans, April 1977.

12. Donovan, WL, Leavitt, LA, & Balling, JD: Maternal physiological response to infant signals. *Psychophysiology, 15,* 68–74, 1978.

13. Drillien, CM: *The growth and development of the prematurely born infant.* Baltimore: Williams & Wilkins, 1964.

14. Fantz, RL, Fagan, JF, III, & Miranda, SB: Early visual selectivity. In L. B. Cohen & P. Salapatek (eds.), *Infant perception: From sensation to cognition* (Vol. 1). New York: Academic Press, 1975.

15. Francis-Williams, J, & Davies, PA: Very low birth weight and later intelligence, *Dev. Med. Child Neurol., 16,* 709–728, 1974.

16. Frodi, AM, Lamb, ME, Leavitt, LA, & Donovan, WL: Fathers' and mothers' responses to infant smiles and cries. *Infant Behav. Dev., 1,* 127–140, 1978.

17. Frodi, AM, Lamb, ME, Leavitt, LA, Donovan, WL, Naff, C, & Sharry, D: Fathers' and mothers' responses to the faces and cries of normal and premature infants. *Dev. Psychol., 14,* 490–498, 1978.

18. Frodi, AM, Lamb, ME, & Wille, D: Parents, responses to normal and premature infants. Unpublished manuscript, 1979.

19. Haith, MM, & Compos, JJ: (eds.), *Carmichael's manual of child psychology: Infancy and the biology of development.* New York: John Wiley & Sons, in preparation.

20. Harris, RJ: *A primer of multivariate statistics.* New York: Academic Press, 1975.

21. Heise, DR: *Causal analysis.* New York: John Wiley & Sons, 1975.

22. Hunt, JV, & Rhodes, L: Mental development of preterm infants during the first year. *Child Dev. 48,* 204–210, 1977.

23. Illsley, R: Early prediction of prenatal risk. *Proc. Royal Soc. Med., 59,* 181–184, 1966.

24. Klaus, MH, & Kennell, JH: *Maternal-infant bonding.* St. Louis: C. V. Mosby, 1976.

25. Knobloch, H, & Pasaminick, B: Prospective studies on the epidemiology of reproductive casualty: Methods, findings and some implications. *Merrill-Palmer Quarterly, 12,* 27–43, 1966.

26. Lewis, M: (Ed.), *Origins of intelligence.* New York: Plenum, 1976.

27. Lewis, M, & Goldberg, S: Perceptual-cognitive development in infancy: A generalized expectancy model as a function of the mother-infant interaction. *Merrill-Palmer Quarterly, 15,* 81–100, 1969.

28. McDonald, AD: Intelligence in children of very low birth weight. *Brit. J. Prev. Soc. Med., 18,* 59–74, 1964.

29. Olson, GM, & Sherman, T: Attention, learning and memory. In M. M. Haith & J. J. Compos (Eds.), *Carmichael's manual of child psychology: Infancy and the biology of development.* New York: John Wiley & Sons, in preparation.

30. Osofsky, JD (ED.): *Handbook of infant development.* New York: John Wiley & Sons, 1979.

31. Parke, RD, & Sawin, DB: Infant characteristics and behavior and elicitors of maternal and paternal responsivity in the newborn period. Paper presented at the meeting of the Society for Research in Child Development, Denver, April 1975.

32. Parmelee, AH, Jr., & Sigman, M: Development of visual behavior and neurological organization in pre-term and full-term infants. In A. D. Pick (Ed.), *Minnesota symposia on child psychology* (Vol. 10). Minneapolis: University of Minnesota Press, 1976.

33. Ploof, DL: Effect of temperament on maternal perception of young infants. Paper presented at the meeting of the Eastern Psychological Association, New York, April 1976.

34. Sameroff, AJ: Paper presented at the meeting of the ACP, Philadelphia, July 1974.

35. Sameroff, AJ, & Chandler, MJ: Reproductive risk and the continuum of caretaking casualty. In F. D. Horowitz (Ed.), *Review of child development research* (Vol. 4). Chicago: University of Chicago Press, 1975.

36. Sigman, M, & Parmelee, AH, Jr: Longitudinal evaluation of the high-risk infant. In T. Field (Ed.), *The high risk newborn.* Jamaica, N.Y.: Spectrum, in press.

37. Stevenson, MB, & Lamb, ME: The effects of social experience on cognitive competence and performance. In M. E. Lamb & L. R. Sherrod (Eds.), *Infant social cognition: Theoretical and empirical considerations.* Hillsdale, N.J.: Lawrence Erlbaum Associates, in press.

38. Stewart, AL, & Reynolds, EOR: Improved prognosis for infants of very low birthweight. *Pediatrics, 54,* 724–735, 1974.

39. Thomas, A, Chess, S, & Birch, HG: *Temperament and behavior disorders in children.* New York: New York University Press, 1968.

40. Thomas, A, Chess, S, Birch, HG, Hertzig, M, & Korn, S: *Behavioral individuality in early childhood.* New York: New York University Press, 1963.

41. Tulkin, SR, & Covitz, FE: Mother-infant interaction and intellectual functioning at age six. Paper presented at the meeting of the Society for Research in Child Development, Denver, April 1975.

42. Tulkin, SR, & Kagan, J: Mother-child interaction in the first year of life. *Child Dev. 43,* 31–41, 1972.

43. Yarrow, LJ, Rubenstein, JL, Pedersen, FA, & Jankowski, JJ: Dimensions of early stimulation and their differential effects on infant development, *Merrill-Palmer Quarterly, 18,* 205–218, 1972.

Chapter 5

DEVELOPMENTAL SEQUENCES IN INFANTS AT HIGH RISK FOR CENTRAL NERVOUS SYSTEM DYSFUNCTION

The Recovery Process in the First Year of Life

Suzann K. Campbell, Ph.D.
Irma J. Wilhelm, M.S.

INTRODUCTION

The attempt to understand any medical condition usually includes a description of the natural history of its evolution or resolution. Such a description is considered essential to prognosis, development of therapeutic measures, and assessment of the effectiveness of treatment. Yet when one searches the literature on central nervous system (CNS) dysfunction in children, only Paine et al.[37] appear to have followed the natural history of a large number of abnormal infants. Retrospective studies have, from the beginning when Little described cerebral palsy in an 1862 paper, emphasized the presence of a history of pre- and perinatal complications, including prematurity.[13,15] The presence of a number of abnormal neurological findings in the neonatal period,[13,41,56] abnormal tone and maintained primitive reflexes,[27,28,37] failure of development of the postural reflex mechanism and, sooner or later, delayed developmental milestones[5-8,28,37] are suggested as usual precursors or indicators of the diagnosis of CNS dysfunction, but few specific details and no longitudinal studies performed prospectively with frequent assessment of multiple dimensions of development can be found in the literature. Retrospective data on cerebral palsy can be seriously misleading because such studies include only children with poor outcome. We cannot ascertain from retrospective study of abnormal children how many infants may have manifested similar early symptoms and developmental deviance but later recovered fully or exhibited less serious sequelae.

Modern neonatal care has also altered the outlook for numerous categories of high-risk infants such that older studies are inadequate to describe the sequelae of perinatal events which earlier contributed to high mortality and morbidity rates, especially for those infants with low birth weight.[50] For example, prior to the advent of intensive care management of immature neonates, the incidence of intellectual and neurologic deficits in survivors ranged in numerous reports from 10 to 85% for infants at highest risk, including major neurologic defects in up to 28%.[21,50] Current figures for major neurologic deficits are 25% in survivors of severe birth asphyxia,[46] 8% of a similar group in another study,[16] 25% of infants with serious perinatal complications,[15] 17% of infants surviving severe idiopathic respiratory distress syndrome (IRDS),[30] 13% of infants with weight average for gestational age (AGA) but under 33 weeks gestational age (GA),[20] no infants with intrauterine growth retardation (IUGR),[34] and no infants experiencing a terminal episode of intrapartum asphyxia.[33] These rates were even more impressive when one realizes that many of these infants would not have survived a few years ago. In addition, some causes of serious neurological sequelae, such as rubella in the first trimester of pregnancy and erythroblastosis fetalis, have been significantly reduced, resulting in fewer numbers of handicapped children from these causes. In general, serious sequelae appear to result from the stress of experiencing multiple insults rather than from any single factor. For instance, Fitzhardinge[20] reports that many of the very young premature infants with serious sequelae also experienced severe birth asphyxia. Outcome in high-risk infants appears to be highly dependent on the quality of immediate attention to developing problems, and outcome remains better in infants born in hospitals with intensive care units than in infants transported to them after birth.[50] The large increases in numbers of infants surviving traumatic conditions in early life do not appear to have resulted in an increase in morbidity in terms of serious neurological handicap.[2,50] Amiel-Tison[1] has even shown a 3- to 4-week *acceleration* in neurological development in newborns subjected to the stress of prenatal placental function of a degree insufficient to produce IUGR.

Vulnerable infants still exist, however, and we cannot prognosticate successfully to long-term outcome from the continuum of perinatal casualty alone. A critical element in the ability of an infant to recover from early insult appears to be the ecological context in which s/he is nurtured.[45] Overall socioeconomic status (SES), the stability of the family, and the quality of mother-infant interaction have been shown in various studies to have powerful effects on amelioration or prevention of early deviance from the course of normal development, though none of these studies has specifically documented recovery from CNS dysfunction.[43,47,53,54] The mother's willingness to continue interaction with a "difficult" infant and the degree to which she avoids the permanent labeling of this child as deviant, the more opportunity the infant has to "self-right," compensate, or recover from early deviance.[45] The marvel of the human organism is the drive to function; if any way at all exists to accomplish the developmental tasks of childhood, any but the most grossly retarded appear to manage them. Lipsitt[32] suggests that infant imperturbability in the face of disturbing handling and "hedonistic receptivity," the ability to experience pleasure, may be two of the most important factors in infant temperament leading to successful amelioration of early deviant patterns. Most researchers now believe that both infant and caretaker make contributions to developmental outcome and that the interaction of the two must be taken into account in attempting to assess or predict the outcome of early less than optimal events.

In the literature on the effect of brain lesions on behavior, recovery is typically defined as return to normal or near-normal function following the initially disruptive effects of injury to the nervous system.[31] Such a definition is difficult to apply to the study of infants at risk for CNS dysfunction because one does not know, except in the most grossly defective infants: (1) when, or even if, an insult to the brain has actually occurred; (2) whether the insult has produced only transient, reversible dysfunction, or a permanent insult; (3) where the damage is; or (4) the potential for development of the infant *prior* to the insult. Also, in the developing organism, many behaviors are not yet present that might be affected by lesions in particular brain areas. Thus deficits may become apparent in individuals at different times during the early maturation of the nervous system, and longitudinal assessments may contribute to the study of brain-behavior correlations, especially when coupled with computerized tomographic studies to reveal damaged neural areas.

In summary, longitudinal prospective studies with frequent assessment of children at high risk for CNS dysfunction are needed to document the natural history of both recovery sequences and of permanent deviance in those children who do not recover. Such investigations must take into account the quality of the environment into which the children are born, as well as the temperament of the individual infant which will interact with his or her unique life events. This research will be useful for:

1) developing cumulative risk indices for neuromuscular development similar to those devised for cognitive

development by Parmelee et al.[38] and Field et al.[19] for preterm and IRDS or postmature infants, respectively;

2) identifying, through multiple assessments, the specific details of deficits common to children in whom outcome is poor;

3) establishing baseline data on the natural history of recovery against which the effectiveness of treatment may be compared;

4) informing parents about continuing risk status in individual children; and

5) developing theories regarding the nature of recovery that may be tested in experimental animal models of CNS dysfunction in infancy.

The study to be reported here is an initial attempt to assess a small group of children who are at high risk for CNS dysfunction on the basis of serious medical problems in the prenatal, perinatal, and early postnatal period, including the presence of several conditions or symptoms shown in the literature to be frequently related to poor neurological outcome.[13,35,41,56] The study involves longitudinal assessment at numerous points in the first year of life, beginning in the neonatal period, and using multiple measures, particularly of motor and neurologic functioning. Also included are assessments of cognitive and affective development and of the home environment. The results in the first seven high-risk infants studied for an entire year will be presented. No conclusions can yet be drawn from a study of only seven subjects, but, in addition to comparing our infants with other previously studied samples, this chapter will attempt to present the possibilities of such a continuing study and our speculations about the data currently available.

CONCEPTS BASIC TO THE STUDY

The design of our study is based on several concepts of infant development. Infant development takes place within the context of an infant-environment interaction which is unique for each individual. The infant brings into the world his or her own genetic potential and basic temperament style, but the environment is a powerful shaper of the individual's ability to achieve his or her potential in cognitive, affective, and motor development. In most of the studies that have been done, socio-economic status and all that it encompasses is the strongest single predictor of infant cognitive development, and the infant cannot be seen apart from the circumstances in which s/he is reared. We also see the development of the high-risk infant in a framework of the continuum of development wherein initial early insult results in the potential for severe limitation of developmental outcome but is not sufficient to predict final outcome without additional data collection of a cumulative nature. As more is known about delays, aberrant patterns, and the quality of the environmental transactions in which the infant participated, the better one should be able to predict status at one or two years of age. We are interested in looking at the value of cumulative data from prenatal factors on into the assessment of multiple developmental functions for predicting recovery or nonrecovery from early traumatic medical events.

STUDY DESIGN

Sample Selection and Assignment

A group of 20 very high-risk and a group of 10 low-risk infants are being identified using the Problem Oriented Perinatal Risk Assessment System (POPRAS) of Hobel.[25] This system includes assessment of prenatal, intrapartum, and neonatal risk factors resulting in a total score which is used medically (if $\geq$ 10) to determine the need for special medical attention, but in our study is used to determine degree of potential insult to the brain on the basis of large numbers of serious conditions. To be designated very high risk in this study, an infant must achieve a score of 50 or more on the POPRAS *and* have at least *four* of the following symptoms or conditions: (1) 5-minute

Apgar score less than or equal to 5; (2) asphyxia; (3) need for resuscitation at birth; (4) repeated periods of apnea; (5) persistent cyanosis, (6) hyperbilirubinemia necessitating transfusion; (7) generalized sepsis; (8) meningitis; (9) positive TORCH (Toxoplasmosis, Rubella, Cytomegalic inclusion disese, Herpes) or (10) syphilis; (11) CNS depression lasting more than 24 hours; (12) seizures; (13) jitteriness or hyperactivity not associated with a metabolic imbalance; (14) CNS bleeds or infarcts; and (15) skull fractures. Infants with genetic disorders or birth defects are excluded from consideration. To be a low-risk control subject, an infant must have a POPRAS score of less than 10. Infants are recruited into the study using methods approved by the School of Medicine Committee on the Protection of the Rights of Human Subjects with full information about the neonatal assessments to be performed and the repeated tests to be administered during the first 12 months of life (with adjustments for premature birth).

Infants are divided into three groups for assessment (Figure 5–1). Ten infants comprise a high-risk group to be evaluated at monthly intervals; 10 infants who are low-risk are matched to these infants on the basis of sex, race, and family socioeconomic status; and 10 high-risk infants are assessed at quarterly intervals. Assignment to monthly or quarterly high-risk groups is at random.

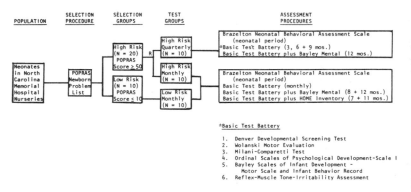

Figure 5–1

Neonatal Assessment

Following recruitment, the infants are assessed using the Brazelton Neonatal Behavioral Assessment Scale[10,48] as soon as they are medically stable (off oxygen and on oral feedings) and then again just prior to discharge from the hospital or near to term-equivalent age for prematurely born infants. This examination results in an infant profile reflecting the baby's ability to interact with events and objects presented during the course of the examination, control motoric processes, and maintain an organized state, both physiologically and behaviorally.

Developmental Assessments

Developmental assessments are then carried out at monthly or quarterly intervals until the infants reach 12-months postconceptional age. We also hope to continue following these infants at yearly intervals following the completion of their participation in the current study. The assessments used for this battery reflect the developmental areas of interest, assess the home environment, include both comprehensive and screening tests, both highly objective and more subjective, and are found frequently in the literature of child development and physical therapy so that comparisons with the work of others can be made.

In defining recovery, one must study both the attainment of goals by the subject, i.e. developmental milestones, and the *means* by which these goals are achieved, i.e. the quality of movement patterns, postural tone and reflexes, and the compensatory mechanisms which are activated by the persistent organism. Many valid and reliable instruments are available for the assessment of developmental milestones which are routinely used in studies found in the literature on other types of infant populations. But almost none of these studies uses assessments aimed at tapping the means to achievement of motor developmental goals, for the obvious reasons that few such tools exist. Neither clinical nor research tools are available for assessing quality of postural tone and movement across the first year of life and which are quantitative and investigated with respect to reliability and validity. Our choice of measures will, then, be most conducive to studying the sequence of developmental milestone acquisition during the first year of life.

Cognitive Development

Cognitive development is assessed at 8 and 12 months with the Mental Scale of the Bayley Scales of Infant Development (BSID)[3] and monthly or quarterly with the scale for The Development of Visual Pursuit and the Permanence of Objects from the Ordinal Scales of Infant Psychological Development.[52] The BSID Mental Scale is a well-standardized test designed to assess (1) sensory-perceptual abilities; (2) early acquisition of memory, learning, problem solving, and generalization; and (3) initiation of vocalization and verbal communication. Results can be expressed as a standard score, the Mental Developmental Index (MDI), for comparison with a normative group mean of 100 and standard deviation (SD) of 16. The Ordinal Scales are based on the work of Piaget;[39,40] the scale used in this study evaluates the infant's ability to follow objects visually and to search for objects that are hidden in sequentially more complex ways.

Affective Development

After each test session, the Infant Behavior Record (IBR) of the BSID[3] is scored to assess affective behavior, including attention, activity, muscular tension, reactivity, social orientation, and goal directedness.

Motor and Reflex Development

Several assessments of motor development are included in order to allow comparisons among them. They include: the

Motor Scale of the BSID,[3] the Wolánski Motor Evaluation,[55] and the Milani-Comparetti Developmental Examination.[36]

The BSID Motor Scale assesses gross and fine motor milestones and coordination. Results can be expressed as a standard score, the Psychomotor Developmental Index (PDI), with a normative mean of 100 and SD of 16.

The Wolánski Motor Evaluation is a standardized screening test of gross motor development normed on 212 Polish children 3 to 13 months old. Development in four areas is assessed: head and trunk movements, sitting, standing, and locomotion. Scores are compared with a developmental grid of percentiles for normal Polish male or female children.

The Milani-Comparetti Developmental Examination is a screening tool for assessment of motor milestones and reflexes in children zero to two years. This test was developed after observation of the temporal relationship between motor milestones and reflex behaviors in "several hundred babies seen for long periods" (*personal communication,* Milani-Comparetti, 1969). No standardized scoring system is provided.

In addition to the reflex assessments included in the Milani-Comparetti tool, a battery of quantitative reflex items is scored. Rating scales used were taken from the work of Beintema,[4] Brazelton,[10] Carter and Campbell,[12] Cupps et al.,[14] Graham,[24] Prechtl,[41] Prechtl and Beintema,[42] Rosenblith,[44] and Twitchell;[51] additional rating scales were developed and pretested by Donatelle.[17]

Assessment of the Environment

The quality of the home environment is assessed at 7 and 11 months of age using the Home Observation for Measurement of the Environment (HOME) Inventory.[11,18] The inventory is scored from a parent interview and observation of mother-infant interaction and measures six factors related to the quality of the home environment: emotional and verbal responsivity of the mother, avoidance of restriction and punishment, organization of the environment, provision of appropriate play materials, maternal involvement with the child, and opportunities for variety in the daily routine.

In addition to the tests described, the Denver Developmental Screening Test (DDST) is scored at each visit.[22,23] The DDST is a widely used screening test of overall development which was standardized and normed on 1,036 Denver children aged zero to six years. Areas of behavior assessed include: personal-social, fine motor and adaptive, language, and gross motor. Results are expressed based on the number of items failed (delays) which were passed by 90% of the normative group at that particular age. Outcome is expressed only as normal, abnormal, or questionable; no numerical scores are obtainable.

While working at the Division of Physical Therapy as a postdoctoral fellow, Dr. Janet Donatelle developed the reflex items and a master test, encompassing most of the items from the standardized motor and reflex tests into a compact checklist which contains no information about ages at which the items should be passed. The master test both increased efficiency and helped to control tester bias toward expected infant performance. A new checklist is used each time the child is assessed to eliminate all information about previous performance. The master test can be administered in 45 minutes. When either the BSID Mental Scale or HOME is added, the testing takes about 90 minutes. Dr. Donatelle also developed a pictorial diary to be completed by the parents to fill in details about items and quality of movement not available on the test battery and to provide the parents with a record of their child's first year that they could keep after the study was over. Examples of diary pictures can be found in Appendix A.

RESULTS

The experiences of the seven children recruited between July and December 1977 will first be presented, outlining maternal and neonatal medical and social data, results of newborn testing, and events taking place in the family during the course of the study that may have an impact on the course of infant development. Next, group outcome will be compared with data obtained in other studies of high-risk infants. Finally, individual performance on quarterly standardized motor and cognitive tests and on selected reflexes will be presented. The home assessment, affective development, and parent diaries are not discussed.

Selection of infants on the basis of medical symptoms results in a heterogeneous group on numerous variables. Common to our group, however, are evidences of difficulty at birth expressed in need for resuscitation and low Apgar scores, worrisome results on at least one neonatal exam, and low SES. Tables 5–1, 5–2, and 5–3 provide a summary of parental factors, neonatal factors, and medical problems, respectively. The details of individual case histories can be found in Appendix B.

Table 5–1   Parental Factors

Subject no.	Race	Marital status	Age of mother	Mother's education	Mother's occupation	Father's occupation
002	B	M/Sep.	16	11	HS student	Maintenance man
003	B	U	17	11	HS student	City worker
004	W	M	24	10	Millworker	Maintenance man
005	W	M	29	9	Waitress	Electrician
006	B	U	16	10	HS student	Millworker
007	W	M/Sep.	18	12	Housewife	Foreman
008	W	M	31	?	Housewife	Truckdriver

Group Outcome

Table 5–4 presents a comparison of performance at 6 and 12 months on the PDI and at 12 months on the MDI to that of other high-risk infants studied in recent years. Our sample includes one infant (02) who is definitely abnormal (spastic quadriplegic with microcephaly), one infant (06) still at risk at one year of age (PDI and MDI both between −1 and −2 SD below the mean), and five infants considered within normal limits for overall development at one year (both PDI and MDI between −1 and +1 SD from the mean). It is interesting to note that our two poor outcomes are in term male infants while the presumed normals are preterm males or term females. Our sample means are lower than all but the RDS group of premature infants, but like all the other groups studied, PDIs at six months are slightly higher than can be expected for the same group of children at 12 months. In each study, mean MDI is higher than mean PDI at the same age.

Performance on Standardized Tests

Figure 5–2 presents the BSID Motor Scale standard score (PDI) for each subject at 3, 6, 9, and 12 months (ages adjusted for prematurity for infants 03, 04, and 05 who were born before term). At all ages, including the 3-month assessment, the ab-

Table 5–2   Neonatal Factors

Subject no.	In/ Outborn	Sex	EGA (wks.)	Birth wgt. (g)	Wgt./ GA	Apgar scores 1, 5 min.	Resuscitation
002	O	M	38	3290	AGA	5, 6	No record of this
003	I	M	30	1140	AGA	1, 2	Intub., bag, O_2
004	I	M	35	1450	SGA	6, 9	O_2
005	I	M	33	1720	AGA	4, 9	Mask, bag
006	O	M	40	3430	AGA	1, 5	Yes, but 12 mins. to breathe
007	O	F	40	3920	AGA	2, ?	Bag, O_2, but 10–12 min. to breathe
008	O	F	40	3680	AGA	3, 7	O_2, suction

Table 5-3 Medical Problems

Subject no.	Prenatal problems	Intrapartum problems	Cardio-pulmonary problems	Metabolic problems	Hematological problems	Neurological problems	Days in hospital
002	Minor problems only	Fetal bradycardia, O_2 given to mother	Apnea and bradycardia (CPAP), mild respiratory distress (TTNB)	Persistent metabolic acidosis	Anemia	Subarachnoid hemorrhage, CNS depression, seizures, rigidity/opisthotonos	21, NICU-4 ICN-17
003	Gonorrhea, minor problems	PROM, amnionitis, premature labor, fetal bradycardia	Apnea and bradycardia, two cardio-pulmonary arrests, GC pneumonia, persistent cyanosis, patent ductus arteriosis	Persistent metabolic acidosis, hypocalcemia	Anemia, hyperbilirubinemia (phototherapy)	Hypothermia	48, NICU-31 ICN-17
004	Severe preeclampsia, Rh neg. and minor problems	Induced premature labor, PROM, fetal bradycardia	Heart murmur	Late metabolic acidosis	Hyperbilirubinemia (exchange transfusion and phototherapy), polycythemia	Jittery/hyperactive	13, NICU-7 ICN-6
005	Rh neg., sensitized, intrauterine transfusion. Previous infant: C/S for CPD, Rh incompatibility, died 8 mos—meningitis	Transverse lie C/S delivery	Severe RDS (CPAP, ventilator), mild apnea and bradycardia, persistent cyanosis, patent ductus arteriosus	Persistent metabolic acidosis, hypocalcemia	Anemia, hyperbilirubinemia (two exchange transfusions and phototherapy)	Jittery/hyperactive, hypothermia	35, NICU-10 ICN-25
006	Active TB—mother and grandmother	Scanty record— none recorded	Mild apnea and bradycardia, small VSD	Hypoglycemia	None	Seizures, CNS depression, cerebral edema, and possible infarcts, hypothermia	23, NICU-6 ICN-17
007	Scanty records— minor problems	Transverse lie, forceps rotation, meconium-stained fluid (light), heavy medication (Demerol 225 mg.)	None	None	Anemia	IC hemorrhage, Jittery/hyperactive	13, NICU-11 ICN-2
008	Scanty record— mild preeclampsia	Fetal bradycardia, meconium-stained fluid (heavy)	Meconium aspiration, pneumothorax, pneumomediastinum, persistent cyanosis, persistent fetal circulation	Hypocalcemia, hyponatremia	None	Seizures, hypotonia	17 in NICU

Table 5–4   Comparison of Bayley Scales Outcome in
Studies of High-Risk Infants

Study	Subjects	6-Mo. PDI		12-Mo. PDI		12-Mo. MDI	
		$\bar{X}$	SD	$\bar{X}$	SD	$\bar{X}$	SD
Campbell and Wilhelm, 1979	7 infants at high risk for CNS dysfunction	89.57 (96.17)	24.53 (21.00)	86.57 (92.67)	18.71 (13.63)	94.86 (102.33)	23.15 (17.02)
Field et al, 1978 19	46 preterms with RDS			80.11*	—	89.91*	—
Low et al, 1978A 33	42 infants with intrapartum fetal asphyxia	111.3	17.1	98.2	13.5	108.1	13.5
Low et al, 1978B 34	86 IUGR infants	119.5 [99.7*]	—	99.5* [88.2]	—	112.3* [99.6*]	—
Tilford, 1976 49	20 "normal" pre-term infants					104.03	19.03

( ) Statistics recalculated omitting one child with diagnosed cerebral palsy.
[ ] Statistics recalculated on subgroup with significant asphyxia.
*Significant difference between experimental group and normal full-term controls or other comparison group.

normal child (02) is clearly outside the range of normal scores. Only the Bayley Motor Scale clearly shows his abnormal performance this early. Subject 06, though gaining new motor milestones each time, fell further below average performance on each successive test through 9 months, but then dramatically improved on the 12-month assessment. The fact that this child was in one foster home until shortly before the 6-month assessment and then in a second foster home until shortly before the 9-month assessment at which time he went to his own home may be highly significant. For the other children, who were doing well at 1 year, the frequency of higher performance at 6 and 9 months which is not maintained at one year is interesting to note. Though not enough data are available to interpret the meaning of this, of clinical importance is the fact that standard scores for individuals changed as much as two standard deviations over repeated testing during the first year. Those children who remain below average at one year are not yet walking alone although all except 02 and 06 were cruising around furniture holding on with one hand or walking with one hand held. Subject 06 was cruising sideways along furniture.

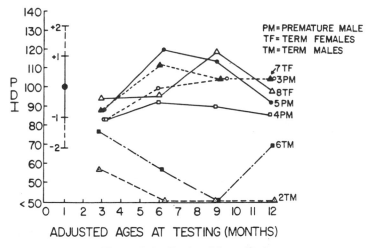

Figure 5–2 Bayley Motor Scale

Figure 5–3 illustrates the importance of adjusting for prematurity. When PDIs are calculated for chronological age, all three premature infants appear to be performing in the below average range throughout the entire first year. In contrast to the subjects doing poorly throughout the first year, however, PDIs do gradually rise for each premature subject. This reflects the fact that scores for the original standardization sample showed increasing variance after six months of age so that performing two months below age level at 3 months is a more unique event than performing two months below age level at 12 months. For example, according to Hunt and Rhodes,[26] an infant who consistently scores 2 months below chronological age from age 3 months to 15 months will show an MDI that increases from 61 to 80.

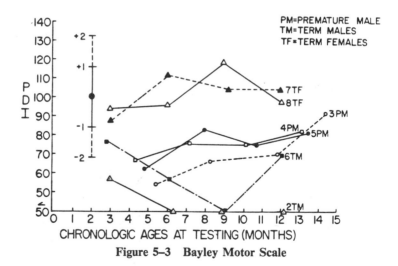

Figure 5–3   Bayley Motor Scale

On the Object Permanence Scale (Figure 5–4), all subjects except 02 showed gradually increasing ability to search for hidden objects, but considerable variability among subjects was present at 1 year. The best performer, 03, was able to follow successive invisible displacements under three screens, while subjects 04 and 06 were at the level of pulling a screen off a completely hidden object in two or three different places. The abnormal child, 02, actually showed regression on this test. At 3 months, he visually followed objects 180 degrees, but by 6 months, his lack of head control and increasingly strong asymmetrical tonic neck reflex did not permit following an object across the midline.

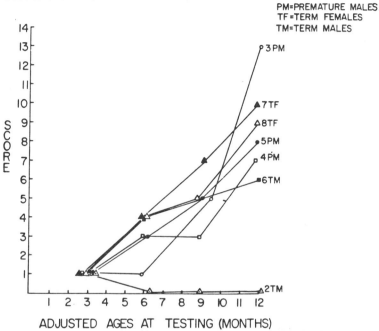

Figure 5–4   Hunt-Užgiris: Scale I—Object Permanence

The rankings of the individual subjects on the Object Permanence Scale are identical to those on the BSID Motor Scale except that subjects 03 and 07 had exactly the same PDIs (Table 5–5). The very high performance on the Object Permanence Scale of subject 03 may reflect an influence of experience. Subject 03 was the only very young premature in the study and was already more than 14 months old at the last test session. The rankings are *not* the same as the MDIs, perhaps reflecting

an important motor component in the Object Permanence Scale
not present in the BSID Mental Scale.

Table 5–5   Individual Rankings on Object Permanence (OP)
Scale, Bayley Motor (PDI), and Bayley Mental (MDI) Scales
at 12 Months Postconceptional Age*

	OP		PDI		MDI	
Subject	Rank	(Score)	Rank	(Score)	Rank	(Score)
3PM	1	(13)	1.5	(105)	2	(115)
7TF	2	(10)	1.5	(105)	1	(119)
8TF	3	(9)	3	(98)	4	(112)
5PM	4	(8)	4	(92)	5	(89)
4PM	5	(7)	5	(86)	3	(103)
6TM	6	(6)	6	(70)	6	(75)
2TM	7	(0)	7	(50)	7	(50)

*r_s = .99 p < .01 (two tailed test) (OP, PDI); r_s = .86 p < .05 (two tailed test)
(OP, MDI); r_s = .88 p < .02 (two tailed test) (PDI, MDI).

In Figure 5–5, raw score performance of the subjects is
illustrated against the Wolánski examination grids. The central
hatched area represents the average range of performance (35th
to 65th percentiles) for the Polish standardization sample, while
the outermost solid lines represent the 5th and 95th percentiles.
As in the Bayley scales, group variance increases with age.
Performance of our sample on the Wolánski scale is similar to
that on the Bayley Motor Scale with performance of children
with good outcome falling within the average range at 6 months
but typically slightly below the mean at 9 and 12 months. The
rankings of the individual children are essentially the same as
on the Bayley Motor Scales and on the Object Permanence
Scale.

The two children with poor outcome at 12 months have
scores of 0, reflecting poor head and trunk control, at 3 months,
but are clearly far outside the norms and different from the rest
of the sample only at the 6-month assessment. Subject 06 sneaks
above the 5th percentile at 12 months, thus showing his marked
improvement at the last testing.

Figure 5–6 presents the Wolánski data in a slightly different way. Here adjusted age (AA) at testing is plotted against the motor development age (MDA) obtained by finding the age for which the subject's obtained score would be at the 50th percentile. If AA = MDA, the points would fall along the solid line on the graph. Again, in the good outcome group, generally above average performance is found up to 9 months with all subjects falling below the mean at 12 months. This method of graphing results gives a better picture of the gradually decelerating rate of development of subject 06 before his apparent recovery at 12 months. Both methods show an actual decrease in performance in subject 02 which is reflected in Bayley raw

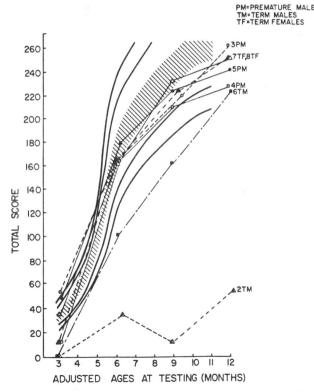

Figure 5–5   Wolánski Evaluation of Motor Development

scores, but not standard scores since these are not calculated when below 50. Other scores for this subject at the 9-month session, with one exception, were also depressed relative to 6-and 12-month performance. No specific explanation can be given, but this infant was on phenobarbitol and drug-level changes are one possible cause.

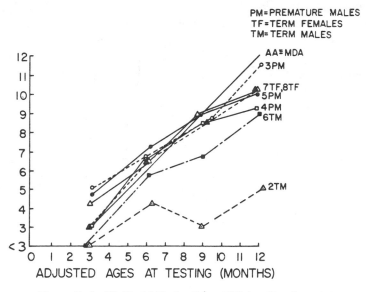

Figure 5–6   Wolánski Evaluation of Motor Development: Motor Development Age (MDA)

Figure 5–7 illustrates the gross motor development on the Wolánski evaluation for the two monthly subjects who have been followed for 1 year. Both show the apparent slowing of developmental rate beginning around 9 months, but both are walking independently at 1 year. Subject 03, a premature male, demonstrates the high performance others have reported in premature infants during the 2- to 4-month period.[9] This apparent acceleration seems to be due to the relative dominance of extensor over flexor tone seen in premature infants during this period and does not appear to be indicative of later superior performance.

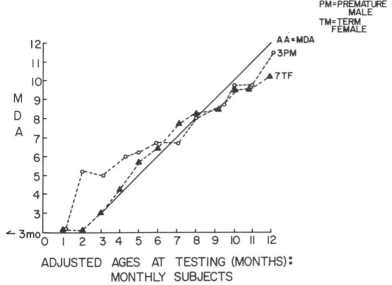

Figure 5–7 Wolánski Evaluation of Motor Development: Motor Development Age (MDA)

A graph of the results on the Denver Developmental Screening Test (Figure 5–8) illustrates the strengths and the weaknesses of a screening test. The DDST identifies the abnormal child as "questionable" (and therefore in need of further testing) as early as 3 months and as "abnormal" by 6 months. All of the other children, including subject 06, identified as still at risk on other tests, achieve normal scores throughout the first year. Even if one does not adjust for prematurity, only one of the three premature infants ever received an abnormal score, subject 05 at 3 months. By 6 or 9 months, all premature infants received normal scores even without adjusting for early birth.

Because no standard scoring scheme exists for assessing results on the Milani-Comparetti Developmental Examination, we decided to count number of delayed behaviors and number of aberrant evoked responses, i.e., primitive reflexes present that should not be, or more advanced responses not yet demonstrated that were age-appropriate. Delay was assessed relative to the age line drawn on the graph at the child's adjusted age.

Figure 5–9 shows the number of delays in spontaneous behaviors found with this method. All children show one or more delays throughout the first year. The trend to 9 months appeared to show gradually decreasing numbers of delays, or perhaps recovery. At 12 months, however, the increasingly difficult tasks against gravity faced by the children seem to present a large hurdle.

Unlike other tests, the charting of aberrant evoked responses (Figure 5–10) clearly shows the increasingly abnormal reflex development of the child with cerebral palsy; however, he is not notably different from the other children at 3 months when only primitive reflexes are assessed. As primitive reflexes fail to be overcome by voluntary activity, and protective, righting, and equilibrium responses do not develop, his number of aberrant items rise dramatically. The large number of aberrant responses shown by the other children should also be noted,

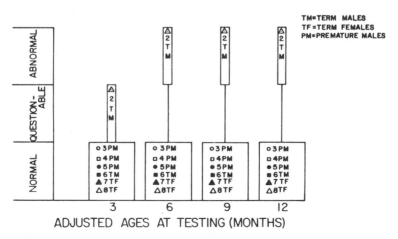

Figure 5–8   Denver Developmental Screening Test

however, since many showed at least vestiges of retained primitive reflexes for many months. Subject 06 shows the second highest score at 9 months, reflecting mostly delayed development of higher level reflexes rather than retention of many primitive responses. At 12 months, he does not appear to be different from the children who are doing well which is reflective of what is probably generally delayed performance rather than clearly evident CNS dysfunction which would be expressed in abnormal patterns of posture and movement. He did show poor trunk posture in sitting at 1 year, but otherwise no notably abnormal quality of movement. We do, however, consider him still at risk for CNS dysfunction as well as for mental and motor retardation.

Performance on Selected Reflex Items

Of the many reflexes tested, only a few will be illustrated here. The rating scales for each can be found in Appendix C. Although exaggerated and prolonged appearance of primitive

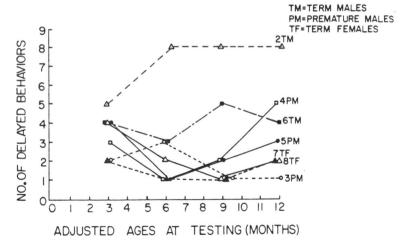

Figure 5–9   Milani-Comparetti Test: Spontaneous Behaviors

reflexes is apparent in the abnormal child, major differences between his performance and that of the other children are not obvious until the 6-month test. As noted before, some of his reflexes were also markedly different at 9 months than at either 6 or 12 months. The most consistent and interesting early differences are found in the emerging righting reflexes.

Figure 5–11 illustrates the relatively precocious, though asymmetrical, head righting (holding head in line with body as tipped) of subject 02 at 3 months, but then only weak attempts at later test sessions. At 6 months and 9 months, subject 06 shows relatively poor performance compared with other children and only demonstrates consistently good head righting at 12 months. Most other children (the very young premature 03 is the exception) show perfect head righting responses in all directions by 6 months.

Body righting when one leg is rolled over the other in a supine position (Figure 5–12) shows a similar but later pattern

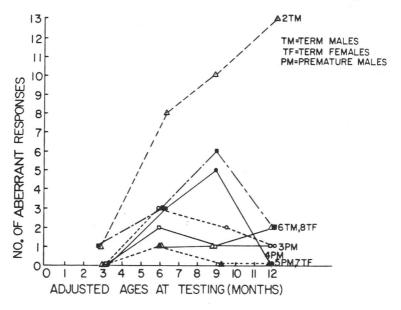

Figure 5–10   Milani-Comparetti Test: Evoked Responses

of development for the group. Even at 12 months, the abnormal child only rolls to prone after a long latency while most of the other children are already able to voluntarily inhibit the reflex response by counterrotating the upper trunk.

On the Landau reaction (Figure 5–13), subject 02 shows consistently poor performance but the differences are not as remarkable as for the righting reactions. The fact that subjects 02, 04, and 06, the poorest performers on the BSID Motor Scale at 12 months, have the poorest Landau responses at 9 months is interesting. Each of these infants (and subjects 05 and 08) were not walking independently at 1 year.

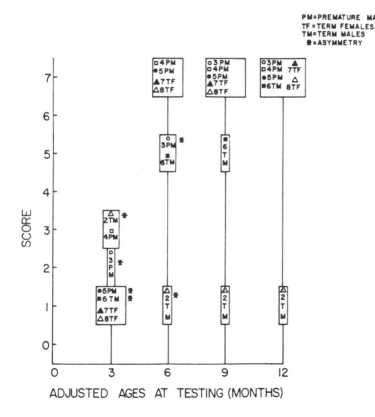

Figure 5–11   Head Righting in Space

The primitive reflexes were maintained for long periods of time in many of the children in our sample. For example, the asymmetrical tonic neck reflex (Figure 5–14) was observed upon passive or active neck rotation at 6 months in five of the seven children (subjects 05 and 07 showed partial overt posturing during active head rotation not shown in the Figure 5–14 graph of passive elicitation). However, only the two subjects with poorest outcome demonstrated overt, full-blown, though not obligatory, postures at the 6-month testing. By 9 months, the abnormal child has not changed while all other children show no response to passive neck rotation.

The Moro response data (Figure 5–15) are interesting in that only the premature infants show a reaction at 6 months. The abnormal child had increased muscle tone that proba-

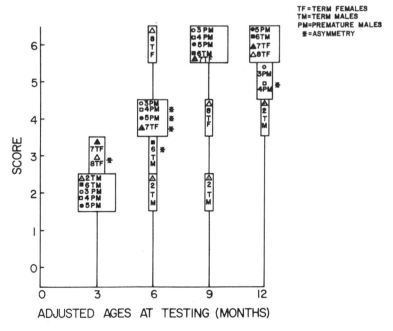

Figure 5–12   Body Righting on the Body

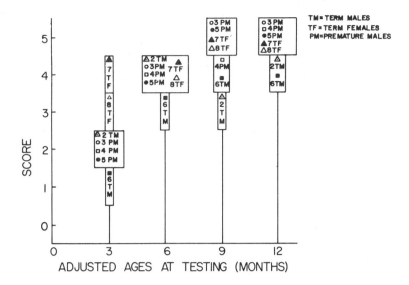

Figure 5–13   Landau Reaction

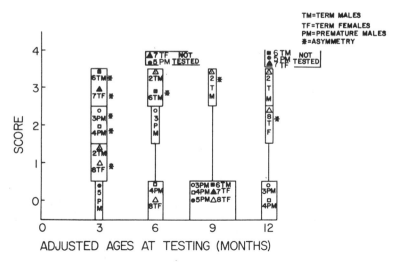

Figure 5–14   Asymmetrical Tonic Neck Reflex—Passive

bly prohibited obtaining enough head movement to elicit a full response except at the 9-month test session when he gave the overall impression of depressed performance but exhibited active Moro and asymmetrical tonic neck reflex responses.

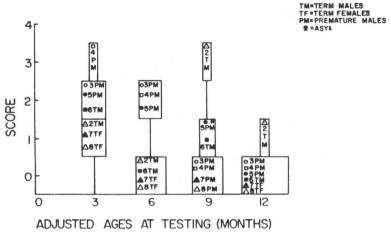

Figure 5–15   Moro Response

The Galant response (Figure 5–16) was maintained across much of the first year for most of our sample, including a number of children with excellent outcome. Considerable variability appears to exist for individual children from one test session to the next, suggesting a possible problem with administering a standard stimulus across repeated tests since precise pressure and placement are difficult to control when using digital stimulation.

Palmar grasp (Figure 5–17) decreased gradually for all children across the first year but was still present at 9 months in two children with good outcome. One of these children was very premature. The abnormal child continues to show a palmar grasp at 12 months after having only a slight reflex response at 9 months.

The maintained primitive reflexes exhibited by the subjects in our study coexist with overall muscle tone that is higher than the BSID mode for muscle tension in the first year (Figure 5–18). Except at 6 months, most infants were rated to have higher muscle tone than the modal child in the standardization sample. The scores received by all of the children with good outcome, however, were in a range suggesting that high tone was only occasionally, not continually, present. Both children with poor outcomes were consistently ranked as having more increased tone than the others in the sample. Subject 06 exhibited increased tone up to half the time while the abnormal subject, 02, was always outside the range of normal with no ability to achieve a relaxed state even momentarily during a testing situation.

DISCUSSION

Of seven children selected for the presence of serious medical problems in the neonatal period, at 1 year of adjusted age

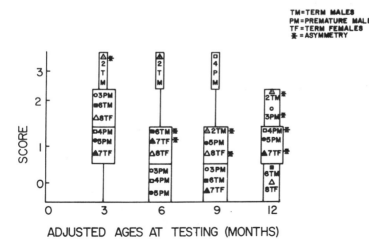

Figure 5–16   Incurvation of the Trunk (Galant's Response)

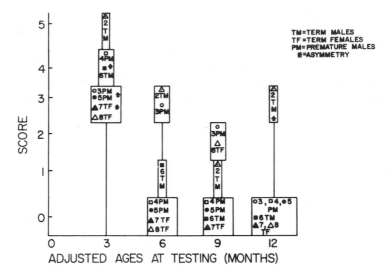

Figure 5–17   Palmar Grasp

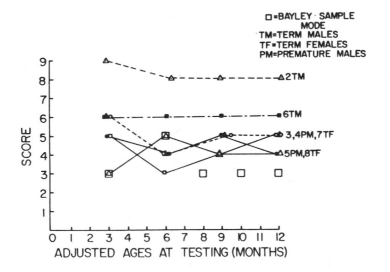

Figure 5–18   Bayley Scales: Infant Behavior Record
#6—Tension

one has cerebral palsy with inability to roll or sit, one is functioning in the below average range on both cognitive and motor tests but does not have evidence of significant problems with quality of movement, and five are functioning within the average range on mental and motor, including reflex, assessments. The two subjects with poorest outcome were transported in after delivery elsewhere (as were two subjects with excellent outcome) and both experienced disruptive home conditions, one (02) a parental separation between 9 and 12 months, the other (06) three different primary caretakers during the first year. All three of the premature infants performed within the average range at 1 year, with the most premature being among the top performers despite considerable delay in suppressing primitive reflexes. Although too little data exist at present to make definitive conclusions, performance of these children appears to be comparable to other groups that have been studied. More variance seems to be present but we cannot yet tell whether this is related to small sample size or the heterogeneity of the sample. Our results do appear to be a compliment to the modern neonatal intensive care practiced at North Carolina Memorial Hospital (NCMH), where medical problems received prompt attention from NCMH nursing and house staff, at least after transfer to their care. Even these minimal results point up the inability to predict outcome successfully from only early medical data, but we hope that continued work with repeated assessments can lead to cumulative risk indices for assessing degree of continuing risk for poor developmental outcome in the first year. Further investigation is also needed to assess outcome in terms of less severe problems identifiable only after one year of age.

Working Hypotheses

The following hypotheses are presented for future consideration based on our currently available data:

1.   Many infants can recover from serious insult or illness

in the prenatal, intrapartum, or neonatal periods with those showing average performance on standardized developmental tests at 12 months having already achieved that level of performance by 3 months.

2. Infants with less than optimal performance at 12 months already show deficits on the BSID Motor Scale at 3 months and lack adequate head righting in space at 6 months and body righting (rotation) at 9 months.

3. Primitive reflexes and increased tone may be evident for long periods of time in high-risk infants but may not be related to motor outcome at 12 months unless very strong or very delayed in resolving.

According to the Paine et al.[37] studies of primitive reflexes in 66 normal children:

1. Twenty percent have a Moro response at 5 months, none at 6 months.

2. Asymmetrical tonic neck reflex was found in none at 7 months.

3. Neck righting (defined as rolling with trunk rotation, equivalent to our score of 4 or 5) was present in all by 10 months.

4. Landau was complete (including concave spine) in all by 10 months.

5. Pincer grasp was present in all by 12 months.

By contrast, in our five high-risk children with good outcome:

1. Three (all premature infants tested at adjusted ages) had a Moro response at 6 months.

2. Three showed an ATNR at 6 months.

3. All achieved neck righting as defined by Paine et al.[37]

by 6 months. (Neither child with poor outcome achieved this milestone at 6 months.)

4. Four of five achieved a full Landau at 9 months.
5. Neat pincer grasp (Bayley Motor #41) was present at 12 months in four of five. The other child had achieved inferior pincer grasp (Bayley Motor #35).

As indicated above, the appropriate appearance of motor milestones and emerging postural reactions in high-risk infants may be more important predictors than the failure to suppress primitive reflexes as early as this is accomplished by low-risk children. The presence of significant primitive reflex activity, however, is certainly of use in differentiating children with delayed development from those with CNS dysfunction and is essential for planning management of developmental problems.

Theories of Recovery

Discussions of the effects of brain lesions in infancy usually include the assumption that the infant brain is more plastic than that of the adult, i.e., that a lesion in an infant produces less permanent deficit than the same lesion in the adult organism.[29] This assumption is based on the finding that the *acute* effects of lesions in the infant are never as devastating as those in adults, but Johnson and Almli, in a review of the literature on this question fail to find support for differences in the long-term outcome. The idea that significant neural reorganization can occur in the immature dynamic brain is, therefore, coming under increasing scrutiny. There certainly is evidence that neural reorganization can occur, but it usually results in *abnormal* patterns, not recovery of the original function. Johnson and Almli[29] quote Alfred Binet as having said, "Tell me what you are looking for and I will tell you what you will find." They suggest that we have looked for enhanced recovery in infants and have found it! New data also suggest that the brain is far more susceptible to permanent damage from early nutritional, hormonal, and environmental deprivation influences than to damage from single insults. This is probably true because growth of the whole brain is retarded by such continuing deprivation whereas single insults may result in more circumscribed lesions. No studies to date have been specifically designed to show whether alternative behavioral strategies are developed to deal with the functional problems caused by brain lesions and how much so-called recovery in both adults and infants is really compensation. To develop appropriate studies of recovery from brain dysfunction, the various theories current in the experimental literature on animals must be considered in order to design studies from a theoretical rather than empirical base.

Theories of recovery include von Monakow's diaschisis theory, neural redundancy or substitution hypotheses, vicariation or equipotentiality, regeneration, collateral sprouting, denervation supersensitivity, and behavioral strategy change or compensation.[29] They are not necessarily mutually exclusive as neural mechanisms may operate differentially throughout the life span of an organism or in the presence of various environmental conditions. Each of these theories will be briefly discussed.

(1)   Diaschisis is an acute functional shock occurring after a lesion to the nervous system. Its causes are not totally known, but appear to include temporary disturbance of areas not directly affected by the lesion as a result of vascular disturbances, edema, and loss of regulation of areas connected to the damaged areas. Restitution, or true recovery, of function can be expected as vascular disturbances and edema subside, but recovery from the loss of inputs to distant structures must be explained in terms of one of the other theories unless the damaged area is only partially destroyed by the lesion. Diaschisis is believed to be least disruptive to functioning in the infant and may be primarily responsible for the apparently

greater recovery of function after lesions in the infant when compared with the adult.

(2) Neural redundancy or substitution theory postulates that when one area of the brain is damaged, another area can take over the functions of the former. Performance of the function need not necessarily be accomplished in the identical manner to that of the normally used system, but it must perform the same job. Evidence suggests that the ability of other systems to take over is more limited when damage occurs to highly topographically organized areas,[27] such as the motor cortex and subcortical areas, whereas loosely coupled areas like association cortex can demonstrate much recovery, at least early in development. Damage to areas like association cortex early in life, before they are committed to specific functions, may however, result in the *delayed* appearance of deficits when that area should become committed to a function and no other "plastic" area remains uncommitted to assume its usual function. The development of fine motor control, a function normally delayed until the second half of the first year of life in human infants, may also be such a system wherein cortical areas no longer remain available to take over for the motor cortex at the time that fine motor skills should be developing.

(3) Equipotentiality is closely related to the idea of redundancy but refers to neurons in a given region of the brain possessing the capability to assume all of the normal function of a certain region when part of it is destroyed. Thus the ability to recover from a lesion is seen under this theory to be more related to the size of the lesion than to the specific placement of the lesion in a given locus.[31]

(4) Regeneration implies the reestablishment of the original connections leading, when successful, to total res-

titution of function. Regeneration is quite successful in the peripheral nervous system, but to date has been difficult to demonstrate in the CNS. Why such differences should occur is not totally clear, but extensive scarring preventing reestablishment of the complex connectivity in the CNS is implicated.[31]

(5) Collateral sprouting refers to the idea that undamaged neurons may develop sprouts forming new connections or synapses with neurons that have been deprived of their normal connections due to damage of systems afferent to them. Such sprouts have been observed experimentally and may be a major occurrence in spinal cord lesions. They frequently are responsible for the development of new function, but it is usually abnormal. Sprouting then may be seen as essentially maladaptive for the organism and, therefore, actually detrimental to recovery.

(6) Denervation supersensitivity refers to the phenomenon of increased postsynaptic responsiveness to neurotransmitter substances after input to a neural area has been destroyed.[31] Thus compensation or apparent functional recovery of an area can occur because of increased sensitivity of postsynaptic membranes to the decreased amount of transmitter substance released from damaged neurons. Supersensitivity does indeed occur, but how much it contributes to recovery of function in the whole organism is unknown.

(7) A theory of compensation implies that the organism seeks to use undamaged areas and experience to find alternative means of achieving developmental tasks. The patterns used may or may not appear normal to the observer.

Although most of the experimental work to be done in attempting to test these various theories must be done in the laboratory with animal models, we believe that clinical research can make important contributions. Repeated assessments of children who have experienced multiple insults will be useful in documenting recovery from initial neural shock or diaschisis, and longitudinal assessments are needed to document the natural history of recovery, of nonrecovery, and of the appearance of delayed deficits. The use of multiple assessment procedures may be useful in revealing specific areas of deficit related to particular early events and may aid in the exploration of the ability of the infant to seek compensatory means for achieving desired developmental ends. Finally, the trauma inflicted on the family by the event of having a very sick baby may lead to altered environmental interactions between parents and infant thus interfering with development and learning. Family stresses added to the overwhelming daily task of dealing with poverty and inadequate support systems lead to an even more vulnerable child. Very little research exists on the interactional problems of stressed infants and their equally distressed families, and almost none on whether environmental manipulations can be effective in helping either the family or the child. Since a large economic investment is being made annually in the management of such children, we owe them and their families more intensified efforts to study these problems and their management.

ACKNOWLEDGMENTS

This project has been supported in part by the following grants to the principal investigator: research grant from the American Academy for Cerebral Palsy and Developmental Medicine; Grant 149, Maternal and Child Health Services, Bureau of Community Health Services, DHEW, USPHS; University of North Carolina School of Medicine Faculty Research Grant; Division of Physical Therapy Research Travel Grant; and a Postdoctoral Research Fellowship to Janet M.

Donatelle from the American Association of University Women.

Project staff performing Neonatal Behavioral Assessment Scale examinations were trained in administration and scoring of the Scale by the staff of the Child Development Unit, Boston Children's Hospital (Campbell, DeSantis, Provost, Wilhelm) or the Department of Human Development, University of Kansas (Donatelle).

We are indebted to the following persons at the University of North Carolina School of Medicine for many hours of assistance with project development and data collection: Ernest N. Kraybill, Associate Professor of Pediatrics and Director of Nurseries; Janet M. Donatelle, Darlene DeSantis, Susan Attermeier, Nancy Niparko, John Scholz, Elizabeth Provost, Kristi Morse, Darlene Slaton, Jeanne Strozier, and Kathleen Hogan, Division of Physical Therapy, Department of Medical Allied Health Professions. The following persons provided assistance with graphics: Cedonia Edwards, Gayle Lawson, and Steve Rizzuto. The manuscript was typed by Shirley M. Taylor.

REFERENCES

1. Amiel-Tison, C: Acceleration of cerebral maturation following high risk pregnancy. Paper presented at the biennial meeting of the Society for Research in Child Development, March 17, 1979.

2. Baum, D et al: The benefit and hazard of neonatology. In T. Chard, PM Richards (Eds), *Benefits and hazards of the new obstetrics.* Clinics in Developmental Medicine #64, Philadelphia: Lippincott, 1977.

3. Bayley, N: Revised manual for the Bayley scales of infant development. New York: The Psychological Corporation, 1969.

4. Beintema, DJ: A neurological study of newborn infants. *Clin. Dev. Med.* (No. 28). Philadelphia: Lippincott, 1968.

5. Bobath, B: The very early treatment of cerebral palsy. *Dev. Med. Child Neurol.* *9:*373–390, 1967.

6. Bobath, B: *Abnormal postural reflex actitivy caused by brain lesions,* 2nd ed. London: Heinmann, 1971.

7. Bobath, K: The normal postural reflex mechanism and its deviation in children with cerebral palsy. *Physiotherapy, 57:*1–11, 1971.

8. Bobath, K., & Bobath, B: The diagnosis of cerebral palsy in infancy. *Arch. Dis. Child, 31:*408–414, 1956.

9. Brandt, I: Physical neuromotor and intellectual development of preterm and fullterm infants from birth to five years. Paper presented at the biennial meeting of the Society for Research in Child Development, March 16, 1979.

10. Brazelton, TB: Neonatal behavioral assessment scale. *Clin. Dev. Med,* No. 50. Philadelphia: Lippincott, 1973.

11. Caldwell, B: HOME inventory: Home observation for measurment of the environment. Unpublished instructional manual. Little Rock, Arkansas: Center for Early Development and Education, N.D.

12. Carter, RE, & Campbell, DK: Early neuromuscular development of the premature infant. *Phys. Ther, 55:*1332–1341, 1975.

13. Crothers, B, & Paine, R: *The natural history of cerebral palsy.* Cambridge, Mass.: Harvard University Press, 1959.

14. Cupps, C, & Plescia, MG: The Landau reaction: A clinical and electromyographic analysis. *Dev. Med. Child Neurol., 18:*41–54, 1976.

15. del Mundo-Vallarta, J, & Robb, JP: A follow-up study of newborn infants with perinatal complications: Determination of etiology and predictive value of abnormal histories and neurological signs. *Neurology, 14:*413–424, 1964.

16. DeSouza, SW, & Richards, B: Neurological sequelae in new born babies after perinatal asphyxia. *Arch. Dis. Child, 53*(7):564–569, 1978.

17. Donatelle, JM: NIH postdoctoral research fellowship application, 1977.

18. Elardo, R, & Bradley, R: The relation of infants' home environments to mental test performance from six to thirty-six months: A longitudinal analysis. *Child Dev, 46:*71–76 1975.

19. Field, T, & Hallock, N: A first-year follow-up of high-risk infants: Formulating a cumulative risk index. *Child Dev., 49:*119–131, 1978.

20. Fitzhardinge, PM: Early growth and development in low-birthweight infants following treatment in an intensive care nursery. *Pediatrics, 56:* 162, 1975.

21. Franco S, & Andrews BF: Reduction of cerebral palsy by neonatal intensive care. *Pediatr. Clin. North. Am., 24:*639–49, 1977.

22. Frankenburg, WK, & Dodds, JB: *Denver developmental screening test manual,* revised edition. Denver: University of Colorado Medical Center, 1970.

23. Frankenburg, WK, & Goldstein, A: The revised Denver developmental screening test: Its accuracy as a screening instrument. *J. Pediatr., 71:* 988–995, 1967.

24. Graham, FK: Behavioral differences between normal and traumatized newborns: I. The test procedures. *Psychol. Monogr., 70:*1–16, 1956.

25. Hobel, CJ, & Hyvarinen, MA et al: Prenatal and intrapartum high-risk screening. I. Prediction of the high-risk neonate. *Am. J. Obstet. Gynecol., 117:*1–9, 1973.

26. Hunt, JV, & Rohdes, L: Mental development of preterm infants during the first year. *Child Dev., 48:*204–210, 1977.

27. Illingworth, RS: The diagnosis of cerebral palsy in the first year of life. *Develop. Med. Child Neurol., 8:*178–194, 1966.

28. Ingram, TTS: The new approach to early diagnosis of handicaps in childhood. *Dev. Med. Child Neurol., 11:*279–290, 1969.

29. Johnson, D, & Almli, CR: Age, brain damage and performance. In S. Finger (Ed), *Recovery from brain damage: Research and theory.* New York: Plenum Press, 1978.

30. Kamper, J: Long-term prognosis of infants with severe idiopathic respiratory distress syndrome I. Neurological and mental outcome. *Acta Paediatr. Scand., 67*(1):61–69, 1978.

31. Lawrence, S, & Stein, DG: Recovery after brain damage and the concept of localization of function. In S. Finger (Ed), *Recovery from brain damage: Research and theory.* New York: Plenum Press, 1978.

32. Lipsitt, LP: Infancy and life-span development. Paper presented at the biennial meeting of the Society for Research in Child Development, March 17, 1979.

33. Low, JA et al: Intrapartum fetal asphyxia: A preliminary report in regard to long-term morbidity. *Am. J. Obstet. Gynecol., 130*(5):525–533, 1978.

34. Low, JA et al: Intrauterine growth retardation: A preliminary report of long-term morbidity. *Am. J. Obstet. Gynecol., 130:*534, 1978.

35. Mednick, BR: Intellectual and behavorial functioning of ten- to twelve-year-old children who showed certain transient symptoms in the neonatal period. *Child Dev., 48:*844–853, 1977.

36. Milani-Comparetti, A, & Gidoni, ES: Routine developmental examination in normal and retarded children. *Dev. Med. Child Neurol., 9:* 631–638, 1967.

37. Paine, RS, Brazelton, TB et al: Evolution of postural reflexes in normal infants and in the presence of chronic brain syndromes. *Neurology, 14:* 1036–1048, 1964.

38. Parmelee, AH, & Sigman, M: The concept of a cumulative risk score for infants. In N.R. Ellis (Ed), *Abevant development in infancy: Human and animal studies.* Hillsdale, N.J.: Erlbaum, 1975.

39. Piaget, J: *The origins of intelligence in children.* Trans. by M. Cook. New York: International Universities Press, 1936.

40. Piaget, J: *The construction of reality in the child.* Trans. by M. Cook, New York: Basic Books, 1937.

41. Prechtl, HFR: Prognostic value of neurological signs in the newborn infant. *Proc. R. Soc. Med., 58:*3–4, 1965.

42. Prechtl, HFR, & Beintema, D: The neurological examination of the full term newborn infant. *Clinics in Developmental Medicine* (No. 12). Philadelphia: Lippincott, 1975.

43. Rockwell, RC, & Elder, GH, Jr.: Economic deprivation and problem behavior: Childhood and adolescence in the Great Depression. Paper presented at the biennial meeting of the Society for Research in Child Development, March 17, 1979.

44. Rosenblith, JF: Manual for behavorial examination of the neonate (unpublished), 1961.

45. Sameroff, AJ: Theoretical and empirical issues in the operationalization of transactional research. Paper presented at the biennial meeting of the Society for Research in Child Development, March 17, 1979.

46. Scott, H: Outcome of very severe birth asphyxia. *Arch. Dis. Child, 51:* 712–716, 1976.

47. Sigman, M, & Parmelee, AH: Evidence for the transactional model in longitudinal study of preterm infants. Paper presented at the biennial meeting of the Society for Research in Child Development, March 17, 1979.

48. St. Clair, KL: Neonatal assessment procedures: A historical review. *Child Dev., 49:*280–292, 1978.

49. Tilford, JA: The relationship between gestational age and adaptive behavior. *Merrill-Palmer Quarterly, 22:*319–326, 1976.

50. Thompson, T, & Reynolds, J: The results of intensive care therapy for neonates. *J Perinat. Med., 5:*59–75, 1977.

51. Twitchell, FE: Reflex mechanism and the development of prehension mechanisms of motor skill development. In K.J. Connally (Ed), New York: Academic Press, 1970.

52. Uzgiris, IC, & Hunt, J: *Assessment in infancy: Ordinal scales of psychological development.* Chicago: University of Illinois Press, 1975.

53. Vietze, PM, & Sandler, HM: Transactional approach to prediction of child maltreatment. Paper presented at the biennial meeting of the Society for Research in Child Development, March 17, 1979.

54. Werner, E: The transactional model: Applications to the longitudinal study of the high-risk child on the island of Kauai. Paper presented at the biennial meeting of the Society for Research in Child Development, March 17, 1979.

55. Wolánski, N, & Zdanska-Brincken, M: A new method for the evaluation of motor development of infants. *Polish Psychol. Bull., 4:*43, 1975.

56. Ziegler, AL, Calme, AG et al: Cerebral distress in full-term newborns and its prognostic value. A follow-up study of 90 infants. *Helv. Paediatr. Acta, 31:*299–317, 1976.

APPENDIX A

Example From Parental Diary

My baby first lifted and held his head, arms, and legs up all at the same time on _____.

(date)

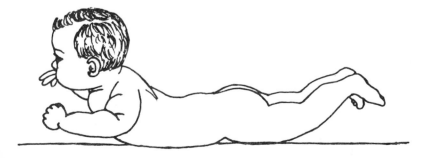

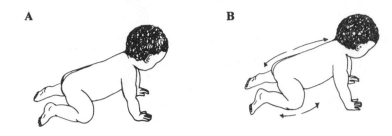

(A) My baby first got onto his hands and knees on _____.
                                             (date)

(B) My baby first rocked back and forth while on his hands and knees on _____.
        (date)

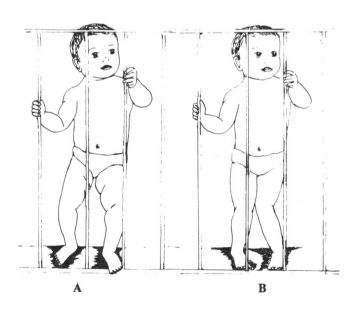

After my baby has pulled up into standing he looks more like
_____baby A   _____baby B
(check)

APPENDIX B

Case Histories

002 TM BD 7/21/77

Social History: Parents are a black couple, unmarried
                                   at time baby was conceived, but were
                                   married during the pregnancy. Mother
                                   was a 16-year-old high school student;
                                   father was a 20-year-old high school
                                   graduate, working as a maintenance
                                   man.

Family Medical
History: Unremarkable
Mother's Past
Medical History: Unremarkable
Parental History: $Gr_1 P_{0000}$. Minor problems only: mild
                                   anemia, treated urinary tract infection
                                   (UTI), and persistent low blood pres-
                                   sure throughout pregnancy.

Intrapartum
History: Fetal bradycardia (down to 80/min. for
                                  10 mins.)

Neonatal Course: Estimated gestational age (EGA) of
                                  38 weeks, birth weight (BW) 3,290
                                  g., AGA, male, Apgar scores 5,6.
                                  This baby was born at a small, rural
                                  primary hospital, transferred to a
                                  secondary hospital at two days of
                                  age and to the tertiary facility at age
                                  three days. At age four days a suba-
                                  rachnoid hemorrhage was confirmed
                                  by skull X-rays. The infant was unre-
                                  sponsive to stimuli and hypotonic, al-
                                  ternating with rigidity and opisthoto-
                                  nos. Seizures were confirmed by EEG
                                  (diffuse slowing pattern) and treated
                                  with   Dilantin   and   Phenobarbi-
                                  tol.

                                  In the first week of life the infant also
                                  had persistent metabolic acidosis, mild
                                  respiratory distress (TTNB), and early
                                  apnea   and   bradycardia   (requiring
                                  CPAP, but not a ventilator).

                                  The Brazelton Neonatal Behavioral As-
                                  sessment Scale (NBAS) was adminis-
                                  tered two times during the hospital
                                  stay:

                                  (1) At CA of 13 days: Dimensions I
                                       (Interactive Processes), II (Mo-
                                       toric Processes), and III (State
                                       Control), were worrisome; Di-
                                       mension IV (Response to Stress)
                                       was average.
                                  (2) At CA of 18 days: No change
                                       from first test.

The infant was discharged at CA of three weeks and has subsequently been diagnosed as spastic quadriplegia with microcephaly.

Other Events: The marital relationship has been tenuous. The parents were at first each living with his/her own parents. They moved into their own home when the baby was between five and six months of age. They were separated some time between his 9- and 12-month evaluations. The mother has the baby and is again living with her parents.

003 PM BD 8/5/77

Social History: Parents are a black, unmarried couple. Mother was a 17-year-old high school student, father was a high school graduate, city worker.

Family Medical
History: Positive for twins, hypertension, heart disease, and epilepsy.

Mother's Past
Medical History: Unremarkable

Prenatal History: Gr_1 P_{0000}. Mother was severely anemic and had a positive GC screen (treated), both within 2-months of the delivery date.

Intrapartum
History: Premature rupture of the membranes (PROM) and premature labor requiring pitocin augmentation. Monitoring showed fetal bradycardia; maternal amnionitis was evident after delivery.

Neonatal Course: EGA of 30 weeks, BW 1,140 g., AGA, male, Apgar scores 1, 2. The infant was resuscitated (intubation, bagging). He was apneic with persistent cyanosis from day one, and at eight days had a cardiopulmonary arrest and again required resuscitation. Apnea, bradycardia, and cyanosis persisted and he had a second arrest at age 34 days. GC pneumonia was diagnosed at 10 days, and the baby also had a persistent ductus arteriosus (PDA), hypocalcemia, persistent metabolic acidosis, hyperbilirubinemia requiring phototherapy, GC eye infection, and iatrogenic anemia.

Two Brazelton examination results were as follows:

(1)   At postconceptional age of 37 weeks (CA 49 days)—Dimensions I (Interactive Processes) and III (State Control—flat, depressed) were worrisome. Dimensions II (Motoric Processes) and IV (Response to Stress) were average;

(2)   At postconceptional age of 37.5 weeks (CA 53 days)—Dimensions I, II and IV were worrisome; Dimension III was average.

He was discharged at CA of two months (about term age).

Other Events: Mother moved from her mother's home to her own mobile home when infant was between six and one half and seven and one half months CA (four and five months AA). She moved back to her mother's home when he was between eight one half and nine and one half months CA (six and seven months AA). When the baby was about 13 and one half months CA (11 months AA), the mother returned to finish high school and the infant was being cared for by his MGM. When he was seventeen months old (CA), his mother gave birth to a full-term baby girl.

004 PM BD 8/23/77

Social History:

Parents are a white, married couple. Mother was a 24-year-old textile mill worker with a 10th grade education; father was a maintenance man, also with a 10th grade education. Parents had their own trailer, but were living with the PGPs at the beginning of the study, with plans to remove to the trailer the following spring.

Family Medical History:

Positive for twins, diabetes, and a neurophychiatric disorder (mother's sister).

Mother's Past Medical History:

$Gr_2 P_{1001}$. Mother had one other child as a teenager which was placed for adoption. The child was full-term and with no known problems.

Prenatal History:

Mother is Rh negative and received Rhogam after her first delivery. Early in pregnancy she had some vaginal spotting, mild anemia, a flu-like episode with fever, and low blood pressure. Later she developed severe pre-

eclampsia (BP at least 160/110 with >
2 + proteinuria), and the fetus was
growth retarded.

Intrapartum
History:

PROM occurred and premature labor
was induced with pitocin because of the
severe preeclampsia. Fetal monitoring
showed severe fetal bradycardia with
decreased baseline variability.

Neonatal Course:

EGA of 34 to 35 weeks, BW 1,450 g.,
SGA, male, Apgar scores 6,9. He received some O_2 at delivery, but his lungs
were mature and he never had respiratory problems. The major complication
was RH incompatibility and hyperbilirubinemia requiring an exchange
transfusion at age two days. He was
suspected of being a FLK because
of slightly low-set ears and a split
xyphoid, but no syndrome was ever
diagnosed. The infant also had poly-
cythemia (Hct 75) at age one day,
was jittery and hyperactive without
metabolic problems, and had an episode of late metabolic acidosis at
age one month which delayed his discharge.

His Brazelton NBAS results were as
follows:

(1)   At nine days CA (36 weeks postconceptional age), Dimension III
was worrisome (State Control—
flat, depressed); all others were average;

(2)   At 26 days CA (three weeks postconceptional age), Dimensions I

(Interactive Processes) and II (Motoric Processes) were worrisome; Dimensions III and IV were average.

He was discharged at CA of one month, five days (about at term age).

Other Events: Mother was supposed to be hospitalized for eye surgery in the fall. Our records do not show if this was done. Parents continued to live with the PGPs throughout the study.

005 PM BD 8/29/77

Social History: Parents are a white, married couple. Mother was a 29-year-old waitress with a 9th grade education; Father worked as an electrician.

Family Medical
History: Unremarkable

Mother's Past
Medical History: Mother listed as GR_3 P_{2000}. She apparently had two previous infants by C-section because of cephalopelvic disproportion (CPD). There is no information on one; the other was apparently transfused twice (perhaps exchanged) and later died of meningitis at age eight months.

Prenatal History: Mother smokes (lppd). Mother is Rh negative and was sensitized. The fetus received an intrauterine transfusion about 2 weeks prior to delivery.

Intrapartum
History: Infant presented in transverse lie. De-

livery was by C-section (but probably for rising titer).

Neonatal Course: EGA 32 to 33 weeks, BW 1,720 g., AGA, male, Apgar scores 4,9. The baby required resuscitation by bag and mask. He developed severe RDS and by age two days was on CPAP, and later on a ventilator. At age one day he required an exchange transfusion for hyperbilirubinemia, and later required a second. He also had hypocalcemia, persistent metabolic acidosis, anemia, and was jittery and hyperactive during his first week of life, and had hypothermia, and persistent cyanosis during the 2nd week. At age one month a PDA was diagnosed. IIe was difficult to wcan from O_2 to room air because of apnea, bradycardia, and cyanosis.

His Brazelton NBAS results were as follows:

1) At CA 32 days (37 weeks postconceptional age), Dimensions I (Interactive Processes) and II (Motoric Processes) were worrisome; Dimensions III and IV were average.

2) At 35 days CA (37.5 weeks postconceptional age), Dimension IV (Response to stress) was worrisome; all others were average.

He was discharged at CA of one month, five days (about 38 weeks postconceptional age).

Other Events: After discharge (about 1–2 weeks) the baby had an apneic spell at home. He was rehospitalized at another hospital with a special care nursery and eventually discharged with an apnea monitor for home use. When seen for his 1st quarterly session in January 1978 (AA of 3 months; CA 4 months, 24 days), he had been off the monitor without problems for about a month. Just before the 1st quarterly visit, the father fell off a roof while working and suffered a broken leg. He was unable to return to work and was present at the 1st, 2nd, and 3rd quarterly sessions. He was not present at the final session (presumably had returned to work).

006 TM BD 9/26/77

Social History:

Parents are a black, unmarried couple. Mother was a 16-year-old 10th grade student; father was a 23-year-old mill worker.

Family Medical History:

Positive for active tuberculosis. MGM was in a sanitorium and the mother was on INH. Several other family members had positive skin tests.

Mother's Past Medical History: Unremarkable

Prenatal History: GR_1 P_{0000}. Active Tb in mother.

Intrapartum History: Unremarkable

Neonatal Course: EGA 40 weeks, BW 3,430 g., AGA, male, Apgars 1, 5. Baby was resuscitated, but took 12 mins. to breath. On day one he began having seizures (treated with phenobarbitol, dilantin, valium) and was still unresponsive to pain stimuli and arreflexive by day 3. He also had some periodic apnea and hypoglycemia. A CT scan done on day 2 was somewhat inconclusive (probable cerebral edema and possible infarcts). An echocardiogram done at about one week revealed a small VSD (not expected to affect function).

Brazelton NBAS results were as follows:

(1) At 11 days CA, Dimensions I (Interactive Processes) and II (Motoric Processes) were worrisome; Dimensions III and IV were average;

(2) At age 21 days CA, Dimensions I (Interactive Processes) and III (State Control) were exceptionally good; Dimensions II and IV were average.

The decision was made not to send this infant home (because of the Tb and mother's youth) until the MGM was back in the home. The baby was discharged to foster care at CA of three weeks.

Other Events:
The infant was in two different foster homes; the first until he was about five months old, and the second until he was about eight months old. At that time he was returned to his natural mother's care.

007 TF BD 10/4/77

Social History:	Parents are a white separated couple. Mother was an 18-year-old high school graduate; father had a 10th grade education and was employed as a foreman at a furniture company. Mother was living at the home of her older married sister since the separation.
Family Medical History:	Unremarkable
Mother's Past Medical History:	Unremarkable
Prenatal History:	Gr_1 P_{0000}. Positive only for persistent low blood pressure during the 2nd trimester.
Intrapartum History:	Infant presented in transverse lie, requiring forceps rotation. Amniotic fluid was lightly stained with meconium. Mother was heavily medicated with Demerol (225 mg.).
Neonatal Course:	EGA 40 weeks, 3,920 g., AGA, female, Apgars 2, ?. The baby was resuscitated, but took 10 to 12 minutes to breath spontaneously. An IC hemorrhage was diagnosed via lumbar puncture on day two of life (? if secondary to forceps rotation). The infant was jittery and hyperactive during the first week of life. Hydrocephalus was suspected, as she had a rather large head, but a CT scan ruled this out, and confirmed the hemorrhage. A second CT scan, done on day 10 of life, showed the hemorrhage to be almost resolved.

The Brazelton NBAS results were as follows:

(1) At CA of nine days, all dimensions were worrisome (III was very labile);

(2) At CA of 12 days, only dimention II (Motoric Processes) was worrisome; Dimension I (Interactive Processes) was exceptionally good, Dimensions III and IV were average.

The infant was discharged at 13 days CA.

Other Events: Mother had moved into an apartment by the time the baby was between six and seven months of age, but the baby continued to spend the day with her maternal aunt, as mother had also started to work. A new boyfriend appeared on the scene, approximately when the baby was 10 months old and was present at several of her testing sessions.

008 TF BD 10/16/77

Social History: Parents are a white married couple. Mother was a 31-year-old housewife; father was a truck driver.

Family Medical
History: Unremarkable
Mother's Past
Medical History: Unremarkable, GR_2 P_{1001}—first child alive and well.
Prenatal History: Postive only for mild preeclampsia.

Intrapartum
History: Fetal monitoring showed severe fetal bradycardia. Amniotic fluid was heavily stained with meconium.

Neonatal Course: EGA 40 weeks, 3,680 g., AGA, female, Apgars 3, 7. Infant was resuscitated with O_2 and suctioned for meconium. She developed meconium aspiration syndrome and required CPAP and a ventilator by day two. During the first week of life she had a pneumothorax, pneumomediastinum, persistent cyanosis, persistent fetal circulation, hypocalcemia, hyponatremia, and seizures confirmed by EEG and treated with phenobarbitol and valium. Decreased muscle tone was consistently noted. By age two weeks, her lungs were almost clear, she had a normal EEG, but was still hypotonic.

Brazelton NBAS results were as follows:

(1) At CA of 15 days, Dimension I (Interactive Processes) and II (Motoric Processes) were worrisome; Dimension III (State Control) was exceptionally good and IV (Response to Stress) was average.

(2) At CA of 15 days, only Dimension II (Motoric Processes) was worrisome; all others were average.

The infant was discharged at 17 days CA.

Other Events: Unremarkable.

APPENDIX C

Rating Scales for Selected Reflexes

Head Righting—In Space

PROCEDURE: Hold child vertically in space. Tilt child's body laterally from the vertical 45°. Hold at least 10 seconds. Max. no. trials each side—3. Give highest score.

to right	to left	
_____	_____	0—head passively hangs, no attempts to right*
_____	_____	1—head hangs, attempts to right
_____	_____	2—head moved so in line with body
_____	_____	3—head righted, briefly (1–2 seconds)
_____	_____	4—head righted after tilt, maintained
_____	_____	5—head righted *as* infant tilted side-to-side
_____	_____	6—head *either* remains in line with body

*righted—vertex up, mouth horizontal

axis *or* is righted as infant tilted
forward, backward, then side-to-side

_____   _____   7—head righted as infant tilted forward,
backward, side-to-side

Body Righting On The Body

POSITION: Supine, head in midline

PROCEDURE: Flex one leg and rotate across pelvis to opposite
side. Response—turn prone, segmentally, with rotation, first
trunk, then pectoral girdle, then head. Maximum number of
trials to each side is 3.

SCORING:

to right   to left

_____   _____   0—no response
_____   _____   1—some movement trunk, but roll onto
side not completed
_____   _____   2—infant rolls onto side without rotation
within the body axis
_____   _____   3—infant rolls onto side with rotation
within the body axis
_____   _____   4—infant rolls onto stomach with
rotation, hips before shoulders,
slowly, long latency
_____   _____   5—infant rolls onto stomach with
rotation, hips before shoulders,
rapidly, short latency
_____   _____   6—infant voluntarily inhibits rolling

Landau Reaction

PROCEDURE: Examiner supports child horizontally in air in
prone position with one hand under lower part of thorax.

SCORING:

_____ 0—head below horizontal and spine markedly convex upward

_____ 1—head below the horizontal and spine slightly convex upward

_____ 2—head and spine both horizontal

_____ 3—head less than 45° above the horizontal and spine straight

_____ 4—head greater than 45° but less than 90° above the horizontal and spine slightly concave upward

_____ 5—head 90° above horizontal and spine concave upward (thoracolumbar extension present)

Asymmetrical Tonic Neck Reflex

POSITION: Supine head in midline

PROCEDURE: First try to elicit rotation of the head with visual or auditory stimuli. If not possible, the examiner will passively rotate the head so the jaw is over the shoulder. The head should remain rotated a minimum of 5 seconds (ideally 10 seconds). Maximum number of trials to each side is 3. Give highest score.

SCORING: Score during active and passive neck rotation

To Right				To Left			
Face Extremities (R)		Skull Extremities (L)		Face Extremities (L)		Skull Extremities (R)	
Elbow ext.	Knee ext.	Elbow flex.[+]	Knee flex.	Elbow ext.	Knee ext.	Elbow flex.[+]	Knee flex.

0—no response
1—tone change only, no observable response
2—partial flexion or extension
3—full flexion or extension
4—full flexion or extension, obligatory, cannot be broken by infant

[+] Must be scored.

Moro Response

POSITION: Supine

PROCEDURE: Support child's head and shoulders with hand, allow head to drop back 20–30 degrees with respect to trunk. Repeat 3 times.

SCORING:

Score each trial

Trial   R   L
1_____
2_____
3_____

0—no response
1—extension of fingers and/or elbow only
2—partial abduction and extension of arms
3—full extension and abduction of arms
4—any handling elicits a startle

Galant's Reflex

POSITION: Prone suspended over examiner's hand

PROCEDURE: Firmly stroke the paravertebral muscles in a cephalocaudal direction from approximately midthoracic area to lower lumbar area. Maximum number of trials to each side— 3. Record the highest score.

SCORING:

R   L
_____ _____   0—no response
_____ _____   1—slight incurvation of spine and wrinkling of skin
_____ _____   2—Good incurvation, modulated, with hip swing
_____ _____   3—exaggerated response, with excessive hip swing

Palmar Grasp

POSITION: Supine, symmetrical, head in midline, arms semi-flexed

PROCEDURE: Put fingers (usually index finger) from the ulnar side into the hands and press the palmar surface. Maximum of 3 trials on each side.

SCORING: Note highest score

R	L	
___	___	0—no response
___	___	1—incomplete flexion of fingers, not touching examiner's finger throughout test
___	___	2—complete flexion of fingers, but only lightly touching examiner's fingers through full test (examiner may easily remove finger from infant's grasp)
___	___	3—full flexion, but maintained for less than 10 seconds (examiner may raise infant's arm off mat before infant's grasp releases)
___	___	4—full flexion maintained for longer than 10 seconds (infant's arm and shoulder can be raised off mat)
___	___	5—fingers strongly flexed and have to be retracted by the examiner

Tension (Item 6, BSID Infant Behavior Record)

Tenseness of body (Circle one)

Rating

1   Inert; may be flaccid most of the time
2   Between 1 and 3

3   Body has tone and is generally relaxed
4   Has bounce
5   Becomes tense at times although body has relaxed quality;
    subsequent quick return to supple, relaxed condition
6   Between 5 and 7
7   Body is tense more than half the time; may be stiff or tight
    in one or more areas; startles, quivers, or trembles easily
8   Between 7 and 9
9   Body is predominantly taut or tense

Chapter 6

THE PSYCHOTIC CHILD

Early Identification of Psychosis in the First Years of Life

B. Kay Campbell, Ph.D.
Henry N. Massie, M.D.

INTRODUCTION

In this International Year of the Child it is appropriate to consider how we might better serve the needs of children everywhere. The special child offers us passage into the world of scientific inquiry and knowledge. Although special children are brought to us for help, they excite our curiosity as well as our concern. We become perplexed by our insufficient knowledge and seek further training and opportunities to learn; in the process of understanding the problems of one child, we learn how to help many others.

The psychotic child is found throughout the world, just as blind, deaf, crippled, and deprived children are. Historically, many children with severe handicaps have endured periods of scientific neglect due in part to gaps in our knowledge of developmental deviations, genetic interferences with normal processes, and environmental effects on the growing child.

I want to employ a particular convention for this chapter. I will be writing about the behavior of infants and the behavior of parents. I first wrote the chapter using "he or she" in reference to the infant and that became grammatically confusing. So I tried "babies" (plural: "they"), and I had so many children I didn't know what to do. Next I tried "the infant, it," which was dreadfully impersonal. I finally settled on "he" for the infant because it saved "she" for the mother. That's the next point. "Mother" in this chapter refers to any person who nurtures or protects another. Now, if I say "she picked him up" you'll know I'm referring to a mothering person—of either sex —holding another in her arms.

Erik Erikson[15] wrote in *Childhood and Society* "to come face to face with a schizophrenic child is one of the most awe-inspiring experiences a psychotherapist can have. . . . The total impression immediately convinces the observer that the right person and the right therapeutic regime could bring the child back on the road to coherent progress. This conviction has the more or less explicit corollary that the child has been in the wrong hands and in fact has every reason to mistrust his neglectful and rejecting parents. Our occupational prejudice is the 'rejecting mother' " (p. 169).

Not so many years ago people believed infants in their first year of life were in a period of maximal physical change with minimal mental awareness.[1,5,42] The healthy newborn was thought to neither see nor hear. He was characterized by marked passivity, helplessness, and vulnerability. It fell upon the parents to structure reality for the baby, to control his environment, and to shape his behavior.[39,44] Consistent with this view it was also clearly the parents' fault if the baby turned into a less than perfect child: rebellious, stubborn, selfish, and spoiled.

. In the last decade, however, there has been a tremendous expansion of research in infant development. We now have data documenting the neurophysiologic changes in infancy, the development of perception, the complexities of cognition, the intricacies of growth, and subtleties of emotion. We are learning how infant and parent jointly create the unique relationship they share between them. We've begun to appreciate the reciprocal process of attachment and the evolution of love.

In infancy, as well as throughout life, the process of normal development and the range of normal behaviors must be understood before the process of abnormal development and the range of abnormal behaviors can be understood.

Growth, indicated by pounds and inches or kilos and centimeters, makes it simple to document physical development. Gross motor achievements such as rolling over, sitting alone, crawling, standing, and walking give evidence of maturing muscles and bones that we can touch and feel.

It is more difficult to assess fine motor development and to infer from it visual-motor coordination, although we can observe a baby reaching, holding a raisin, or turning a page. We assume the visual-motor system is maturing on the basis of accuracy and speed: we can time how quickly a baby puts yellow pegs in a board or little blocks in a box.

Intrapsychic processes are still more difficult to document and to study. We cannot see them or feel them or weigh or measure them. We can only infer their presence and we often do so using an "if, then" model of causality. That is, *if* the baby smiles at us *then* it must mean something. But what? What does the baby feel? What does the baby think? How do we know? How can we know?

We answer these questions in terms of the theories and the convictions we bring to the situation. The meaning of the smile is determined by our capacity to organize and make sense of it. Various levels of inference or abstraction allow us to understand the first social smile in increasingly complex and theoretical ways. We can postulate an emotional meaning to the smile, "He's happy" or a communicative meaning, "He smiles because he wants something." Or the smile may have an interpersonal meaning, "He likes me" or a magical meaning, "He smiles because he knows what I'm thinking." We can consider that smile a neurophysiological indicator: nearly all babies of 46-weeks gestational age develop the smiling response when presented with a facial gestalt.[6,40] In a more abstract way the smile may indicate to us the capacity of the infant to intentionally engage his human partner in social interchange. This intention marks a new level of psychic organization and according to Spitz[40] is the first organizer of intrapsychic structures.

Yet, as we move farther away from what we can actually see to theories and ideas, to interpretations and inferences, we run a greater risk of inaccuracy. Inferential statements consist not of raw observations but of conclusions, judgments, and predications. Inferences always involve a leap in the dark—into the unknown and the unobserved.[3]

And so we have two tasks: the first is to learn to see what is there before our eyes, and the second is to know what it means and to relate it to that which we cannot see but can only speculate upon—the developing intrapsychic world.

The healthy neonate is not only capable of focusing his eyes and following a moving figure; he has a preference for the human face,[16,17,40] for colors,[2] and for patterns.[16] In fact, the visual acuity of a newborn is sufficient for him to look, to see, and to visually engage his human partner.[12,25]

Newborns can hear despite an apparent disregard for noise. The fact that they can sleep through the telephone ringing, radio blaring, and the dishwasher roaring gives evidence of their capacity to habituate and retreat from excessive stimulation.[5,24,43] On the other hand, neonates have indicated they prefer the sound of the human voice, sounds as soft as those between 60 and 90 decibels and tones that correspond to those known to come from females generally and from their own mothers specifically.[7,9]

The young infant, if placed face down, will shift his head sufficient to permit breathing. When spoken to, the apparent random movement of an infant's arms and legs have been demonstrated by Condon and Sander[11] to be synchronous with the speed and rhythm of the speaking partner's voice. The infant can deliberately reach for things it finds attractive or interesting, but because the nervous system mediating the visual-motor coordination matures over time the early reaching efforts appear aimless and random. If the baby actually reaches what he sought we may be tempted to say, "Well, he did it by accident."

The newborn's sense of touch is well developed. A baby is capable of being felt and of feeling; of being touched and of touching. In the process of touching the infant experiences skin-to-skin stimulation, whether it is its own hand stroking its own face or the hand and face of another. Touch is something one may initiate as well as receive. We speak of a tactile sense referring to perception by way of touch. We also speak of tactile receptivity, the willingness to be touched. The infant both touches and seeks to be touched; the mothering partner similarly touches and seeks to be touched. Montague[34] writes, "although touch is not itself an emotion its sensory elements induce those neural, glandular, muscular, and mental changes which in combination we call an emotion. Hence, touch is not experienced as a simple physical modality but affectively as emotion." Through touch, the infant, the child, and even the adult reaches, clings, and molds to its loving partner.

Vocalizing, initially by crying, is the primary distal communication system available to the neonate. All babies cry when they are hungry or in pain but they also cry for unexplained reasons. Bowlby[6a] has suggested that crying ensures the continuing closeness of the mother at times not taken up with feeding or instrumental activities. Crying seems to decline according to an internal program and the development of other responses and communicative behaviors takes its place.[13]

One of these is the smile. There is the neonatal smile that may first occur as a reflex but that shortly becomes associated with some internal pleasurable state.[45] It has been noted, however, that a newborn who smiles tends to evoke sensitive and tender feelings in the viewers of that smile and may elicit vigorous social stimulation.[13] For the most part, mothers tend to make light of these early smiles and to ignore them or refer to them as "talking with the angels" or less poetically, "gas expressions."[14] Then there is the social smile, a joyfully anticipated event that occurs when the baby is about two months old. When the infant begins to smile regularly in response to an external stimulus, such as the vivacious face of another person, "then his social life takes a leap forward."[13]

By three months of age babies become more selective about what makes them smile. At four months they generally smile less at unfamiliar people, but stare at them more. They begin to compare mother with nonmother, something Pacella[35] refers to as "comparative scanning." The baby becomes interested in "mother" and seems to compare her with "other," the unfamiliar with the familiar, feature by feature. The baby begins to discriminate between mother and nonmother, a precondition and a step on the road toward the eventual distinction between self and nonself.

Sometime between six and nine months the ready smile becomes more reserved and strangers are greeted with a somber expression that may give way to either tears or laughter. The infant takes a little more time deciding whether to smile a welcome or cry a rejection.

With the advent of crawling and scooting the infant becomes physically able to move away from the mother. With walking comes an enchantment with life. Greenacre[21] says the toddling infant enjoys "a love affair with the world." The plane of his vision changes. Now from his upright vantage he finds new pleasures and new frustrations.[26] As the toddler experiences the world with this new mobility, he confronts a harsh reality. Mother isn't always there when he falls and when he gets hurt her presence alone doesn't always make it better. The toddler begins to suspect that he is not a part of his mother and she is not a part of him. If the mother leaves at this time the toddler cries for her, searching in old familiar places. His behavior gives evidence that in her absence he has a longing for her and a memory of where she might be. If she is too long in returning—too long being a relative term, for each baby's needs are different—upon her return she may be pointedly ignored.

The toddler will not look at her or talk to her. "No!" becomes a favorite word.

The emergence of symbolic language marks another leap in development of the toddler's mind. He begins to use language in the processing of ideas and in the service of social relationships. In the second year of life the toddler's vocabulary grows from single words with multiple referents (when "ta" means bottle, bye-bye, teddy bear, or hold me) to many words with specific referents.[4,8]

Language, smiles, and touches can easily be observed. Thinking, however, cannot be seen. It can only be inferred by observing certain behaviors considered indicators of cognitive processing.

In 1882, Sir Francis Galton believed that complex mental functioning could be studied by measuring simple sensory processes. People flocked to his laboratory to have their sight and color sense tested, their hearing checked, the speed of their reactions calculated, and their muscles measured. Galton reasoned that if one gained knowledge of the world through the perceptual senses, then the better the senses were the greater one's knowledge would be. By the early 1900's this idea was no longer so enthusiastically supported and the original Stanford-Binet Test of Intelligence was designed. This test also infers mental functioning by observing performance. By understanding, however, the way in which problems were solved and questions answered it became possible to devise a model of mental functioning which allowed us to appreciate the integrative capacity of the mind.[22]

Piaget[36] demonstrated the unfolding of cognitive abilities. He delineated stages of intellectual development. As a developmental concept, a "stage" usually defines a set of behaviors that occur together. As a group, they characterize a quality of behavior that differs appreciably from the quality of behavior in earlier and later stages. Stages follow each other in an orderly sequence and the transition from one stage to another usually involves a process of integration whereby the behavior from the earlier stage is transformed into the next along with new elements.

Affective or emotional development cannot be directly observed either, although there is little question when a healthy baby is happy and content or cross and angry. As the baby grows, it becomes clearer that his emotional state seems tied to the availability of his mothering partner. The baby laughs in response to social excitement; the baby cries when alone and seeking company and interaction.

Affective development also progresses through stages. Rene Spitz[40] believed there were three psychic organizers in the first year of life critical to the development of socialized behavior: the smile, the emergence of stranger anxiety, and the beginning of verbal communication. These behaviors we can see and we know when they should appear. They allow us to assume the child is developing a meaningful relationship with another human being. That is, the child's special smile for the mother which appears at about three months signifies his beginning preference for one person above all others; the fear of strangers and the beginning of symbolic speech are outward indicators of further intrapsychic processes. We may begin to think that the baby is developing an intrapsychic internal presence, a memory, and an image of his loved partner. That important first relationship with another person is the model for all future relationships with people. The individual who cannot love, cannot trust, cannot share his joys and pleasures, his pain and sorrows is too often isolated, lonely, and unhappy. "Life," wrote Spitz,[40] "has to be quickened; the vital spark has to be conferred through exchanges with another, a partner, a mother. Nothing less than a reciprocal relationship will do."

In the first year of life and in those that follow there is a physiological maturational timetable and there are various cognitive, motor, and emotional lines of development that should progress in concert, each contributing to and each partaking of the other. Physical, cognitive, motor, and emotional functioning intertwine. The integration of all these lines is critical to the continuing healthy development of the infant.

If the infant successfully establishes and consolidates each developmental task at the appropriate time, then development proceeds evenly. However, when the consolidation, the integration, of the various developmental lines miscarry, development is disintegrated. The impaired lines of development that should have been integrated with other developmental thrusts remain at preceding and less mature levels.[18]

PSYCHOSIS IN EARLY CHILDHOOD

Psychosis in infancy and early childhood is a disorder manifested by such disintegrations. Development may be impaired in sensory processing (a psychotic child may not respond to pain); in communication, both verbal and nonverbal; and in the ability to form relationships, and to manipulate and enjoy objects. Psychosis is characterized by disruptions, disharmonies, and disorders.

Psychosis is a form of mental disorder associated with severe personality disorganization. There are marked disruptions in thinking, in relating to others, and in adaptation to reality. Because self-regulation[37] is impaired, it is difficult to tolerate waiting, to endure disappointments, to consider appropriate outlets for excitement, and to find joy and pleasure. Defensive functioning is disturbed. Perception, intention, and motivation are confused. Language and intelligence may be disarranged. In short, the synthetic, integrating, and organizing functions of the personality are fragmented.

By the time psychosis is apparent, certain mental changes in the personality have already taken place through maturation and development. These changes have caused fundamental distortions in the basic personality itself. There is a failure of developmental lines to converge and the psychotic child often appears at the same time both precocious and retarded. The distortion, the depth, and the permanence of developmental impairment distinguishes psychosis from simpler developmental delays or emotional regressions.[27]

The personality structure is weakened. It is as if in the building of a skyscraper wood was substituted for steel, plastic for porcelain. The pressures, the stresses compromise the integrity of the materials and they give way in particular ways: there is buckling of joints, corners aren't plumb, fixtures crack and plumbing leaks, the windows jam, and the elevator works in fits and starts. These are the indicators of internal disorder. The outside of the building looks fine but the way it works is impaired. This is the problem we face then: Must we wait until the walls are up and the paint applied before we know something is terribly wrong?

In 1971, a three and one-half-year-old girl was referred to Dr. Henry Massie for diagnosis and treatment. The girl was found to be autistic. In taking her history, it was learned that the family had made over 2,000 feet of home movies, beginning at the daughter's birth. The films were borrowed and analyzed frame by frame in an attempt to learn about the child's infancy and evolving social relationships.[28]

Behind this close study was the intuition that patterns of interaction between mother and child, as well as between other family members, might be captured on film. It was hoped that if one could look closely enough at the flow of events then features of social interaction and early development might become evident—features that could help explain the subsequent tragic course of the child's life. The study of the films reveal the little girl's early muted visual and motoric activity; her lack of excitement about persons or things. By six months of age she made little eye contact, seemed self-absorbed, had a constricted affect, and displayed neither pleasure nor displeasure. By nine months of age she was more involved with her internal experiences than with those of the world; autistic hand-flapping was well established and eye contact severely impaired.

At the same time, the film analysis revealed the mother's tendency to look away, to hold herself reserved and distant. She was often filmed laughing and smiling, seemingly unaware of the meaning of her daughter's withdrawal or even of her importance to her baby. The film documents a remarkable early sequence: in a brief moment the baby tries to look at her mother, the mother counters the child's efforts, and the daughter becomes dejected while the mother is unaware of what has happened.

Mother and infant each brought to their relationship a propensity for certain behaviors which were then woven into their many contacts with each other. The girl's failure to maintain visual contact became the hallmark of her illness. She turned away and inward. The mother's need for interpersonal distance and her preoccupation with her own shyness may have prevented her from recognizing the child's emotional retreat as potentially pathological.

This discovery of early precursors to severe emotional disorder led to an extensive study—The Early Natural History of Childhood Psychosis Project—of home movies made by the parents of children who were later diagnosed as psychotic.[28–31] It was hoped that other indicators of psychopathology might be found, signs that would herald the impending disaster of psychosis. Eventually, more than 20 families contributed films they had taken of their children before psychosis was apparent. These films were compared by independent raters with those of normal children in an effort to see what distinguished the infant who became a psychotic child from the infant who did not. Differences were found, particularly in patterns of interaction and notably in the behaviors Bowlby[6a] identified as essential to the attachment process: clinging, following, crying, smiling, and sucking. The childhood psychosis film study revealed repeated failures in attachment, but the failures did not seem to come only from the infant. It became clearer that the irregularities of attachment processes evolved within the relationship of the mother with the baby and of the baby with the mother.

An elaborate rating system was developed to permit objective analysis of the films. The attachment behaviors of feeding, gazing, touching, holding, and vocalizing were operationally defined. These behaviors were then reduced to their component parts to be graded according to the intensity of their display. The scales of behaviors provide a means of quantifying interaction between parent and infant.

The disturbed relationship between parent and infant became the sign of the unfolding pathology.

This is not to say that infant mental illness is caused by an interactive event but rather it is signaled by interactive failure. There may be within the infant an intrapsychic inability to perservere and to negotiate certain developmental stages. The infant may not be able to use the mother as an ally in development, as a "beacon of orientation."[26] The mother may not be able to provide her child with appropriate support and protection when it is needed. Together they present a disharmonious social unit. That is something we can see. I would like to share with you three edited cases from the Early Natural History of Childhood Psychosis Project. I will not provide you detailed case histories in this chapter. We will focus on the interactional behavior of parent and infant revealed in the films. When the outcome is known it's always easier to trace the steps backward to where they began. In psychotherapy such reconstructions sometimes go awry and like Hansel's breadcrumbs the evidence is lost. The retrospective Childhood Psychosis Project was blessed in that the evidence remained to be found.

The question of whether home movies can capture the ordinary daily "real" behavior of a parent and infant is important. One may be tempted to feel that being "on stage" demands a performance. Experts[10,38,41] believe the nonverbal behavior is both culturally determined and highly individualized. It is repeatably, predictably, and unavoidably embedded in one's responses to social situations. Kerlinger[23] reminds us that while we may wish to perform well before an audience we cannot do what we cannot do. We cannot act in a way we do not act.

The first case, which was the original one, demonstrates a passive young girl, Joan, who ineffectively attempts to engage her mother face to face. In aberrant fashion, the mother does not respond. Eventually, Joan gives up and withdraws into her own private world; her mother, by her behavior, appears to deny their distance and separation. An illustrative sequence seen in Figure 6–1, revealed Joan's abortive efforts to engage her mother visually.

A: Mother and child are relaxed. Mother touches baby's cheek.

B: Child turns her head and eyes toward mother's face. Mother's expression tenses and her eyes shift away from child's face. Child tenses.

C: Mother shifts her head backward and to the side of the child's face, blocking child's facial approach and obstructing eye contact. Mother relaxes. Child appears dejected.

D: Mother and baby resume original postures, not in eye contact. Child's expression shifts from dejection to pleasure and drooling appears when mother pats child's head.

Figure 6-1 Sequential Drawings of Dyadic Gaze and Facial Interaction between Mother and Infant at Four Months in Films of Case 1. (*Journal of the American Academy of Child Psychiatry,* vol. 14, 1975, p. 691.)

Joan did not develop stranger anxiety or separation anxiety. She rarely showed either pleasure or displeasure. She became increasingly indifferent to people around her and eventually was diagnosed as autistic and is now in day treatment. The case demonstrates how early in life aberrant gaze existed between mother and infant. This may have been a contributory factor to the later autism or a sign of an organic process in the child that meshed with the mother's characterologic difficulties with eye gaze.

The next case demonstrates the inability of the infant, Ann, to elicit from her mother appropriate attention. Ann's mother fails to be "in tune" with her needs. Ann cannot use mother predictably to either gratify or to frustrate her wishes. The mother's potential empathic understanding of Ann was lost as she struggled with her own sense of inadequacy and inability to satisfy her intrusive mother-in-law. This grandmother was not able to empathize with Ann either and so could not offer a mothering role model for Ann's mother. Figure 6–2 shows Ann when about nine months old. She was not yet able to walk alone and her mother was supporting her from behind. Ann's initial pleasure in walking gave way to fatigue and panic. Her mother, concerned with her own need to demonstrate her child's precocity, did not see Ann desperately reaching for her. The mother kept walking the faltering girl forward.

Ann suffered severe separation anxiety that became apparent when her mother tried to leave her in nursery school. She entered treatment at age four and was diagnosed as autistic with symbiotic features. Ann is now eight years old and is making some progress in day treatment.

The third case begins with a strained but socially attentive infant whose mother seems not to know her baby could be an interactive social partner. Consequently, the mother's attention toward her baby—we'll call him Steven—was sporadic, dysrhythmic, and insensitive. These behaviors are consistent with what we might infer were her beliefs about infant sociability. This little boy did play peek-a-boo, a game facilitating the acquisition of object constancy, and he did have a "security blanket," which offered some of the functions of his mother in her absence. Both of these activities suggest certain developmental levels were achieved before they were lost to the psychotic process which eventually predominated. Steven's fragile but appropriate early social efforts eventually failed and

Figure 6–2   Ann at Nine Months. Mother Walks Child Forward by Standing behind Child and Holding Her Hands from above. Unable to Support Her Weight, the Baby Panics and Reaches Desperately for Mother's Body and Tries to See Her Face. Unaware, Mother Keeps Walking the Child Forward. (© *Child Psychiatry & Human Development,* vol. 7, 1977, p. 220.)

he became regressively psychotic. He was diagnosed at 10 years of age as schizophrenic.

The parents and children in these films demonstrated deviations from normal expected social behaviors. Visual disturbances were indicated by gaze avoidance and aversion. Difficulties with touching became apparent and we saw tactile inhibition. Holding patterns appeared awkward and uncomfortable for parent and child alike. Facial expressions were inappropriate: infants were somber and pleasureless; mothers were disengaged or preoccupied.

The Childhood Psychosis Project allowed us to go backwards in time, beginning with the psychotic disorder and attempting to reconstruct its evolution through time. The early signs of psychosis seemed inextricably bound to early signs of social dysfunction. Observable interactive components were invariably present as the process of psychosis progressed. If it is true that psychosis and social dysfunction occur together, concurrently and in parallel, then can we assume that one signals the presence of the other? If that be true, then would it be possible to identify infants at risk for psychotic disorganization by assessing their ability to interact socially with their mothering partner?

EARLY DIAGNOSIS OF PARENT-INFANT DISTURBANCE

In contrast to the retrospective film study we began a prospective study. We wanted to serially assess and document mother-infant interaction along the lines that had appeared critical in the development of interactional process. We hypothesized from the social behavior we were able to observe that intrapsychic processes (which we could not see) would nonetheless be unfolding in particular ways.

We developed the experimental single-page Scale of Mother-Infant Attachment Indicators During Stress Scale (AIDS Scale),[32] modeling it after the more elaborate rating scales used in analyzing the childhood psychosis films. The

AIDS Scale (which is reproduced in a later chapter) quantifies the reciprocal process of mother-infant interaction while the baby is under the stress of an ordinary pediatric examination. The stress of the examination is not necessarily a function of the clinician's style. A typical examination includes being undressed, weighed and measured, and poked and prodded, usually in the presence of strangers in a strange room and under a bright light. It is the threat of the unfamiliar and the fear of the unknown that makes the physical examination suitable for evaluating mother-infant interaction under stress. When cold, frightened, and uncomfortable a healthy infant turns to his mother for comfort and reassurance. Clinical observations during stress periods may reveal the mother's ability to empathically meet those needs (Bowlby[6a]).

The assessment of an infant's capacity to socially engage the attention and care of his mothering partner should be as much a part of the well-baby examination as assessing the child's eyes, ears, nose, and throat. The mother who leaves the room while her baby is being examined is a different mother than the one who remains within arm's reach of her infant. The infant who stares at the ceiling, ignoring mother and clinician alike, is a different baby than the one who constantly compares mother's face against the clinician's. These are clues to developing intrapsychic processes and they can be appraised.

The AIDS Scale, still in its research edition, is an effort to objectively judge such behaviors. There are six attachment modalities on the Scale: gazing, vocalizing, touching, holding, affect, and proximity. Each is scored on a scale from 1 to 5 according to the intensity of the behavioral display. Each is scored with reference to the infant's behavior toward his mother and the mother's behavior toward her infant.

The AIDS Scale was specifically designed to be consistent with good pediatric practice. It requires only a few minutes to administer and interpret and is easy to use within the context of the pediatric setting. It can, however, be adapted for other settings where infant and mother are stressed sufficiently to mobilize attachment behaviors revealing their quality to the practiced eye.

The following is a case vignette of a film of a well-baby examination conducted at Children's Hospital in San Francisco.

The baby is a four-month-old girl, the breast-fed and firstborn child of an intact middle-class family. Although her growth has been excellent, her mother brought her to this examination concerned because the baby seemed to be increasingly fussy and was waking up more than usual during the night. The father, who was in attendance, also complained that he thought his daughter no longer liked him because she had begun crying when he held her.

This film was fairly typical of a well-baby examination and showed an alert, active, and curious baby girl who frequently glanced at her mother and occasionally reached toward her. This little girl was able to vigorously kick against the examining clinician, clearly demonstrating her desire not to be examined. Her mother remained within arms reach throughout the exam; constantly monitoring her baby and attentive to the process. The mother perceived Catherine's hands to be in the way of the examiner. She slipped in and held Catherine's hands briefly and then released them. She didn't abandon Catherine to the clinician. She was available and at the same time nonintrusive. In dressing Catherine she looked at her and talked with her. Catherine actively waved her arms and, when the mother completed the dressing of Catherine, she picked her up.

Remember that the parents were concerned about their daughter's increased fussiness prior to this visit. The clinician could find nothing physically wrong and reassured the family. A few days later Catherine rolled over, became more sociable with her father, but with a clear preference for her mother; the fussiness and crying resolved and she returned to sleeping through the night. These signal multiple lines of development converging and thrusting this child into a new level of organization. Her fussiness may have been an indicator of a reorganization in preparation for a higher state of development.[13] This film offered a marked contrast to the films of the somber, woeful, apathetic, and socially disordered infants from the Childhood Psychosis Project.

Our studies began with a curiosity about psychopathology in the very young child. Our investigations took us to the first months of life and we began to look at infants in a different way: we learned to appreciate their interactive qualities and to respect what they could bring to a relationship.

We found infants and parents showing disturbances in basic communication modalities through which interaction takes place. Whether dysfunctional social patterns contributed to the later mental illness of the children is unclear, but it was apparent that overt emotional disturbances were preceded by inappropriate and dyssynchronous social involvement.

Establishing a nourishing, loving relationship is essential to the well-being of infant and parent; disturbances within that relationship have repercussions in other relationships and can effect all members of a family. We need to know how to understand what is being revealed. The heartbeat, heard through the stethescope, is a signal to the clinician; the ease with which a child settles into a school routine is a signal to the teacher; the joy with which a child experiences life is a signal to the parent. Perhaps the capacity of the mother and infant to engage each other in mutually adaptive social interaction can become a new signal to the infant mental health professional.

ACKNOWLEDGMENTS

For their helpful criticism appreciation is extended to Dean Barnlund, Linn Campbell, Mary Lamie, Ginnie Adamson, Nina Knox, and Justine Riskind. Research described in this report has been supported by grants from the L.J. and Mary C. Skaggs Foundation, Oakland, California and from Children's Hospital of San Francisco.

REFERENCES

1. Aries, P: *Centuries of childhood: A social history of family life.* Trans. by R. Baldick, New York: Knopf, 1962.

2. Barnet, AB: Visual responses in infancy and their relation to early visual experience. *Clin. Proc. Child Hosp. 22*:273, 1966.

3. Barnlund, DC, & Haiman, F: *Dynamics of discussion.* Boston: Houghton Mifflin, 1960.

4. Bee, H: *The developing child.* 2nd Ed. New York: Harper & Row, 1978.

5. Biehler, RF: *Child development: An introduction.* Boston: Houghton Mifflin, 1976.

6. Bower, TG: *Development in infancy.* San Francisco: Freeman, 1974.

6a. Bowlby, J: Attachment and Loss (Vol 1- Attachment). London: Horgarth, 1969.

7. Brazelton, TB, Koslowski, B, & Main, M: The origins of reciprocity: The early mother-infant interaction. In M. Lewis & L. A. Rosenblum (Eds), *The effect of the infant on its caregiver.* New York: Wiley, 1974.

8. Brown, R: *The first language, the early stages.* Cambridge, Mass.: Harvard University Press, 1973.

9. Carpenter, G: Mother's face and the newborn. In R. Lewin (Ed), *Child alive.* London: Temple Smith, 1975.

10. Condon, WS: A primary phase in the organization of infant responding behavior. Paper presented at Conference on Recent Advances in Patterns of Infant Development: Relevance for Later Life. Costa Mesa, Ca., Feb. 24–26, 1978.

11. Condon, WS, & Sander, L: Neonate movement is synchronized with adult speech: Interactional participation and speech acquisition. *Science, 183*:99–101, 1974.

12. Dayton, GO, Jr. et al.: Developmental study of coordinated eye movements in the human infant. *Arch. Opthal., 71*:871, 1964.

13. Emde, R, Gaensbauer, TJ, & Harmon, RJ: *Emotional expression in infancy: A biobehavioral study.* New York: IUP, Inc., 1976.

14. Emde, RN, & Koenig, KL: Neonatal smiling, frowning, and rapid eye movement states, II sleep-cycle study. *J. Am. Acad. Child Psychiatry, 8*:637–656, October 1969.

15. Erikson, E: *Childhood and society.* New York: Norton, 1963.

16. Fantz, RL: Visual perception from birth as shown by pattern selectivity. *NY Acad. Sci., 118*:1965.

17. Fantz, RL, & Miranda, SB: Newborn infant attention to form of contour. *Child Dev, 46*:224–228, 1975.

18. Freud, A: *Normality and pathology in childhood assessments of development.* New York: IUP, Inc., 1965.

19. Freud, S: *New introductory lectures on psycho-analysis and other works,* (Vol 22). London: Hogarth, 1936.

20. Fantz, RL: Pattern vision in newborn infants. *Science, 40*:296–297, 1963.

21. Greenacre, P: The childhood of the artist: Libidinal phase development and giftedness. *PSOC, 12:*27–72, 1957.

22. Guilford, JP: *The nature of human intelligence.* New York: McGraw-Hill, 1967.

23. Kerlinger, FN: *Foundation of behavioral research.* New York: Holt, Rinehart & Winston, 1966.

24. Kessen, W, Haith, M, & Salapetek, P: Infancy. In P. H. Mussen (Ed), *Carmichael's manual of child psychology.* 34d Ed. New York: Wiley, 1970.

25. Klaus, MH, & Kennell, JH: *Maternal-infant bonding.* St. Louis: Mosby, 1976.

26. Mahler, M, Bergman, A, & Pine, F: *The psychological birth of the human infant.* New York: Basic Books, 1975.

27. Mahler, M: *The viscisitudes of separation-individuation. Infantile psychosis* (Vol. 1). New York: IUP, 1968.

28. Massie, H: The early natural history of childhood psychosis. *J. Am. Acad. Child Psychiatry, 14*:683–707, 1975.

29. Massie, H: Patterns of mother-infant behavior and subsequent childhood psychosis: A research and case report. *Child Psychiatry Hum. Dev., 7*:211–230, 1977.

30. Massie, H: The early natural history of childhood psychosis: blind ratings of mother-infant interaction in the first 6 months of life in home movies of subsequently psychotic children and controls. *Am. J. Psychiatry,* 135:1371–1374, 1978.

31. Massie, HN: The early natural history of childhood psychosis: 10 cases studied by analysis of family home movies of the infancies of the children. *J. Am. Acad. Child Psychiatry,* 17:29–45, 1978.

32. Massie, HN, & Campbell, BK: *The scale of mother-infant attachment indicators during stress (AIDS scale).* San Francisco: Children's Hospital and Medical Center of San Francisco, 1977.

33. Meltzoff, AN, & Moore, MK: Imitation of facial and manual gestures by human neonates. *Science, 198*: October 7, 1977.

34. Montaque, A: *Touching, the human significance of skin.* San Francisco: Harper & Row, 1971.

35. Pacella, BL: Early ego development and the dijavu. Paper presented at the New York Psa Society, New York, May 30, 1972.

36. Piaget, J: *The origins of intelligence in children.* New York: Norton, 1952.

37. Sander, L: Neonatal state regulation and the integration of action in early development: A consideration of the matu of organization in development. Costa Mesa, Ca.: 1978.

38. Sheflen, A: *Body language & the social order.* Englewood Cliffs, N.J.: Prentice-Hall, 1972.

39. Skinner, BF: *Science and human behavior.* New York: Macmillan, 1953.

40. Spitz, R: *The first year of life.* New York: International Universities Press, 1965.

41. Stern, DN: A micro analysis of mother-infant interaction: Behavior regulating social contact between a mother and her 3½ month old twins. *J. Am. Acad. Child Psychiatry, 10*:501–517, 1971.

42. Sunley, R: Early nineteenth-century American literature on child rearing. In M. Mead & M. Wolfenstein (Eds.), *Childhood in contemporary cultures.* Chicago: University of Chicago Press, 1955.

43. Tennes, K, Emde, R, Kisley, A, & Metcalf, D: The stimulus barrier in early infancy: An exploration of some formulations of John Benjamin. *Psychoanalysis and contemporary science.* New York: Macmillan, 1972.

44. Watson, JB: Psychological care of infant and child. New York: Norton, 1926.

45. Wolff, P: The early development of smiling. In B. M. Foss (Ed.), *Determinants of infant behavior* (Vol. 2). New York: Wiley, 1963.

Chapter 7

THE AIDS SCALE

The Massie–Campbell Scale of Mother-Infant Attachment Indicators During Stress

Henry N. Massie, M.D.
B. Kay Campbell, Ph.D.

Preface

In Chapter 6 we discussed some of the initial behavioral signs in very young children that may be associated with subsequent psychopathology. There were also illustrations of pathological social interactions occuring between parents and their infants that have been correlated with later emotional disturbances in the children. Data for these descriptions came from a series of clinical research projects that the chapter briefly summarized.

As our research studies progressed, it became clear that the findings should be applied to the critical task of identifying abnormalities of mother-infant dyadic behavior at the earliest possible age. If identification can take place, intervention strategies may be instituted that might reduce the risk of severe developmental disturbances eventuating in the child. To this end we adapted in the form of the AIDS Scale what we had learned to be core bonding behaviors and their components in which a mother and infant reciprocally engage.

The Scale is a 5-point metric scale that is constructed with descriptions of behaviors drawn from our clinical and investigational experience with the range of major ethnic and socioeconomic groups in the United States. The descriptions grade the intensity with which a mother and her infant respond the one to the other during situations of mild to moderate stress. For the pediatrician, psychiatrist, or other childcare specialist who seeks to ascertain the adequacy of a particular parent-child pair, a stressful event is an especially important one to view for two reasons. It heightens and clarifies the capacities and incapacities of mother and child to give care and respond to care that may restore an emotional and physiological homeostasis. Also stresses recur frequently, if not daily, in the home and are the particular events and crises in which psychological (and sometimes physical) trauma to child and parent are likely to occur. A parent and child may also successfully master these events which then become nontraumatic but growth enhancing frustrations.

The AIDS Scale has been designed for easy and rapid use during the infant's pediatric examination which is the time when professionals most often first see parents and infants. It may also be used in other childcare settings to assess the relative normalcy of caretaker and baby response. In such settings, the examiner may construct a mild standardized stress such as a brief mother and child separation or use the Scale in an open-ended, nonstructured fashion. The Scale consists of one page which contains the graded descriptions of behavior. A second page provides the instructions for use which include a list of the Scale's applications, guides to administration, scoring and interpretation, and a list of operational definitions.

In the future, we anticipate publishing the AIDS Scale in a monograph that will detail the findings from its use with large numbers of infants. However, the results of these studies are not yet available.

INTRODUCTION

The AIDS Scale is to be used with infants from birth to 18 months of age to detect aberrant mother-infant responsiveness in stressful situations. The Scale quantifies the reciprocal process of mother-infant attachment while the infant is under the stress of an ordinary physical examination. The Scale can also be used in other situations that produce tension in mother and baby. When stressed, infants normatively seek out their mothers; mothers normatively seek out their infants when they perceive them to be in danger or suffering. Such interactions fall within the general category of attachment behaviors. The Scale includes six basic attachment modalities: gazing, vocalizing, touching, holding, affect, and proximity. These modalities are subdivided into component behaviors and correspond to mother and infant responses clinically seen in stressful situations which arouse tension and anxiety in mother and/or infant. The responses in each attachment modality are graded from 1 to 5 to indicate the increasing intensity of mother-infant involvement that may occur during a stress episode. Generally, behavior at the low end of the Scale (1) indicates abnormal isolation or avoidance of attachment, and responses at the high end (5) indicate abnormally anxious attachment behavior or clinging. The top half of the single-page Scale quantifies the infant's behavior with its mother, and the bottom half quantifies the mother's behavior with her infant during the stressful situation.

APPLICATIONS

The AIDS Scale is for use during the pediatric examination as well as other situations where a relatively standardized stress occurs for parents and babies. For example, it can be used by mental health or childcare workers to assess mother-infant attachment at the moment of reunion following the stress of a brief separation between mother and child. In whatever setting it is used it may serve some or all of the following functions:

1) To record the clinician's assessment of the adequacy of maternal-infant dyadic responsiveness.
2) To document the need for developmental and psychological care to prevent the crystallization of pathological modes of social interaction.
3) To document the efficacy of early intervention efforts by registering improvement in the clinical indicators of attachment when used longitudinally during the first 18 months of life with deviant mother-infant pairs.
4) To teach by heightening the clinician's awareness of parameters of mother-infant interaction central to psychological development.

INSTRUCTIONS FOR ADMINISTRATION AND SCORING

The clinician conducting the examination or an independent observer can administer the AIDS Scale. Generally, the mother should not be alerted to the details of the observation so that she does not modify her usual style; and for the same reason the examiner should not suggest to the mother that she either hold the baby or place the baby on the examining table, but instead leave the decision with the mother.

To use the Scale, observe the interaction between mother and infant *while* the infant is being physically examined (the stress episode) and *immediately afterward* (the reunion and recovery episode). In many pediatric examinations the final phase is the inspection of the head, eyes, ears, nose, and throat. This usually takes about 3 minutes and is often the most difficult for mother and infant. The period immediately following this (about 3 minutes) is the time when mother and infant reunite and tension subsides. Similarly, in nonpediatric settings there is a corresponding rise and fall of tension around a stressful event. Assessment is made by focusing on the period of most heightened stress (the final 3 minutes of the physical examination) and the period of tension decline (the first 3 minutes of the recovery phase). *Immediately after the observation of the recovery episode* circle the behavior description that best fits the mother's and infant's response in each attachment modality during both stress and recovery episodes. If a particular attachment modality, such as holding, has not occurred, circle "not observed" so that an entry is made in every category.

OPERATIONAL DEFINITIONS

Holding: the mutually reciprocated posturing of the infant and mother while the infant is supported in the arms of the mother.

Gazing: the eye-to-face contact within a dyad and the maintenance of this contact.

Vocalizing: the making of vocal sounds for the benefit of the partner in the mother-infant dyad. The infant's crying is considered a vocal signal of dismay during stress which alerts the mother to its tension.

Touching (a): the making of skin-to-skin contact initiated by either the mother or the infant.

Touching (b): the withdrawal from skin-to-skin contact initiated by either the mother or the infant.

Affect: the facial expressions signaling emotional states. A bland expression is considered typical of the individual under stress and is appropriate.

Proximity: the state of being near, close to, or beside another. In the context of the AIDS Scale it refers to the infant maintaining either physical or visual contact with the mother, and to the mother maintaining physical contact or being immediately accessible to her infant.

Rarely: the behavior occurs once in a while, or seldom; it doesn't happen often during the observation period.

Occasionally: the behavior occurs from time to time, now and then during the observation period.

Frequently: the behavior happens often but not all the time during the observation period.

INTERPRETATION OF SCORING

Normal behaviors will usually rate at 3 and 4. When an infant or a mother rates at 1 or 2 it suggests that the infant or mother may be either avoiding contact or not responding to the other's display of tension or attempts at attachment. When there are scores of 5 it should raise concern that there is an overanxious intense attachment or an unusually strong reaction to stress. Further, in dyads where one member rates at 1 or 2 and the other at 5, there is a dissynchrony of interaction which may also have pathological significance. To derive a single or "correct" score is not the proper use of the Scale. The most productive way to interpret the ratings is to use the attachment indicators as a guide to the adequacy of interaction in a given mother-infant pair. Studies indicate that deviant attachment is associated with subsequent psychomotor developmental delays, pathological intrapsychic management of tension and aggression, and inability to postpone gratification—all with their attendant behavioral disturbances. When behaviors of 1, 2, or 5 occur in two successive episodes, there should be a diagnostic workup, for, once established, unhealthy patterns of mother-infant interaction show little change without therapeutic intervention. The exception occurs with some very young or premature infants who show a normal dampened responsiveness. They may rate 2 for gazing, vocalizing, touching (a), and proximity in the first weeks of life. Mother-infant affect at 5 at any age is not necessarily clinging but is aberrant.

AIDS SCALE
THE MASSIE-CAMPBELL SCALE OF MOTHER-INFANT ATTACHMENT INDICATORS DURING STRESS
For Use During the Pediatric Examination and Other Stressful Childcare Situations

| | *Infant's behavior during stress event* | | | | | |
	(1)	(2)	(3)	(4)	(5)	X
Gazing	Always looks away from mother's face.	Rarely searches out mother's face. Fleeting looks at mother's face.	Occasionally looks at mother's face.	Frequently long & short gazing at mother's face.	Rivets gaze on mother's face for long periods.	Behavior not observed.
Vocalizing	Quiet. Never vocalizing.	Rarely vocalizing or whimpering.	Occasionally vocalizing or mild crying.	Frequently vocalizing or intense crying.	Uncontrollable, intense crying much of time.	Behavior not observed.
Touching	(a) Never touches or reaches toward mother.	Rarely touches mother.	Occasionally touches mother.	Frequently reaches toward & touches mother.	When close, always touching mother.	Behavior not observed.
	(b) Always pulls away from mother's touch.	Frequently pulls away from her touch.	Occasionally pulls away from her touch.	Rarely pulls away from her touch.	Never pulls away from her touch.	Behavior not observed.
Holding	Violently resists holding; always arches away from mother.	Does not relax in mother's arms. Frequently pulls away.	Rests in mother's arms and against her shoulder. Occasionally pulls away.	Body molds to mother's. Rarely pulls away.	Actively turns & arches body toward mother's. Clings strongly. Never pulls away.	Behavior not observed.
Affect	Always intensely anguished & fearful.	Frequently irritable & fearful.	Largely unclear, constricted, or bland expressions.	Frequently content & smiling.	Always full smile & content.	Behavior not observed.
Proximity	Never follows mother bodily or with eyes; goes to far corner or out of room.	Rarely follows mother bodily or with eyes; often at far corner of room from mother.	Intermittently follows mother bodily or with eyes.	Frequently follows mother bodily or with eyes.	Always follows mother bodily or with eyes.	Behavior not observed.

Mother's response to infant's stress

Gazing	Always looks away from child's face.	Rarely looks at child's face. Fleeting looks at child's face.	Occasionally looks at child's face.	Frequently long & short gazing at child's face.	Rivets gaze on child's face for long periods.	Behavior not observed.
Vocalizing	Quiet. Never vocalizing.	Rare words, cooing, or murmuring.	Occasionally vocalizing to child.	Frequently speaks, murmurs, coos.	Intense vocalizations throughout exam.	Behavior not observed.
Touching	(a) Never touches or reaches toward child. (b) Always pulls away from his touch.	Rarely touches child. Frequently pulls away from his touch.	Occasionally touches child. Occasionally pulls away from his touch.	Frequently reaches toward and touches child. Rarely pulls away from his touch.	When close, always touching child. Never pulls away from his touch.	Behavior not observed.
Holding	Pushes upset child away, or holds away from body.	Holds child stiffly & awkwardly. Not relaxed.	Supports child relaxedly against her chest or shoulder briefly.	Body molds to child & maintains contact until child quiets.	Body inclines toward child, followed by prolonged holding with molding.	Behavior not observed.
Affect	Always intensely anguished & fearful.	Frequently irritable & fearful.	Largely unclear, constricted, or bland expressions.	Frequently content & smiling.	Always full smile & content.	Behavior not observed.
Proximity	Leaves examining room.	Frequently out of reach of child; or at far corner of room from child.	Intermittently standing or seated within arm's reach of child.	Frequently holding or touching child.	Always holding or touching child.	Behavior not observed.

Growth and development: normal _____ abnormal   *Explain:* _____

Social behavior appears: normal _____ abnormal   *Describe:* _____

Unusual circumstances today: No _____ Yes _____   *Describe:* _____

Infant's name: _____ *Infant's age:* _____ *Date:* _____ *Observer:* _____

© 1977 Henry N. Massie, M.D. and B. Kay Campbell, Ph.D.

Variables

Relatively standardized stress situations may be affected by several variables. An infant's ability to tolerate tension or respond to comforting may be affected, for example, by concurrent illness or hunger. Likewise, a mother's capacities may be affected by concurrent disturbances in her life. History taking should elicit this; and the AIDS Scale can then assist in assessing the capacity of the mother and infant to compensate for additional stress, or their liability for decompensation and the traumatic behaviors that follow. Additionally, a disturbing examining situation or other unusual circumstances can intensify the stress of customary events. If there are unusual occurrences when the rating takes place explain briefly in the space provided at the bottom of the Scale.

Fathers accompany infants less frequently than mothers, but the AIDS Scale can be appropriately used to assess father-infant interaction. When infants are older than 18 months their behaviors have become so increasingly complex that the AIDS Scale is less useful.

Acknowledgment

Development of the AIDS Scale has been supported by a grant from the L.J. and Mary C. Skaggs Foundation, Oakland, California.

Chapter 8

AN ASSESSMENT AND TREATMENT PARADIGM BASED ON THE COGNITIVE, SOCIAL, AND EMOTIONAL DEVELOPMENTAL CHARACTERISTICS OF THE YOUNG AUTISTIC CHILD

Linda Kreger, Ph.D.

CHAPTER FRAMEWORK

This chapter is organized into the following topical areas. First, a brief review of some of the more prevalent views on the etiology of autism will be described. Next, typical characteristics of these children will be summarized and followed by a portion of the developmental assessment scale, which is based upon a synthesis of the theories of Piaget, Erikson, and Freud. Finally, an intervention model will be described which is based upon the needs of these children in the realms of affect, cognition, and related domains of growth.

ETIOLOGY

Most widely published have been the various views on the cause(s) of autism, ever since Leo Kanner[3] first described the syndrome. Two of his most "telling" signs of early infantile autism were: (1) excessive self-isolation, present from infancy, and (2) obsessive insistence on the preservation of sameness. Bernard Rimland[5] has researched autsim for many years and has devised checklists for parents and professionals to contrast autism from other related disturbances. He has recently written about defects in these children's reticular activating system that can explain their inability to receive stimuli adequately. Bruno Bettleheim[2] is characteristic of the psychogenic view which theorizes that the cold, verbal, rejecting parental style encourages this syndrome. He now suggests that a constitutional vulnerability may also be present. Bergman and Escalona[1] describe hypersensitivities of these children that could elicit defensive styles toward adversely perceived stimuli. Schopler[7] thinks that a lack of sensory and perceptual integration is an important factor in the disorientation of these children. Some view an organic defect in biochemical or physiological development as encouraging the phenomena of autism. Michael Rutter[6] proposes an explanation favoring perceptual and cognitive defects. Others find that a congenital organic defect, such as infection with Rubella *in utero,* highly correlates with the incidence of autism.

There are numerous studies documenting findings regarding the etiology of autism. These views may fall under neurobiological, genetic, or biobehavioral theoretical orientations.

A total emphasis on one factor may oversimplify a disability the causes of which may (1) vary from child to child, and (2) be a complex combination of factors which is difficult to assess under current research designs.

It is easy to cite case after case of rejecting, unstimulating parents of autists. It is difficult to note whether this stance was caused by initial rejection by a baby that always screamed, did not mold to the adult's body, and averted gaze and whether attempts to reorient the child toward associating pleasure with human contact would have helped. Only a close study of infants exhibiting autistic-like behavior receiving early stimulation would help clarify this issue. A valiant attempt by an accommodating set of parents and professionals at least should be tried no matter what intervention model one would follow, be it educational, milieu, psychoanalytic, behavioral, or organic.

CHARACTERISTICS

Traits of autistic children when excessive and in combination with one another, typify the syndrome. A list of traits includes: aloofness from humans, need for sameness and repetition, response to frustration by rage or withdrawl, gaze aversion, bizarre movements (twirling, swaying, tapping, etc.), severe communication and learning disabilities, and occasionally an unusual rote memory for certain facts.

These evaluations identify *unusual* behavior. They lack in putting this handicapping condition into a *developmental* perspective, showing either delay and/or aberrance, pointing out quantitative and/or qualitative deviations from the *norm*. Such a perspective would seem to have more usefulness for those living and/or working with these children. Such people need a point at which to launch appropriate interventions that consider the actual functioning level of the individual child. Regardless of chronological age or etiology such a descriptive, developmental assessment would be focused on meeting the child's emotional, social, and cognitive needs in an effort to promote growth along normal lines.

ASSESSMENT

Much of an autist's functioning can be seen in terms of extreme delay and/or aberrance. It is typical for infants to rock, stimulate themselves when people or toys are gone, and repeat old ways to approach new situations. Reflexes exhibit themselves at birth and gradually integrate after both maturation and socialization or learning. Other behaviors develop likewise, i.e., a child will call a dog "dog" but also use this schema in an overgeneralized fashion, calling all four-legged animals "dog." This is one example of overassimilation, the means of adapting reality to oneself rather than accommodating, which is adapting oneself to reality.

This is not to say that the autist is "just like" a normal infant. But when assessing functioning in this manner it is easier to consider needs based on these primitive abilities.

This led Robert Kreger and me to devise a synthesis of the developmental theories of Piaget, Erikson, and Freud. From this design, where both differences and commonalities were designed along various dimensions, we then began devising an assessment and an intervention model based on age norms in realms of emotional, social, and cognitive development.[3] Various operationally defined variables were considered in this assessment and intervention model.

Tables 8-1–2 exhibit two of the variables, and focus on the first two stages of our design. As can be seen, much of the functioning of autists could be described in these terms. (The complete version will include several variables and 0- to 11-year-old norms codified within four stages and three "styles.")

As one can see, at this point we are more concerned with *actual* functioning rather than etiology. The child's stage-related functioning implies certain needs when looked at in such a developmental context.

INTERVENTION

Any approach used with these children must first address their actual developmental level of functioning in the aforementioned realms. The interventions applied will focus on his cognitive, social, and emotional abilities at this time and launch him into progressive, horizontal, and vertical growth.

Table 8-1. Kreger Assessment Instrument Stage 1: Interaction with Other Children—Ages 0-1½

Passive Adaptive Behavior	Normative Adaptive Behavior	Active Adaptive Behavior
Child's play is perserverative with own body or objects, i.e., repetitious and stereotypic twirling or flapping of fingers or objects, stimulation of self by sucking, biting, twirling, rocking.	Most of child's play in this stage is isolative or solitary, i.e., plays by or with self using feet, hands or toys. (His focus is on a *caretaking adult*.)	Child's play is discontinuous. He demands (screams, whines, bangs head) frequent sensorimotor stimulation from numerous objects.
Child derives no pleasure from play with objects. He is apathetic; shows no interest in manipulating objects. He shows steroytpic and reptitious responses to other children or objects, i.e., shaking object with minimal affect.	Mode of child's play involves assimilation of pleasurable affect from manipulation of objects, i.e., "practice plays" with toy to rattle it. He derives pleasure from activity in itself and reflects pleasure, calm, tension, etc., of immediate environment.	Child's play involves intense affect and prolonged responses, i.e., continued tension, etc. Child remains irritable and does not derive pleasure from play.
Child has minimal interaction with other children. He may withdraw, avoid, turn from others, and/or engage in self stimulation, i.e., sucking, biting, twirling.	Interaction with children has caretaking theme, i.e., notices other children if they stimulate him by feeding, holding, playing with him, meeting his needs, or stimulating his interest.	Child engaged in continuous attention-seeking from other children. He imposes self by whining, crying, screaming and otherwise pursuing others to gain response. He may actively reject by biting or spitting at child.
Child has low level of expressing feelings and needs. He is apathetic regarding his inner state and inhibits responding. He uses some primitive movements and sounds in most situations, i.e., flapping hands.	Communication with other children involves gross responses. He communicates feeling states and bodily needs by crying, moving entire body, etc., to show pleasure, fear, discomfort.	Responses of his inner states to other children are intense and frequent, i.e., narcissistic raging, screaming, complaining, biting, spitting at others. He communicates feelings with panic.
Child is unaware of and unresponsive to other children. He is unfocused (not "tuned-in") to outside stimulation.	Child imitates gross movement and responses of children, i.e., smiles, claps, blinks, coos.	The child is overstimulated by other children and their objects. He grabs and take attention and objects from them.

Additional Comments

Table 8–2. Kreger Assessment Instrument Stage I: Interaction with Adults—0–1½

Passive Adaptive Behavior	Normative Adaptive Behavior	Active Adaptive Behavior
Child and mothering figure cannot form bond and attachment. Child does not rely on primary adult to meet his needs but remains detached	Child is totally *dependent on one mothering (primary) figure* for gratification of psychological needs and reduction of discomfort. Child uses her as needfulfilling object. Child depends on the consistency of this caretaker for feelings of trust, security and safety.	Child demands adult responsiveness with intense and prolonged irritability, whining, clinging, etc. He communicates needs quickly and strongly. He may actively shun adult while seeking personal gratification (take object on own with no concern for adult).
Child apathetic, aloof and withdrawn from adult. He does not reach out or provoke caretaking behaviors. Despondency and unattachment dominate his tone of behavior. He doesn't search for adult or attempt to regain attention (by calling, crying, etc.).	Through predicatable and gratifying responsiveness of caretaker, child forms first and primary bond and attachment to external world of people and objects. He fears adult's loss and feels helpless in her absence. He fears strangers (especially at 8 to 10 months) and will retreat from unfamiliar persons at these times.	Child seems panicky and frantic in his attempts for continuous need gratification. He is hard to satisfy and "never has enough . . ." He constantly searches for lost objects (people or other objects).
Child does not express needs or respond to adult nurturance. He avoids and turns away from adults.	Child tries to please caretaker later in stage with smiles, coos and imitated claps, winks, etc. He responds with pleasure to her sensory stimulations (touch, sounds, etc.), reflecting security.	Child responds to adult care with continued demanding, impatient and complaining actions, or orally rejects adult (bites, spits), and attempts to take care of self.
Child responds to adult with passive, inward self-preoccupation.	Child incorporates emotional tone of primary adult, i.e., calm, pleasure, tension or anxiety, sadness, etc. He assimilates "feeling states" of his immediate environment (affective "learning").	Child responds to adult with active, outward preoccupation, using adult as a satisfier of his needs.

Additional Comments

Many interventions seem to force the child to accommodate to what *we* feel is important, i.e., reading or doing math problems. Yet this "splinter skill" may be totally alien and meaningless to the child and force him into more social withdrawal. Many autists' "treatment" consisted of academic tasks or other age-related activities. For example, a boy who did not have a basic identity of who he was or the equality of two halves of an object was kept busy doing long multiplication problems in a "therapeutic" school. Some intervention models propose that focusing on specific, overt task performance is best. However, when one focuses on tasks, even if social tasks, one encourages just the maladaptions that are part of the problem. Concrete, mechanical, and limited functioning is often encouraged when the task becomes more important than the child. The rote, splinter skills so often seen in autists are not integrated nor do they have true meaning for the child. Often, parents and professionals alike are so eager to prove that the autist is not mentally retarded that they push the child to perform for others on useless "intellectual" pursuits which have no meaning to the child. Our first priority should address the basic problem: to first develop in the child a positive attachment to human beings and interest in objects.

The following points speak to psychosocial and cognitive interventions it is felt to benefit the young autistic child. Parents and professionals alike must share in the difficult task of reorienting the child to reality. The theory integrations by R. and L. Kreger[4] speak to these stage needs in more theoretical terms, such as: positive oral incorporations, basic trust of self-others-environment, physical and psychological security, sensory-motor stimulation, predictably permanent objects (humans), and clarification of reality. The following points are more practically oriented, the final model is very specific.

1. *Nurturance* by one constant figure, predictable and consistent care, physical and psychological security, trust of self-others-environment.

2. *Responsiveness* by this (these) nurturing figures, especially during times of feeding, vocalization, crying, and other nonverbal communications.

3. *Good incorporations:* food, touch, and other sensory-motor stimuli, to link pleasure with interactions in the environment and help him assimilate the positive.

4. Adult *assistance* in undeveloped areas of reality testing and right-wrong issues. (For example, the adult needs to define reality and structure; what is safe-unsafe, good-bad, right-wrong, etc., in a nonthreatening manner.)

5. When possible, *explanations* to show cause and effect, reasoning to define situations and help the child anticipate feelings or thoughts or actions.

6. *Experiences* which are concrete (not abstract and/or verbal), here-and-now, appropriately stimulating with people and objects, and sensory-motor in process. (Paper-pencil tasks or leaving the child to his own devices for periods of time will usually initiate self-stimulating, bizarre, or withdrawing behaviors.)

7. Practice with the concept of *object permanence,* with humans and objects. (Hide-and-go-seek, peek-a-boo, and concentration games are helpful.)

8. Offer *yourself* as a permanent object, constant and predictable. (Following through on promises, calling or writing when you are gone, offering photos and other reminders of yourself, and bringing back souvenirs are all important. You don't want his memory traces of you to "fade" and frighten him that you no longer exist when you are not seen.)

9. Offer *alternatives* that all would engage the child in purposeful play, i.e., entice child with desirable musical records, tapes, pattern play, animals, or other indirectly communicative activities; showing him what he *can* do rather than only what he *can't* do.

10. Allow the child *success,* first at his own social level. (Let him isolate until he feels secure, then encourage parallel play beside one safe peer, etc. Don't force or punish his actuarial level.)

11. Permit him both his *own territory and possessions* until he is ready to de-center and give to the nonself world.

12. Offer *help* when needed, even if child had ambivalently "rejected" you previously. (Set yourself up as a need-fulfilling object.)

13. Maintain *constancy* in his life with both other people and situations.

14. Offer *external rewards* to concretely motivate the child away from pure habits, using actions and things he enjoys.

15. Set up situations in which the child can subtly *practice caring,* i.e., feeding an animal, watering a plant; when he is predictably needed by another living thing.

16. Build educational *concepts* of identification (nonverbal), classification (similarities, differences, gross to refined), order of time, spatial relationships, and body image.

17. Provide *sensory-motor learning* through objects and activities where the child's own body is used to see-hear-smell-taste-move in his world. (Present nonadversive stimuli and *gradually* present those he previously would or could not tolerate.)

18. Use music, art, language, puppets, and other *expressive activities* with trusted people, field trips to expose the child to various stimulation and to give opportunities to practice trusting new people and places.

19. *Respond* to any attempts of the child to communicate and offer him nonthreatening verbal communication, i.e., tapes, records, TV, if he is first confused by human talk. (Often, autistic youngsters are puz-

zled by multisensory presentations. If so, you can
expose them to one channel at a time, then two, i.e.,
taste, then taste and sound.)

20.   Offer times for this child to be in *control* actively with
a smaller or less able child. (There he safely can move
out from himself, test reality with another small person and be the "doer", rather than the one "done
to.")

This developmental approach has described children in the
first stage of development. When negotiated, stage-two interventions should be provided. To merely *outline* a few:

Choices, child-directed from alternatives.

Times to express aggressive locomotion and speech, etc.;
times to bind, classify, and clean, etc.

Reflections of worth, praise, reinforcement.

Limits and structure with reasons given to child.

Language activities to help develop internal thought.

Parallel play beside a safe peer.

Decrease of magical thinking by explaining, confronting
misperceptions and mastering fears.

Imitative activities.

Active role with another child to help develop self-esteem
and independence, i.e., help teach another how to do
something.

Conclusion

As the autist increases his basic abilities and affective
schema toward human beings, he will become a more purposeful and certainly a less fearful child. When his *basic* orientations to the outside world are in a more realistic perspective, he
then will be able and willing to respond, organize, and socialize
in a more normal adaptive style.

REFERENCES

1. Bergman, P, & Escalona, S: Unusual sensitivities in very young children. *Psychoanalytic Study Child, 3–4:* 333–335, 1949.

2. Bettleheim, B: *The empty fortress.* New York: Free Press, 1967.

3. Kanner, L: Autistic disturbances of affective contact. *Nerv. Child, 2:* 217–250, 1943.

4. Kreger, L, & Kreger, R: Application of cognitive, psychosocial and psychoanalytic theories in the developmentally integrated assessment and treatment of emotionally handicapped disturbed children. Educational Resource Center, April, 1978.

5. Rimland, B: *Infantile autism.* New York: Appleton-Century-Crofts, 1964.

6. Rutter, M, & Bartak, L: Causes of infantile autism: Some considerations from recent research. *J. Autism Child. Schizophrenia, 1:* 20–32, 1971.

7. Schopler, E: Early infantile autism and receptor processes. *Arch. Gen. Psychiatry, 13:* 327–335, 1964.

Part II

FAMILIES

In our highly specialized professional world we often concentrate so closely on our specific area of expertise or the dysfunction that we are asked to help remedy that we fail to recognize or deal with the broader psychosocial aspects of the problem.

This section looks at the effect the small child's handicap can have on the family—parents and siblings. These chapters highlight the impact on families from such problems as chronic endocrine disease in young children, blindness, and feeding problems, and gives suggestions for teaching families how to cope and/or give special support to these people.

It should be emphasized that we, the caregivers, are also an intimate part of the psychosocial network of the young handicapped child and in addition to paying special attention to helping families cope, we should pay special attention to our own needs and those of our colleagues when dealing with these often heartbreaking problems.

Chapter 9

FEEDING PROBLEMS AND THEIR EFFECT ON FAMILIES WITH HANDICAPPED INFANTS

Sally Atkins-Burnett, M.Ed.

This chapter concerns the family that has an infant with feeding problems. First, consider the cultural significance of feeding in our society. Look in any woman's magazine and almost every other page seems to have some food advertisements. The U.S. fosters one of the most obese cultures in the world. Feelings about being a good mother are strongly influenced by the feeding experience.

When Klaus and Kennell discuss events after birth that are important to attachment, they talk about seeing, touching, and giving care to the baby. In examining attachment behaviors, they choose a feeding time "because of its universality and its central position in the mother-infant relationship" (p. 55).[11] Feeding enhances a feeling of giving life to the infant—of helping to maintain the life given.

Given this background, enter the infant with a feeding problem and, if not adequately handled, you're flirting with an attachment problem as well. The timing of the feeding problem and the severity of it will also affect the extent of its impact on the parent-child relationship.

What is a feeding problem? Rudolph Schaeffer, in his book *Mothering,* discusses the complexity of the initial total feeding act: rooting, opening the mouth, grasping the nipple with the lips, sucking, and swallowing. All these are integrated in sequence, along with breathing, and the infant is able to deal with temperature changes and changes in flow of milk. Schaeffer states that it would make the mother's task "even more complex if she had somehow to teach it" (Schaeffer, p. 32).[13] As the child goes from bottle to solid foods, even more complex skills replace the initial suck-swallow patterns. Appendix A lists the developmental process involved in learning feeding behaviors. I would define a feeding problem as occurring anytime a mother or child experiences more than momentary difficulty during the feeding process. It can be as "minor" as a new mother who has difficulty nursing her infant because she cannot get into a comfortable position, or as "major" as a child born with a severe cleft palate or cerebral palsy. Appendix B lists a variety of feeding problems. No matter how minor a feeding problem might be initially, it has the potential to become a major problem unless resolved.

Most of my contact concerning infants with feeding problems has been with infants three months or older who, in addition to the feeding problem they display, are handicapped in some way.

Before moving to Michigan, I worked in Kansas City, Missouri in a Parent Infant Program (PIP) that was operated by the Regional Center for the State Department of Mental Health. We served families that had handicapped children from birth to three years of age. PIP served seven counties and is a home-based program.

The children we served manifested a wide variety of disabilities: Down's syndrome, cerebral palsy, microcephaly, hydrocephaly, myelomeningocele, Burenstein-Tabey's, epilepsy, and many developmental delays that could not be easily classified.

The staff of PIP included four occupational therapists and two teachers. Each of us carried a caseload of 12 to 15 families. In addition, there were physical therapy, social work, speech therapy, and psychology consultants available to the staff. Each of us was responsible for helping the parents learn how to encourage their child's development in all areas (gross and fine motor, language, sensory, social, self-help, cognitive). We saw most families once a week, Monday through Thursday. Friday was the day we compiled our reports, had in-service training sessions, and met and consulted with each other. These meetings offered us the opportunity to gain support from each other as well as help in áreas in which we were having difficulty. We would invite one family each week to come into the center for all of us to evaluate and review. In addition, each child was seen once a year by the diagnostic team at the center. Parents also had the option of attending one of the parent groups that we organized. I will discuss the program in some depth because I think it is a good model.

The particular advantages of this model to a family with a feeding problem are:

1.   That it is a home-based program. This allows the therapist a full understanding of what is available in the home and what occurs during the feeding times. There are many things that a parent may not notice that a child might be sensitive to. For example, the infant might be startled by the 12 o'clock siren in the middle of his meal or by his three-year-old brother running around.

2.   That there was one person who was aware of all areas of the child's development, who was "assigning tasks or activities for family" and who was thus able to help the family prioritize their needs and the child's needs.

These points are very important. I have known families that have seen different therapists for each aspect of the child's development. They spend most of the week traveling to and from visits to various professionals and they sometimes receive conflicting advice from the different disciplines. If they tried to follow the suggestions of each of the therapists, they would find that there are not enough hours in the day. Feeding alone can take as many as 6 or more hours a day.

When working with a family, it is important to know where their priorities lie. It is the therapist's or teacher's job to supply parents with the information they need to make *informed* decisions about priorities, but the therapists need to be flexible enough to follow the priorities of the parents in giving suggestions, even if these priorities differ from the value system of the therapist. Remember, it is the parents who will be living with this child day in and day out, and it is the parents who will be there to see the consequences of their decisions. Be honest with the parents about both the positive and negative consequences of a decision and about areas in which your knowledge (or knowledge in general) is limited.

In assessing feeding problems, look at a number of things about the environment and the mother-child relationship as well as the actual feeding problem.

QUALITY OF MOTHER-CHILD INTERACTION

What is the quality of the mother-child interaction? Do the infant and mother maintain eye contact? Do they participate in synchronous play behaviors? Does the mother seem to enjoy her infant? How does the mother feel about her ability to mother? Is this a first child or a tenth, and did the other children experience feeding problems? How important is feeding to this family—is food an important issue? Who considers feeding to be a problem and who brought up the issue? These things make a difference in terms of how and when you approach the feeding problem.

Case Study

Matthew was 14 months old when I first visited his family. He and his twin brother had been born at six months gestational age. His twin brother was born "normal"; Matthew experienced respiratory difficulties and spent the first two months of life in the hospital. When he was eight months old, he reentered the hospital for heart surgery. When I began seeing the family, Matthew had been diagnosed as severely mentally retarded, spastic quadriplegic, and cortically blind. His mother had said that she used to have trouble feeding him because he vomited frequently, but that she had medicine to relax his stomach (Mylanta) and he did not vomit as much anymore. I asked to observe his eating behaviors, explaining that an infant learned a lot about the parts of his mouth and how to move them when he ate, and this was important for speech development. When I visited, I observed the following things: When Mrs. M. held Matthew, she had him facing away from her. She fed Matthew, his twin, and herself at the same time. Matthew sat in a "bouncy chair" on the floor on one side of his mother and his twin in a high chair on the other side. Matthew turned his head to the side in order to eat since a very strong extensor pattern predominated when his head was at midline. Mother spoonfed Matthew and his twin alternating their bites with her own. She then laid Matthew in the corner of the couch and propped up his bottle to the side of him. In evaluating his eating behavior, I found that he had a strong primitive sucking reflex, an emerging bite reflex, and a very high, narrow palate. He drooled a lot. His facial expressions were total patterns; if he pursed his lips, his whole face seemed to purse. Matthew's breathing was very shallow. With his head to the side, you could see the influence of the asymmetrical tonic neck reflex (ATNR) on his muscle tone. Also, because of the ATNR Matthew could not bring his hand to his mouth. Matthew startled very easily to sounds and to touch. He was chronically constipated. In short, Matthew had many problems with eating, but this did not seem like the place to start the intervention. Remember that Matthew's mother did not consider feeding a problem and she did not know Matthew as a person. She had been told he could not see; he startled when she talked to him and stiffened when she touched him. He cried but did not babble, and she had been told he was severely retarded. She did not talk to him and play with him. She did not know how. She took care of him—she bathed, fed, dressed, and changed him. I decided that before complicating the feeding process with Mueller's feeding techniques, this mother and child needed to get to know and love each other. We began with lots of activities aimed at relaxing Matthew and helping his mother to cue into his responses to her. Their favorite of these activities was to have Matthew lie on a large, partially deflated ball facing his mother as she bounced him. We talked about positioning; and handling, we stimulated him visually, and tried to desensitize his response to sound and touch. We turned down the thermostat in the house (tactile-defensive children prefer cooler temperatures—about 65 degrees). We developed a form of communication and a bond between mother and child and *then* we talked about those things I perceived to be feeding problems and the techniques used to eliminate them. Mrs. M. opted to try the techniques, and I supported her by visiting (and by sometimes relieving her) during one meal each day for the first week.

Parents learning feeding techniques need a great deal of support and encouragement. The techniques are not always easy to use, and it may be difficult for some people to observe the differences they are making. Parents need assurances when they are correctly using feeding techniques, and assistance when they are not using them correctly or when the technique needs to be adapted for some reason. For some children feeding takes many hours a day. I think the therapist should encourage the parents to find other people who can help feed their child. The family may need assistance in identifying who would be willing to share in the feeding process. Grandparents, relatives, baby sitters, and nursing students are some resources that can be utilized. The parent (mother especially) may need reassurance that allowing someone else to help feed her child does *not* mean she is "failing" her child in any way. Having the mother teach other adults (with you present to support her) allows her to verbalize her understanding of the feeding techniques which may clarify some of the techniques for her.

Lack of bonding alone is not sufficient reason to delay feeding techniques. In some instances the feeding problem might be an obstacle impeding the development of attachment.

Case Study

When I first visited her family, Martha was a four-month-old Down's syndrome infant. She weighed only 6 lb and did not seem to be gaining any weight. Martha was born to parents in their mid-40s in a rural area. She had one brother who was eight at the time of her birth.

Martha's oral muscle tone was very poor. She had a very weak suck with minimal lip closure. Her tongue lagged so much that it was over the edge of her chin most of the time. When her mother held or carried her, she held Martha facing away from her—even when she fed her. For this mother, feeding was a problem. Her child was not gaining weight in the way she wanted. It took a long time for her to feed Martha, and Martha's low muscle tone in the oral area accentuated, for her mother, the fact that this child, this girl they had longed to have, was handicapped.

Martha had developed a tongue thrust when she swallowed. She was being fed with a preemie nipple that was too long for her oral structure and that had an enlarged hole. Her cereal was mixed in with her formula.

I began with this family by talking about how we could eliminate some of the feeding problems by increasing Martha's oral muscle tone and suck and by decreasing her tongue thrust. I attempted to help Mrs. R. find a feeding position that was comfortable for her and that would allow her to be *en face* with

Martha. At first, Mrs. R. resisted positions that involved looking at Martha. As Martha's suck improved and her tongue
lagged less and less, her mother was more and more able to look
at her. While we were working on feeding, I also encouraged
Mrs. R. to do activities to improve eye tracking and thus helped
her to focus on looking at Martha and at her eyes in a more
positive light.

Today, Martha is continuing to gain weight steadily and
to grow and develop. Her parents are very attached to her and
take pride in her accomplishments.

Child's Skills in Reference to Feeding Behaviors

What are the child's skills in reference to a normal sequence of feeding behaviors? Are the "problems" experienced
actually normal occurrences in a developmental sequence or are
they pathological responses?

The most common example of this is spitting up. It is quite
common for infants to spit up some of their food. It is more
common in infants with poor lip closure because they swallow
more air as they eat and as the air comes back up, it also pushes
some food out. It is also very common for infants to experience
a lot of spitting up from the time they begin sitting up and
crawling until they stand up. Infants who are fed too quickly
will often vomit (this elicits the stretch reflex of stomach muscles). Slowing down feeding can prevent this from occurring. If,
however, the spitting up is a projectile vomiting, it is a less
normal, more pathological response. It may be the result of an
allergy, a hyperactive esophogeal reflex, or pyloric stenosis. If
the child is not gaining weight as a result of the spitting up,
feeding problems should be investigated medically even when
the vomiting is not projectile.

Appendix A describes the developmental sequence of feeding behaviors and gives approximate ages at which these behaviors occur. Remember, the ages are approximate. Infants can
vary greatly in when they achieve each step in a developmental

sequence. If a child is delayed in other areas (especially if delayed in motor skills), anticipate that there might be a similar delay in his/her feeding skills. If a parent feels his/her child is experiencing a problem in feeding which is a normal developmental response (e.g., decreased appetite of one- to two-year-olds), I would suggest that you refer them to one of T. Berry Brazelton's books (*Infants and Mothers* or *Toddlers and Parents*).[3,4] He handles discussion of these and other problems in a way that is comforting to parents and assures them that what they are experiencing is OK.

PROBLEMS THE CHILD EXHIBITS

What problems is the child exhibiting? Does the child have a tongue thrust? Does (s)he exhibit a strong gag reflex? Bite reflex? Suck-swallow reflex? Are the child's facial expressions relaxed and symmetrical? Is the facio-oral structure normal? Does (s)he have a cleft palate? A high-vaulted upper palate? What does jaw occlusion look like? How much muscle tone does the child exhibit? Is (s)he hyperresponsive to touch? What is the shape of his/her tongue? (When chewing motions begin, the tongue begins to form a tip, and it is no longer as rounded.) Are the gums inflamed? Is the child drooling? Can the child move food around well in his/her mouth by moving the tongue from side to side? Can the child chew or does (s)he suck food until it is soft enough to swallow? (Appendix B lists a variety of feeding problems.)

I will briefly discuss children with hypersensitive mouths. This is a frequent problem that is often experienced in conjunction with other feeding problems. Children who are gavage fed for a long time are often hypersensitive orally because of lack of stimulation to the tactile nerves. Massage of the lips, gums, and cheeks to help desensitize the oral area is helpful for these children. This may be done with gauze wrapped around a Q-tip or with a finger. One side should be massaged and then the mouth closed for a swallow before the next side is begun. Rub-

208 THE SPECIAL INFANT

bing of the gums stimulates increased salivation, thus by pausing for a swallow, you are encouraging a normal response (to increased salivation). Since the nerves inside the mouth go directly to the brain stem, their influence and your stimulation of them is stronger. Switching sides too quickly could overwhelm the nervous system. In switching from one side of the mouth to the other, your input is changing from one side of the brain to the other. Thus, it is most helpful to massage one side, pause, then massage the other side. Gradually increasing the texture of foods eaten also helps to desensitize the mouth. For some children, the taste of some foods is as alerting as the texture. You can help to decrease this problem by having the child near the area in which the food is cooked so he/she habituates to the smell. Our senses of smell and taste are strongly related.

Many children who are tactile-defensive inside their mouths, may be tactile-defensive elsewhere and so, while desensitizing the mouth, the rest of the body may need to be desensitized as well. It is not unusual for a tactile-defensive child also to be auditorily defensive, so it may be best to feed them at times when the noise level will remain consistent and will be calming to the system rather than alerting. I often recommend that parents play soothing music during feeding to help relax both themselves and their child. Children often sense their parents' anxiety and may respond more to the parents' anxiety than to the feeding technique used, no matter how well the technique is used.

For further discussion of specific feeding techniques and handling and positioning during feeding, you are referred to the notes.

1. Ayres, AJ: Tactile functions. *Am. J. Occup. Ther., 18:* 6–11, 1964.

2. Bosma, J, Grossman, R, & Kavanagh, JF: A syndrome of impairment of oral perception. In *Symptoms on oral sensation and perception.* Springfield, Ill.: Charles C Thomas, 1976.

3. Brazelton, TB: *Infants and mothers.* New York: Dell, 1969.

4. Brazelton, TB: *Toddlers and parents.* New York: Dell, 1969.

5. *Children in contemporary society.* Special Issue: *Nutrition and young children, 12:* November, 1978. (Available from Pittsburgh Association for the Education of Young Children, P.O. Box 11173, Pittsburgh, Pa. 15237.)

6. Farber, S: *Sensorimotor evaluation and treatment procedures.* Indiana University Foundation, 1974. (Order from Fred Sammons, Inc., Box 32, Brookfield, Ill. 60513.)

7. Finnie, N: *Handling the young cerebral palsied child at home.* New York: Dutton, 1975.

8. Gallender, D: *Eating handicaps: Illustrated techniques for feeding disorders.* Springfield, Ill.: Charles C Thomas, 1978.

9. Getchel, & Howard: *Nutrition in development.* New York: McGraw-Hill, 1975.

10. Ingram, TTS: Clinical significance of infantile feeding reflexes. *Dev. Med. Child Neurol., 4:* 159–169, 1962.

11. Klaus, MH, & Kennell, J: *Maternal-infant bonding.* St. Louis: Mosby, 1976.

12. Mueller, H: Facilitating feeding and prespeech. In W. Pearson (Ed.), *Physical therapy services in the developmental disabilities.* Springfield, Ill.: Charles C Thomas, 1972.

13. Schaeffer, R: Mothering. In *The developing child series.* Cambridge, Mass.: Harvard University Press, 1977.

14. Solka, D, & Lowry, M: *Nutrition and feeding techniques for handicapped children.* (Available from Developmental Disabilities Program, Room 892, California State Department of Health, 744 P Street, Sacramento, Ca. 95814.)

15. South Central Regional Center for Services to Deaf-Blind Children: *Problem Feeder Mini-Workshop Proceedings,* May, 1974. (Available from S.C.R.C. Callier Center for Communication Disorders, 1966 Inwood Rd., Dallas, Texas 75235.)

APPENDIX A

Feeding

Approximate Age*
Birth   Rooting reflex present
Sucking reflex elicited by hunger or any stimulation in region of mouth
Swallowing reflex present
Palate aware if temperature changes
Incomplete lip closure
Unable to release nipple
Projectible vomiting may be first sign of allergy

1 Month   Mouth opening reflex cannot be inhibited, will open mouth whether he/she wants the food or not
Opens mouth waiting for food
Better lip closure

*For premature babies, add number of months of prematurity to age listed.

Active lip movement when sucking
Can take cereal from spoon held by parent**

2 Months Cup feeding *may* be *introducing;*
child's need for sucking (both nutritive
and nonnutritive) continues
Can take juice from a cup held by parent: swallows; breast or bottle should be
the way he/she receives major fluid intake
Beginning of other signs of allergy—
colic, diarrhea, constipation, eczema,
head sweating, congestion, etc.

3 Months Sucking and swallowing in sequence
Peristalis in correct direction
Takes several swallows at a time from
a cup held by parent
Anticipates feeding
Salivary glands begin to mature (infant
blows bubbles, mouths or bites objects,
and may appear to be teething)

4 Months Choking is reflexive until chewing is established
Can inhibit biting and sucking reflexes
(inhibits sucking as the nipple refills)
More control and movement of tongue
is handled by child, not by reflexes
Recognizes bottle: puts hands on,
mouth ready for nipple
Strong tongue movement against nipple
producing strong sucking

**Breastfeeding (supplemented by iron and vitamins) fulfills an infant's
nutritional needs for the first 6 to 12 months of life. If the mother's milk
supply is diminished and for the child who has a poor suck, the pediatrician
might recommend supplementing with cereal to increase caloric intake.

Tongue thrust seen more with cupfeeding than spoonfeeding (rooting for nipple)

Anticipates food on sight: arms active at sight, poises mouth, and smacks lips

Appetite is more erratic

Indicates satiation by spitting out food

Can show food preferences as mouth-opening reflex is inhibited

5 Months Has control of neck muscles which makes it easier to close mouth and swallow

Can use hands to draw bottle to mouth, but releases when nipple is inserted if not encouraged to continue holding

Holds bottle in supine position: head flexed

Drinks continuously from an open glass

Mouth ready for spoon

Tongue reversal after spoon removed, ejecting food involuntarily

5½ Months Swallowing is completely voluntary

Good control with lips and tongue

Holds bottle in infant seat (glass bottle might be too heavy)

Beginning definite chewing motion by gumming food

Holds and sucks a cookie

Pulls food off spoon with lips

Eats new foods if introduced regularly in a variety

Prime or optimal time for munching which increases the development of dental structures and desensitizes the gastrointestinal tract and mouth

7 Months	First signs of chewing are observed
	Keeps lips closed while chewing
	Bites off piece of cracker
	Removes food quickly from spoon with lips
	Teeth beginning to erupt (through 18 months)
8 Months	Holds own bottle in high chair
	Drinks from cup with minimal assistance to help hold
	Plays with spoon
	Hands reach for dish out of arms length
9 Months	Finger feeds most of food: picks up with thumb and forefinger
	Helps hold and lick spoon after dipped into food
	Child can be helped to begin drinking through a straw (different suck from suck-swallow pattern—an inverted whistle)
	Finicky about appetite
10 Months	As chewing develops, automatic chew reflex is inhibited.
	Real chew appears as tongue transfers lumps of food from one side to the other: sign of lateral chewing
	Can lick food off lower lip with tongue
	Burps self by rotating to prone position, and in crawling and creeping
	Cup drinking still messy—may want to play with it
	Appetite continues to be sporadic
	Very definite about disliked foods
	Investigative about food—may remove it from mouth several times: food is to

	be felt, tasted, smeared, and dropped on the floor
11 Months	Uses two hands on cup—messy
	Objects if mother tries to help complete feeding
12 Months	Appetite may decrease
	Shows definite preference for foods—more choosy about food
	Lunch is least motivating meal
	Rotary chewing is present
	Holds cup with digital grasp—tilts cup rather than head, still spilling
	Grasps spoon—poor manipulation, spoon inverted before insertion—fills poorly
	Independent about finishing meal—may dump remaining food on floor
	May no longer need bottle
15 Months	Wants to help feed self
	Beginning to independently use spoon—grasps and inserts into dish, occasionally turns spoon before reaching mouth
	Leaves dish on tray when finished
	Shows definite preference for certain foods
	Regular diet
	Lowest point of appetite (until 18 months)
	Discards bottle—may include nighttime bottle
	Children should never be given bottles lying flat on backs, in cribs, especially if anything other than water is in it. "Bottle babies" are prone to dental caries, ear infections, and tongue thrust.

18 Months	Drinks from cup well—adjusts head properly
	Chews meat well
	Grasps spoon with thumb and pincer finger
	Better control with spoon—fills, turns in mouth; spills food to moderate degree only
	Hands empty cup or dish to mother— if she does not see child with, will drop or throw it,
	Child weaned from bottle
21 Months	Handles a cup well—lifting, drinking, replacing
	Distinguishes between edible and nonedible items
	Removes wrappers from food
	Very regimented in eating—wants everything on a routine schedule and presented same way each time
	Wants to play with food, especially stirable food
2 Years	Chewing is becoming more rotary with little effort
	Can handle small glass with one hand, partially filled as drinks
	Inserts food into mouth without turning over spoon—moderate spillage
	Begins fork feeding
	Continues to require supervision with eating, since now apt to play with food —very interested in stirring
2½ Years	Obtains drink from faucet by self
	Fork feeds
	Pours from small pitcher with some spilling

3 Years	Pours well from a pitcher
	Serves self at table with help
	Minimum spilling from spoon
	Cleans up spills with help
	Drinks through a plastic straw using an inverted whistle
	Dawdles at mealtime
	Gets up from table frequently
	Completes a meal
4 Years	Helps set table
	Feeds self quite well
	Beginning to use knife to spread
	Cleans up spills without help
	Clears his/her dishes from the table to kitchen
	Sits at table during length of meal, but may leave for frequent trips to the bathroom

APPENDIX B

Feeding Problems Can Be Related to Physical or Structural Problems Such As:

1. Tongue movements: tongue tied or absent or poor lateral movement
2. (A) Tactile-defensive mouth
    (B) Hyposensitive mouth and face
    (C) Hypersensitive mouth and face
3. Curved or short upper lip which gives incomplete closure for vacuum needed to swallow
4. Enlarged tonsils which fill throat
5. Mouth breathing which causes coordination problems in swallowing and respiration
6. Tongue thrust either learned from poor positioning in feeding or part of the extensor motor pattern
7. High narrow arch in mouth caused by abnormal tongue action or broad swollen gum ridges

Adapted from an outline designed by Mary Benbow, O.T.R.

8. Cleft palate
9. "Reverse swallow" seen in combination with thrust pattern
10. Mal occlusion of teeth; genetic, too long on bottle feeding, behavioral mannerisms
11. Slow eruption of teeth and in irregular pattern
12. Tongue in poor position:
    (A) May be elevated and pressed against front teeth and roof of mouth
    (B) May protrude and seem large
    (C) May lie low and lazy in mouth
13. Gag
    (A) Hyperactive gag due to the late introduction of solid food
    (B) Hypoactive gag due to poor muscle and reflex tone
14. Hyperactive esophogeal reflex
15. Hypertonia
16. Hypotonia

And to Medical Problems Such As:

1. Soft gums due to soft foods in diet and lack of brushing
2. Hard, inflamed, and swollen gums
3. Medications: Always know dosage and side effects
   (A) Dilantin is a drug which depresses the motor centers of the cortex only. Its side effects are hyperplasia of the gingivi, loss of taste, irritability, gastric irritability, and gingivitis
   (B) Ritalin may cut appetite and weight gain
4. Allergies
5. Endocrine system malfunction

And to Emotional Problems Such As:

1. Maternal anxiety
2. Poor mother-infant (parent-infant) attachment
3. Other

Chapter 10

PROFESSIONAL SUPPORT FOR FAMILIES OF BLIND CHILDREN

Strategies for Coping with Inevitable Developmental Lag, Disappointment, and Doubt

Edna Adelson, M.A.

Over the past 12 years I have met many infants and young children who were blind from birth. I have met their parents as well. The one thing I have not met in all these years is any simple formula or test or checklist that would free me and the family from the uncertainty that is a normal part of the early years of a blind child's growth. Nor have I found any way to shorten the time it takes for careful assessment and the planning of individualized intervention and guidance. One way or another the work always involves questions that test my knowledge about the children, and, inevitably, there are tensions that test my partnership with the parents. Teachers, pediatricians, and all who meet blind children and their families can expect to meet similar dilemmas. Any enterprise can be endangered by misunderstood and misdirected doubt, disappointment, and anger. But when the problems are recognized and kept in perspective, then the good work and forward progress can be kept safe.

Blindness has its own special impact on early development. In our research at the Child Development Project we came to understand and appreciate the ways the blind child's early growth was similar to and different from that of the sighted child.* In partnership with the parents we began a slow and systematic process of open inquiry and ongoing assessment. Our best observations came during slow-paced visits that were usually at home. Simple ordinary events let us see the baby's best performance and let us hear the parents' real concerns. What evolved was a flexible program of support and guidance fitted to the needs and pace of each child and his family. We knew that the important influences on a blind child's adequacy lay in the major areas of human attachment, the concept of a permanent object, language and gross motor development, and hand or fine motor development. We learned to record observable behaviors in great detail. The observed behaviors served us as outer clues to the inner mental organization that influenced the parent-child relationship and the infant's understanding of his experiences.

Briefly, we found that the milestones of human attachment should be as they are for any child: smiling, preference for mother, and reaction to a stranger all being shown at the usual times. Sleeping and eating patterns and early speech patterns should also be no different. Creeping and walking are usually delayed, but good control of the body in other ways should not be late. Since touch and hearing do not automatically compensate for the missing sense of sight, special care must be taken to ensure from the start that the hands come together at the midline and that the fingers become adept and alert, and that sounds come to have meaning. An important finding is that reach to sound, which is as important to the blind child as reach

*This research was sponsored by Office of Education, Grant #OEG-0-9-322108-2469 (032) and the National Institute for Child Health and Development, Grant #5R01 HD 01444.

on sight is to the sighted child, may not occur until 10 or 11 months. And until it does occur, the blind child is not tempted to seek something beyond his reach, and thus to begin creeping.

I eagerly offered information to each family as rapidly as the Project studies progressed. And then I made a humbling discovery. The parents chose only what made sense to them, what fit their style. The shy, depressed young mother did not suddenly become vivacious and conversational just because I explained how much her blind baby needed to hear her voice as she tended him. It took time for her to appreciate how much her voice meant to her baby who could not see her. And no matter how ingenious or insistent I was in demonstrating the baby's readiness and ability to get information with his hands, a family that was busily on the go, or a housewife who liked everything neatly in place would probably not remember to keep interesting toys within the baby's reach as often as I would like. But I did know that parents made extraordinary adaptations to meet their blind baby's needs, and I could do no less than make a similar adaptation to their pace and pattern.

Ultimately each baby's progress depends on a combination of his abilities, his parent's readiness to recognize and support small changes, their resourcefulness and mine, and my understanding of their strengths. There is no one right way to raise a blind baby, or any baby for that matter. I keep my eye on the baby's readiness to progress, to return his parent's affection, to reach out for experience. It is the best guide I have to measure how well I am meeting the family's needs. I also have to remember that my expectations are based on the many blind children I have followed; but parents usually know only one blind infant —their own.

Naturally enough their expectations are matched to those we all have for sighted children. The similarities are reassuring. The differences are continually disquieting. It is the unrecognized effect of this chronic disquiet that I would like to discuss.

In periods of slow development there is always the question of whether this delay or that kind of play is a normal part of the blind child's progress, or whether it is an ominous sign of further damage. No one wants to overlook danger signals that require a review of medical, educational, or psychological interventions. But very often what is most helpful is the search for evidence that the baby or child's behavior is still intelligent and purposeful. Is his response related to a period of developmental consolidation, or an outcome of some situational change —illness, holiday travels? Later on are there factors in social or school circumstances that make it more difficult for him to keep to the best level of performance?

For example, during the first year the normal delay in creeping is frequently a period that stresses both the parents and the professional. Unless that tension is understood and attended to, the baby's good progress may falter and his parent's love for him and confidence in themselves may be sorely tried. Our experience with Mark will illustrate this problem.

I met Mark when he was three weeks old. He had infantile glaucoma and his parents were concerned about how to give him a good start. They were wise about babies and for months gave Mark just what he needed. His steady progress showed them how much he was learning from their loving care, their gentle play, and their enjoyment of him despite their natural worries. We met every other week. As the end of the first year approached I knew how impatient the parents would be to have Mark leave infancy behind and enter toddlerhood. The delay that is normal for the blind baby was disturbing to them. Their questions of me became more pressing. It was time for him to get off his plump bottom and start creeping. And besides, he wasn't doing anything new anymore. From what they could see he was just shaking things. And therein lay the worry—their fear that he might be turning off the outside world, heading for the stereotypic repetitive behaviors of the older, disturbed blind child. If only he would creep.

They understood it was not so much a matter of motor coordination but a matter of mental conceptualization for Mark. He had to gain enough experience with what lay within arms' reach to develop an inner idea of the outer world. He needed a little more time to know that what he held and put down was still there—to become so familiar with the unity of the sound and touch of his playthings that the sound alone would help him hold onto the idea of how his toys felt, what he liked to do with them. This inner knowledge would lead him to reach out further and then creep to get what he wanted, and make interesting new discoveries along the way.

But there is small comfort in intellectual explanations when a parent is seriously worried about his or her blind infant's slower and somewhat different pattern of early progress. Mark's parents hoped I could give them some quick and certain exercise or play that would activate Mark and allay their fears. I could not, even though I knew they suffered with mounting doubts about whether Mark was normal, whether they were up to the continuing stress of parenting a blind infant, and whether I knew what I was doing. So far as I could tell Mark was in good health; nothing pointed to physical or neurological change. But his parents were very worried, and they had serious questions about his play, the so-called shaking. His parents were very good observers, and from their reports we were able to consider the world from Mark's perspective. The view was more complex and interesting than it first appeared.

From what his parents described in thoughtful detail, Mark wasn't "just shaking everything." He was tapping or pounding things on different surfaces, or wiggling and waving toys of different weights and shapes, or pushing at the furniture and nearly toppling it. He was getting the feel of his arms in motion, of how things behaved when he acted on them in the space closest to him. And all this was done with intention and fine control. He could rock and tip a wicker stool until it almost fell, but he knew just how far was far enough. He could swing a bell in his fist to make a strong, almost deafening clang—or he could just as easily hold it between two fingers and move it with such delicacy it made no sound at all. This was quite consistent with Mark's earlier style of persistent and thorough explorations of whatever interested him. He was gaining a solid sense of the world around him. He was readying himself, in his way, for the next steps he would take—the steps his parents awaited with such eagerness and anxiety. To me he was the same boy he had always been.

Why then did he appear to be different to his parents? Why did play that was all right one week, appear all wrong to them the next? I think I know the answer. For months and years parents of a blind child have to control chronic worry, and discouragement is never far from the surface. The emotional shock felt when they first learn their baby is blind leaves them wary of hearing that something else may also be wrong. At a time of delay the old doubts and fears surface and call into question all that has happened, is happening, may happen. All that looked good seems faulty.

These are genuine crises. Parents may turn from their baby, or turn on him, to scold and punish because of their disappointment in him and in themselves. They may think less of themselves and expect less of him than he can really do. Teachers face similar distress with the older blind child. The professional's task is a crucial one: to be open to questions and worries without exaggerating or minimizing them; to be alert to signs of change that call for pediatric examination; but first and foremost, to hold onto the good baby. It is essential to keep the baby and his parents, and teachers as well, in touch with their good selves and with each other during troubled interludes.

To Mark's parents I counseled patience, as they knew I would. I documented Mark's adequacy and readiness to creep —still I could not offer a way to make it happen right away. They were skeptical and disappointed. Back at the Project I consulted with the staff to review for myself where things stood. I needed to borrow some calm and patience myself to get through a time when I knew I could not hurry things for Mark and his parents. As it turned out, there was not so long to wait. Within a week there was a phone call with good news: Mark was creeping and he was wonderful. The relief and happiness in his mother's voice told me just how much despair and potential grief had haunted his parent's in the preceding weeks. Now they felt better about Mark, themselves, and me. We had all passed a test and we could go on to wrestle with other quandaries and share the pride of other triumphs as Mark followed the normal pattern of blind development. It is a pattern that can be more calmly viewed in retrospect than when some particularly slow phase is in process.

What happened between Mark and his parents has happened for most of the other families I have known. Whenever their blind child makes ready to step into a new part of the world—out of toddlerhood into the preschool years, from nursery school into the grades, from the grades to junior high school—is a time when his parents have reason to question what will happen. And with the new questions the old doubts and worries return to strain the family ties. Whatever support and guidance we can give through those times is most important.

The nature of the support changes over time. Assessment of the child's development and of his place in the family affections remains central. But other kinds of intervention can also be appropriate. When the family looks at the educational resources of their community, they have to learn to make their own assessments of different programs and staffs. It is the first round for them of the many decisions and judgments they will be making in the years ahead. Whether we stand on the sidelines or join in some school conferences, most parents find it helpful to use someone outside those systems as a well-informed but neutral sounding board. By putting into words just what they have seen and how it meets their view of what their child needs, they become more confident of their ability to take part in the planning. This work anticipates the time when the family will move ahead on its own.

Over the years I got occasional reports of the children I once knew as babies. Most did well in school, some in special classes or in combination with the regular school program, depending on what the community had to offer. The children

were good students, fine sons and daughters. I had not anticipated, however, that I would be called upon for another kind
of assessment and intervention so long after the early years.

I was consulted when bright blind children in the upper
grades in good public school systems hit a slump and nothing
seemed to work out. The slowdown in school performance did
not respond to coaxing, firmness, or punishment—and all
thoughts turned to finding out what was wrong with the child.
The children's previous academic success, which was excellent
by any standard, was suddenly called into question. Doubts and
fears colored everyone's view of the past and the future. When
I met the children, I found them attractive, lively, socially
acute, and self-observant young boys and girls. Looking with a
psychologist's eyes I could also see that they were feeling frustrated, confused, and growing discouraged in a way that bor-
dered on depression. But why? The question arose in the school
setting, and so it was to the school setting I turned. I disclaimed
any expertise as an educator and simply tried to understand
how it was for the blind child in school—by my own visit or
by report.

In one school an experienced teacher had an unusually
unruly class—one she could barely control much less teach.
When young Donald was placed in that class for his fourth
grade, he found it impossible to concentrate. He could not meet
his own high standards, and when he could not keep up he grew
discouraged and silently depressed and stopped trying to complete his assignments. The solution was simple enough. The
problem was redefined; the difficulty lay in the context of the
classroom, not in Donald's blindness. When he was no longer
scolded but shifted to a more stable classroom, he resumed his
good spirits and his good work. But it had been a near miss. If
he had been labeled as damaged and incompetent, it might well
have turned into a self-fulfilling prophecy.

In another state at another good public school, a young girl
in fifth grade fell behind in her work, and again much effort
went into finding out what was wrong with her. This involved

an extensive and expensive battery of tests, and along the way Selma Fraiberg and I were asked to see the child and review the test results. When I met Cynthia she took about 5 minutes to decide I was OK, and I took only a few more to decide she was talented, delightful, and surely reflected the sustained good efforts of her family and school. I visited the school for one morning. In the first period with an experienced teacher the entire class did well, and so did Cynthia. In the second period with a poorly prepared teacher everything fell apart, for the class and for Cynthia. The teacher was irritable and disorganized. Her helter-skelter presentation left the children scrambling for books, notes, and glimpses of the blackboard. The room hummed with their whispers as they tried to help each other and Cynthia. And while all this went on, Cynthia's math tutor arrived to try to work with her at the side of the room. I was frazzled, and Cynthia was exhausted and bewildered. At the end of the hour she was too confused to find her way to the next classroom—no one helped her. Her erratic wandering confirmed everyone's fear that a serious organic problem was finally being revealed and they drew away. In a lengthy report Mrs. Fraiberg and I found a convincing way to reaffirm Cynthia's adequacy with volumes of documentation, to restore her in her parents' eyes, and to help in thinking through a better school plan for the next year.

Similar episodes have accumulated over the years. When they appear in good school systems in different communities, and with bright blind children who have had warm support at home, then I have to wonder what it means. One possible explanation might be that many teachers do not have experience with the blind student, and are doing the best they can. They cannot be faulted for not having training or knowledge that was never given to them. But what catches my attention is the impatience and anger that colors their response to the children's slowed learning—and the alarming way that mood so quickly undermines the family's image of themselves and their child.

This calls for some other explanation and I think it is closely linked to the earlier discussion of Mark and his parent's response to his delay in creeping. I think that answer lies in the everpresent emotional impact blindness has for all of us. It need not be overdramatized, but it merits our recognition. I think there is a chronic disappointment we all feel in some measure. No matter how much we do, how well we do it, and for how long, there is always one thing we cannot do. We cannot undo the blindless itself. It is always there. I believe that when things do not go well for a while, we are vulnerable to a helpless anger at the ineradicable tragedy of blindness—and that anger is sometimes directed at the blind child. It is better to know that the anger will be there occasionally. It would be wiser and safer to voice it to an understanding colleague than to vent it on the child, his parents, or each other. Then we can get on with the good work.

Whenever I meet a new student, teacher, or pediatrician who has questions about a blind infant or young child, I have to remind myself how recent our knowledge is. It is unlikely their training or experience included anything about the early psychological development of infants, or the unique developmental problems of children blind from birth. They usually feel pressured to find quick answers and are given little time in which to work. I have to find a way to let them choose the information that will be most useful, will best supplement their knowledge and expertise. If I am successful in starting them on the path to careful observation and thinking about the psychological development of young blind children, then I am satisfied. Their inquiry, empathy, and support will serve the individual blind child and can also bring us more answers to the questions that still remain. If they can be aware of the inevitable stresses, their work will be well-planned and very satisfying.

REFERENCES

1.   Adelson, E.: Karen: Recovery from a Year's Deprivation. 15 minutes, black and white, sound, 16mm, 1972.

2. Adelson, E, & Chethik, M: A Blind Child and a Sighted Child: The First Year. 25 minutes, black and white, sound 16mm, 1969.

3. Adelson, E, & Fraiberg, S: Mouth and hand in the early development of blind infants. *Proc. Third Symp. Oral Sensation and Perception.* Springfield, Ill.: Charles C Thomas, 1972.

4. Adelson, E, & Fraiberg, S: Gross motor development in infants blind from birth. *Child Dev., 45;* 1974.

5. Blos, JW: Traditional nursery rhymes and games: Language learning experiences for preschool blind children. *New Outlook for the Blind:* 268–275, June 1974.

6. Blos, JW: Rhymes, songs, records, and stories: Language learning experiences for preschool blind children. *New Outlook for the Blind:* 300–307, September 1974.

7. Fraiberg, S: *Insights from the blind: Comparative studies of blind and sighted infants.* New York: Basic Books, 1977.

8. Fraiberg, S: Parallel and divergent patterns in blind and sighted children. *Psychoanal. Study Child, 23:* 1968.

9. Fraiberg, S: The muse in the kitchen: A case study in clinical research. *Smith College Studies in Social Work, 40:* 1970.

10. Fraiberg, S: Intervention in infancy: A program for blind infants. *J. Am.Acad. Child Psychiatry, 10:* July 1971.

11. Fraiberg, S: Separation crisis in two blind infants. *Psychoanal. Study Child,* 26: 1971.

12. Fraiberg, S: Smiling and stranger reaction in blind infants. In J. Hellmuth (Ed.), *Exceptional Infant,* Vol. II, 1971.

13. Fraiberg, S: Blind infants and their mothers: An examination of the sign system. In M. Lewis & L. Rosenblum (Eds.), *The effect of the infant on its caregiver.* New York: John Wiley, 1974.

14. Fraiberg, S: The clinical dimension of baby games. *J. Am. Acad. of Child Psychiatry, 13:* 1974.

15. Fraiberg, S: The development of human attachment in children blind from birth. *Merrill-Palmer Quarterly, 21:* October 1975.

16. Fraiberg, S, & Adelson, E: Self-representation in language and play: Observations of blind children. *Psychoanalytic Quarterly, 42:* 1973.

17. Fraiberg, S, Siegel, B, & Gibson, R: The role of sound in the search behavior of blind infants. *Psychoanal. Study Child, 21:* 1966.

18. Fraiberg, S, Smith, M, & Adelson, E: An educational program for blind infants. *J. Spec. Ed., 3:* 121–139, 1969.

19. Ross, M: Blindness in infancy: The promise of growth and learning. 8 minutes, black and white, sound, 16mm, 1972.*

20. Smith, M, Chethik, M, & Adelson, E: Differential assessments of "Blindisms." *Am. J. Orthopsychiatry:* 807–817, October 1969.

21. Ulrich, S (with S. Fraiberg, & E. Adelson): *Elizabeth.* Ann Arbor: University of Michigan Press, 1972.

*Available on loan from University of Michigan Audio-Visual Center, 416 Fourth Street, Ann Arbor, Michigan.

Chapter 11

DEVELOPING A WORKING ALLIANCE WITH PARENTS OF INFANTS AT RISK

Vivian Shapiro, M.S.W.
Kathleen Tuta, M.A.

Recent theoretical and applied research findings have high-lighted the importance of a wide range of clinical services to infants at risk.* Infant mental health clinicians are developing significant expertise about the interface between medical, psychological, and developmental issues and developing a range of treatment modalities. It is often difficult, however, to engage parents in a constructive long-term treatment alliance on behalf of their babies. The parents may stop coming or even if they do come may not engage in significant work. Clinicians are often left with a sense of urgency and despair, with worry for the baby and the family, and knowledge of what is wrong and what is needed, and yet with a wide gulf and a shaky bridge between themselves and the parents. We will attempt to explore some of the issues involved in developing a treatment alliance with parents of infants at risk.

*See bibliography.

The ideas in this chapter derive from the authors' work at the Child Development Project, a clinical research program with a primary emphasis on infant mental health.** Through grants from the National Institute of Health and the Grant Foundation, since 1972 we have been studying the assessment and treatment of infants at risk. We had the privilege of small caseloads and a research focus that enabled us to look at problems in depth and to provide extensive outreach services. While initially we expected to serve infants who were at risk primarily because of emotional disturbance, the nature of the referrals presented us with a wider range of developmental problems. We saw infants, who because of early neonatal difficulties, had long-term developmental problems. They were at risk in a way which interfaced medical, developmental, and psychological issues. We saw other infants who were at risk primarily because of environmental factors and inadequacies in the parent-child relationship. Our referrals usually came from primary health caregivers, but some came directly from parents. A common thread ran through all these referrals: the wish and hope that some expertise would be brought to bear to understand and ameliorate the specific needs of the child and family. We found that the assessment process was critical, not only in understanding the dimensions of the problem and outlining future needs, but in influencing whether or not the parent would continue to seek appropriate help.

From our own experience and by report from other practitioners, an underlying general problem exists. The clinician seeing infants at risk must be able to develop a treatment alliance with the parents, for it is through them that the real goals of any infant work must be accomplished. It is the parent as a primary attachment figure, the giver of psychological nurturance and physical care, the provider of an appropriate long-term environment where the child can best develop, who will

**University of Michigan, Child Development Project, 201 E. Catherine Street, Ann Arbor, Michigan 48104.

be the central core of any successful therapeutic effort. It is only with the help of the parent that the clinician can complete a good assessment, and it is through the parent that any treatment program must be carried out in its broadest sense.

THE TREATMENT ALLIANCE

The concept of a treatment alliance has a special meaning in traditional psychoanalytic work. In a one-to-one therapeutic realtionship a constructive treatment alliance means that the patient has developed a reasonable, rational rapport with the therapist that enables him to work purposefully in the therapeutic situation. This alliance is based in some part on an effective positive transference (which requires a relatively good capacity to establish object relations), capacity for insight and observation, a capacity to tolerate a certain amount of frustration, and importantly, the existence of a certain degree of basic trust and identification with the aims of the treatment.***

The methodological approaches that have been utilized in traditional psychoanalysis and psychotherapy, which enabled a patient and therapist to slowly develop a functional treatment alliance, needed to be modified in infant-focused therapy. When a baby was in crisis, time was of the essence. The therapist and parent(s) often needed to begin serious work with an alliance that arose out of concern with the baby, but a yet undeveloped parent-therapist relationship. Once the referral crisis was passed, to sustain a meaningful therapeutic relationship to continuing work, the therapist had to attend to the developing fabric of the parent-therapist relationship. The core of the treatment alliance is similar in all therapies, i.e., the development of

***Greenson, RR: *The Technique and Practice of Psychoanalysis. Volume 1.* New York, International Universities Press, 1967. Sander J, Dane C, Holder A: *The Patient and the Analyst.* New York, International Universities Press, 1973.

a positive transference; the mutual clarity of goals; and the development of basic trust. In infant-focused psychotherapy, the process of developing such an alliance is unique.

In a review of the long-term treatment cases at the Child Development Project, we found that a special framework exists at the beginning of clinical work with parents on behalf of their infants. The presenting problem was most often a crisis with the baby: for example, a three-month-old baby born prematurely whose parents just discovered that he was blind from retrolental fibroplasia; a 17-month-old baby boy who had significant neonatal difficulties and now was diagnosed as mentally impaired; a 24-month-old little girl with grave affective and behavior problems whose unwed teenage mother could not take care of her.

The parents we saw came to the agency out of worry, grief, fear, concern, or perhaps even coercion, but certainly not with any well-thought-out idea of what the nature of the work would be. The therapeutic task needed to be to engage the parent in the process of investigating and understanding the problem. A treatment alliance between the parent and the therapist at this early point in the work involved only an understanding that together they would begin to explore the problems that the baby had. It needed to be understood that the therapist did not immediately have the answer to the problem and in fact needed the parents as collaborators in the process. The method of the work was to talk together, to watch the baby, to pull together the medical and developmental picture, and social history that was relevant, and to try to structure some questions so as to have a frame of reference for the baby's problem. This process usually led from present to past and back again. When an initial understanding about the extent of the baby's problems was reached, the therapist and parent together needed to explore the next step, i.e., either referral or continued work, and on what basis.

This process of initial exploration was often very difficult for the patient. As has been stated the presenting conditions were often stressful and the families were in states of crisis.

There was often significant disparity in the way the parent and the therapist initially viewed the problem and the work to be done. Often parents presented the problem as an external one —there was something the matter with the baby. It was frequently far too early and too painful for the parent to look inward and see how he or she may or may not have been contributing to the baby's problems. However, since no baby's problem was only the baby's problem, the parents who came for help soon realized, by virtue of the assessment process and the questions raised, that their own feelings, concerns, fears, and capacities were drawn into the center of the work. It was in this delicate balance of expanding the focus from the baby to the parent and back again that stress often increased. This happened whether the problem lay with a physical impairment with the baby or if the difficulties were of psychogenic origin. At times, appointments were canceled or forgotten and tenacious resistances appeared. The clinicians needed to acknowledge the feelings and distress of the parent without allowing the work to diverge too far from the primary treatment focus: the common concern for the best interests of the baby. It was in the service of helping the baby that the parents could often sustain involvement in the assessment process despite great anxiety. When the parents could trust that the focus of the assessment would remain with helping the baby, this understanding allowed for a variety of explorations and discussions that might otherwise have been too threatening.

As in all therapeutic relationships a treatment alliance could not develop without at least a minimal positive transference and degree of basic trust. But having a baby with a severe problem was a devastating blow to most of the parents and the effects of this crisis often impeded the establishment of a positive transference. Looking further at this, we have found that having a healthy, happy baby was a wish that most of the parents had, even those who had great difficulty nurturing their babies. All parents experienced a sense of loss in acknowledging a serious difficulty with their child. Whether the baby was in difficulty for physiological or psychogenic reasons, the problems evoked a myriad of feelings of grief for the parent, the present pain being reinforced by past losses and difficulties. In order to deal with the painful affects, idiosyncratic defenses were visibly mobilized and denial often made it difficult for the parent to acknowledge that a problem existed or that help was needed. In one family, for example, a mother and father were in different stages of readiness to acknowledge the seriousness of the situation and the need for help. This was evident in the case of Michael, a two-year-old little boy who was finally diagnosed as mentally impaired. What appeared to be monumental resistance on the part of the father to getting help for his son was really a need to deny the painful reality of his baby's problems.

The parents in crises were often emotionally bereft and in a state of personal depletion. There was little left in terms of energy or feelings to enable them to take initiative establishing a working relationship. It was probably no accident then that outreach by our clinic was necessary in establishing and continuing contact with a high proportion of the parents. The therapist could not assume that the parent's hesitancy and apparent resistance was a lack of neither motivation or caring about the baby.

Often other issues impeded the establishment of a positive transference. By the time the parents reached the clinic they had usually been through the mill of professionals. The parents frequently came with a history of heartache, disappointment, and frustration in relation to primary caregivers. This heartache or frustration was either due to real mistreatment or displaced anger because of grief and needing to blame someone for the family's difficulties. Each therapist had to find a way to deal with this inheritance of negative transference feelings, to address them, to clarify his or her own particular role, and to separate himself from the parent's past. In doing this the therapists had to take special care to be sensitive, to be empathetic, and to explain and to acknowledge realities and feelings.

There was more to the difficulty of establishing a positive treatment alliance than simply working through recent negative transference experiences. Not all parents we saw had a capacity to trust and not all could transfer positive feelings of hope, belief, and realistic expectations to the therapist. In many families the parents themselves had a traumatic childhood with no stable relationships, without a history that promoted the capacity to trust, and for these parents it was more typical that the transference to the therapist was primarily negative. Many of the parents of children at risk for psychogenic reasons had great difficulty in personal relations in general and would have been unable to participate in traditional psychotherapy when we first saw them.

There was an additional complication in the establishment of a working relationship between the parent and the infant mental health clinician. In any therapy it is difficult for a patient to believe the therapist is on his side and will be accepting of him. When the patient is a parent seeking help for a child at risk, how does he view the infant mental health clinician's concern? Does he experience the therapist's concern for himself, the adult, or the baby? And in his mind may there not be a conflict between the two? Will the parent be asked to do more than he can, to feel what he does not feel? What will the therapist think of him for having negative thoughts about his child or for evidence of neglect, abuse, etc.? Will the therapist blame him, perhaps as he blames himself? In most cases we attempted to reassure and demonstrate to the parent that our concern included the parent's and the baby's welfare, that those were compatible, and that the work would proceed at a pace the parent could handle as long as this did not endanger the baby. In the most difficult cases of neglect and abuse, where a conflict actually existed, we addressed the problem directly. We conveyed to the parent our efforts to do all that we could to help the baby stay with the parent, but that if necessary we would act to protect the baby in the best possible sense. We found this straightforward but empathically stated approach to be important diagnostically and therapeutically.

The goal of the assessment process was seen as a dual goal: (a) to arrive at a clinical assessment of the baby, and (b) to develop a treatment alliance with the parent that could lead to appropriate intervention. In one case a clinician had achieved these dual goals when a sullen adolescent mother, who had brought her troubled baby girl to a clinic saying the baby was bad, said at the end of the assessment period, "I want to understand her." The delicacy and difficulty of helping the mother consider the possibility that the fault lay not entirely in the baby was profound. In developing this treatment alliance with this parent the therapist and agency had been able to communicate something about the parent's worth as a parent, the therapist's concern for the parent as a person, and the acceptance of the idea that the parent and the baby were involved in a relationship with each other and with the therapist which was important for each of them.

The real relationship in infant-focused psychotherapy, as practiced at the Child Development Project, included concrete attention to the actual medical, nutritional, and developmental needs of the babies and often their young parents. We found that this active and supportive outreach enhanced a sense of caring, and always affected the transference, sometimes positively and sometimes negatively. The therapeutic relationship, therefore, continuously needed to be addressed with the parents, so that the therapeutic purpose and nature of the work was always in the forefront. While sometimes the therapist did what a grandmother might have done, i.e., take the sick baby and mother to the hospital, the therapist's professional role was continuously clarified, and the feelings that the therapist's actions may have evoked in transference with the parents were dealt with interpretively. The unavoidable active involvement of the therapist in a nontraditional role had an impact on the therapeutic process which could be positive when dealt with in therapeutic terms.

Importantly, the treatment of a baby at risk within a family was often a difficult emotional experience for the therapists, and they had to be aware of their own countertransference feelings regarding the dependent baby and the often less than perfect parent. The kind of outreach effort that these families required, and the crisis-oriented focus of the work, made the real relationship of the patient and therapist powerful and difficult in some of the families' day-to-day struggles, not only as observers but as participants. Concern for the at-risk status of the whole family was often great and led to worry about the outcome. There were no miracles to offer and that realization was at times difficult for all of us to accept.

CONCLUSION

The nature of early developmental disturbances and the critical importance of the early parent-child relationship lent to the infant-centered work a great urgency. In general, time was critical. The parents' resistances, the therapists' countertransference feelings, and the infants' neediness combined to make the therapeutic work emotionally and intellectually draining. The success of early intervention gave much hope and promise which supported the therapeutic efforts.

The staff of the Child Development Project has found that the therapist could be greatly helped by supervision and consultation. This was so at all levels of professional development. A consultant who was not directly involved with the case was often able to bring perspective to the relationships among the therapist's countertransference feelings, the parent's dynamics, and the baby's needs. This synthesis and the support granted from talking with another professional about the case often enabled the therapist to reenter a difficult treatment situation with a new sense of direction and optimism.

Unfortunately in some cases the best efforts of the therapist and supervisor were not enough and the parents did not continue their work on behalf of the baby. If the baby was urgently at risk, a referral to a protective agency was made. For others the therapists had to accept the decision of the parents and found it useful to convey to the parents a continuing interest and availability so that the parents could in time find their way back to treatment.

Finally, while this chapter has focused primarily on the development of a working alliance at the beginning of a patient-therapist relationship, the maintenance of the alliance was a challenge that continued throughout treatment. New developments brought new resistances to understanding and new treatment goals for the parents and baby. Sometimes the nature of the working alliance changed so that what started out, for example, as a developmental guidance case, in time became an intensive treatment case necessitating interpretive psychotherapy for the parent.

Let us review the special aspects of a treatment alliance in infant-focused therapy. The alliance, once developed, implies that the parent and therapist share openly a common definition of the problem. A solid treatment alliance is grounded in a positive transference—in increasing trust and mutual respect between the therapist and parent. The positive transference enables the parent to use the expertise of the therapist in terms of developmental guidance and to broaden the focus of treatment when relevant, i.e., the parent is willing to explore his own feelings in relationship to the baby when this is deemed to be part of the problem. Furthermore, there is a tacit recognition that the therapist has allied with the healthy ego of the parent so that together all that is necessary will be done to promote the emotional and physical health of the baby. This is based also on the belief that the therapist will work in the best interest of the parent as well, wherever possible.

REFERENCES

1. Adelson, E, & Fraiberg, S: An abandoned mother: An abandoned baby. *Menninger Bull., 41:* 162–180, March 1977.

2. Ainsworth, MDS, Blehar, MC, Waters, E, & Wall, S: *Patterns of attachment: A psychological study of the strange situation.* Hillsdale, N.J.: Erlbaum, 1978.

3. Aradine, C, Uman, H, & Shapiro, V: Collaborative treatment of infant with a long-term tracheostomy and his parents. *Issues Comp. Pediatr. Nurs. 3:* 29–41, July 1978.

4. Fraiberg, S, Adelson, E, & Shapiro, V: Ghosts in the nursery. *J. Am. Acad. Child Psychiatry, 14:* 387–421, Summer 1975.

5. Greenspan, SI, Lourie, RS, Nover, RA: A developmental approach to the classification of psychopathology in infancy and early childhood. In *Handbook of child psychiatry* (Vol. 2), 157–164.

6. Klaus, MH, Leger, T, & Trause, MA (Eds.): *Maternal attachment and mothering disorders.* Piscataway, N.J.: Johnson & Johnson, 1979.

7. Robson, KS: Development of object relations during the first year of life. *Sem. Psychiatry, 4:* 301–316, November 1972.

Chapter 12

HELPING FAMILIES COPE WITH CHRONIC ENDOCRINE DISEASE IN YOUNG CHILDREN

Nancy J. Hopwood, M.D.
Martha L. Spencer, M.D.

The impact of the diagnosis of a chronic, potentially life-threatening illness on an individual or family is significant at any time of life. The recognition of such a serious medical problem in an infant or young child is particularly stressful to young parents. Strong emotional reactions usually follow. After the initial shock, feelings of helplessness, hopelessness, guilt, fear, and denial are frequent. Some families may avoid facing the serious nature of the problem, certain that in time their child will be once again normal. Juvenile diabetes mellitus and hypopituitarism are examples of two chronic, potentially life-threatening, nonreversible medical diseases which can have an onset in the infant or young child. Although these disorders can be successfully managed medically and result in a long productive life for the child, a thorough understanding of the physiology of the disorder by the family is necessary for adequate daily management. Of paramount importance is the psychological adjustment of the family to the child's illness. The presence of emotional conflicts within the child and his family can offset adequate medical management and

242

lead to permanent psychological as well as physical damage.

Infants and young children will adapt to the diagnosis according to the parents' reaction and adjustment. Vulnerable areas of development such as sex role identity, self-identity, development of self-control, and independence may be affected. Eating problems, toilet training, and behavior commonly are areas of contention between the child and parent. With chronic diseases, these areas may become exaggerated and result in major issues complicating medical management.

Another area of concern is preoccupation of the parents with the child's problems. Exclusion of other members of the family and friends may result and hinder the development of the child and themselves. In this chapter, examples of ways to help families cope with chronic illness such as juvenile diabetes mellitus and hypopituitarism in the very young child will be illustrated. Figure 12–1 demonstrates a number of pathways a family may take.

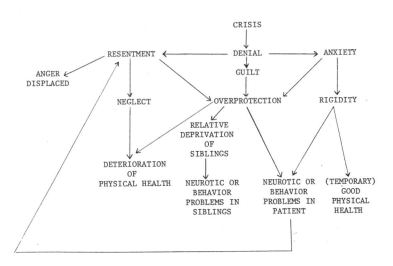

IMMEDIATE FAMILY REACTIONS TO
SEVERE CHRONIC ILLNESS

Figure 12–1 Immediate Family Reactions to Severe Chronic Illness

Juvenile Diabetes Mellitus (JDM)

Although the peak age incidence for the onset of JDM is 9 to 12 years, a significant percentage of a large group (3,538 children) of newly diagnosed diabetics summarized by Fleegler and associates were less than six years of age (40%); approximately 10% were less than three years of age. Despite the fact that JDM in the very young child is not rare, it is unlikely that many physicians have had wide experience in the management of these patients. It is even more unlikely that the parents of a toddler with diabetes will have encountered other families who have to cope with similar problems in the course of their daily activities. Thus, the parents of the infant or young child may have an even stronger feeling of isolation and helplessness than the usual family to the diagnosis of diabetes in their child. Most families are in a semistate of shock the first few days after diagnosis. They are fearful of the consequences because of their own concepts of diabetes from prior experiences. Some will express guilt and feel responsible for such an insult to their child. Some parents may be angry and hostile; usually these feelings are directed at a physician or spouse for not suspecting the condition earlier and preventing its onset. An opportunity for ventilation of these feelings should be provided; repression of them can only be the source of emotional conflict at a later time. It is important for the family to hear that the onset of diabetes in the child is rapid. It is unlikely to have been ignored for a considerable time due to negligence prior to presentation. Likewise, the blame for a child's diabetes cannot be assigned to a single parent as the etiology of JDM still remains unknown and is unlikely to be a single factor. A brief explanation of what to expect, how much time management of the diabetes will take, cost, and limitation of the child's and family's activities will alleviate many fears and clear up misunderstandings.

During the first few days after diagnosis, it is usually helpful to involve the parents in the more technical parts of the child's management, such as urine testing for sugar and ketones and in technique of insulin injections. Rarely are the parents ready to begin education about problems of management, acute illness, regulation of diet or insulin during this period of initial adjustment to the diagnosis when emotions are still very high. An inpatient hospital stay of one to two weeks is usually necessary to accomplish adequate education and achieve self-confidence by the parents. This length of stay also enables the parents to come to know the multidisciplinary team which helps parents care for children with diabetes: physicians, nurse clinician, nutritionist, and social worker. All of these people are thus available during this initial education process and see the child on subsequent visits to the diabetic clinic.

Young children with diabetes have some unique problems. Unable to comprehend that they are sick, suddenly they are faced with painful injections of insulin, first by strangers and then by their own parent. They cannot grasp the seriousness of the situation themselves, but the tension and/or *anxiety* of the parent can be easily sensed and not understood. Many parents express frustration at the inability to adequately explain to their children why they have to hurt them. Helping parents to *share* this responsibility in situations in which the child does not understand is important, as well as making the experience as brief as possible by dealing with injections in a matter-of-fact manner. Urine tests for glucose must also be monitored throughout the day. Young children will rarely urinate on demand and modifications of the usual treatment requirements must be made. Parents are encouraged to feed the child frequently and give many alternatives, such as crackers and juice when the child is reluctant. Food should never be used as a reward. Mealtimes should not become a battle ground. The whole family should be encouraged to be on the same meal plan. Even the young child enjoys participating in selection and preparation of the menu. The young child is also very unpredictable in other ways. There are frequent acute illnesses to contend with, periods of refusal to eat and/or vomiting, and variability of activity level. All the above lead to instability well-known in children with insulin-dependent diabetes.

Frequent episodes of hypoglycemia are a major problem in young children. Inability to recognize and treat early symptoms of low blood glucose adds to the burden of parents of young children. Poor behavior may be an early sign of low blood sugar. Parents question when and if they should discipline a child. Suggestions are made again for shared responsibility and consistency in management. Reassurance is given for their parenting. Allowing the child increasing independence, in spite of parental anxiety, is a problem every family has to face and will be illustrated in subsequent case examples.

It is well-known that many difficulties in diabetic control may arise from emotional stress. In families where there are already disturbed relationships, psychosocial problems become principal causes of poor diabetic control. Metabolic alterations that result from stress or from noncompliance to the necessary dietary and insulin management may cause a confusing clinical picture. Frequent episodes of hypoglycemia and/or ketoacidosis may follow. The presence of a child with diabetes may be an additional stress for a family or become the focal point for other stresses in a poorly functioning family. The child in turn can quickly learn to manipulate the family because of parental fear of hypoglycemia or death. If these conflicts are allowed to persist or grow, the adjustment to diabetes when the child reaches adolescence may be very unsatisfactory and lead to multiple psychosocial and medical problems that are very difficult to resolve.

In spite of the multitude of problems that can face a family with a young child who has diabetes, the large majority of families cope well and the children often do not have serious problems for years. In some respects, management of the young child may be easier than that of a school-age child or adolescent. The young child with diabetes is still largely under his parents' control. Dietary patterns are still flexible to a large degree. Exercise is more frequent. Emotional outbursts are usually brief and quickly forgotten. Peer pressure is minimal. Thus, we often see that for the first two years after diagnosis a two-year-old child may do well. As he begins to increase his independence and be aware that he is somehow different, a new set of problems face the family. Will parental anxiety prevent him from making the necessary steps for independent functioning? Although early management may be smooth in the majority of children, parent attitudes about diabetes and illness are crucial to the future psychosocial development of the child as well as to his future health. The self-esteem and confidence that result from these attitudes may be far more predictive of the child's ultimate adjustment to his diabetes and life in general than his day-to-day diabetic control. Thus, when working with families with young children with chronic illness, it is not without forethought that our major goals are for healthy emotional and physical development.

From our population of approximately 50 children whose diabetes had its onset prior to three years of age, a few typical histories have been selected to illustrate common problems facing families of the young child with diabetes.

Case 1

Kim, age 23 months, was diagnosed to have JDM after several weeks of excessive drinking and urination. An only child, her development and past health had been normal. The parents were noted to respond quickly to diabetes education. Kim was noted to be very independent and coped well with intermittent separation from her parents during the hospitalization. The family seemed to adjust well throughout the first year after the diagnosis and appeared relaxed. No major problems were noted. At age 32 months the parents expressed frustration at attempts to toilet train her because of her increased urination. They also reported that Kim sometimes fought during injections. They were encouraged by the nurse clinician to allow Kim to participate in the procedure, i.e., wiping her leg with alcohol and gathering supplies. When seen four months later, the family reported they had stopped pushing toilet training, and now she was completely trained. She was no longer fighting injections and seemed to enjoy her role as a participant.

Case 2

Johnny, third of three children, ages four, two and a half, and fifteen months, was noted to have increasing thirst and urination. Because of her past experience in helping her own brother with JDM check his urine, Johnny's mother tested his urine and found glucose. Subsequently the diagnosis of JDM was made. After a 12-day hospitalization where the family seemed comfortable and well-educated in his management, Johnny returned home and did well. At age 27 months he was reported to have a variable appetite but it was felt that the mother was doing a good job by avoiding substituting sweet foods when he was not eating well. Toilet training was complete. Diabetic control was repeatedly assessed as good and hypoglycemic reactions absent. He was described as a delightful and cooperative child who by five years of age was spending occasional weekends with relatives. One episode of diabetic ketoacidosis occurred at age six because of suspected excessive insulinization. Adjustment to school was good. By age six and one half years he was participating in the preparation for his injections and unashamed to tell his teachers about his diabetes and his need for snacks. Repeatedly the parents, who shared equally in his management, were noted to be relaxed and encouraged independence.

Case 3

Debbie, a twin, developed JDM at age 13 months and was hospitalized, severely ill with diabetic ketoacidosis. Her family responded with initial shock but quickly were able to respond to the diabetic education. At the time of Debbie's hospital discharge they seemed to have a good understanding of the principles of management and seemed eager to start. At each clinic visit over the next several years, both parents had numerous questions of the staff in spite of Debbie's good control. They seemed to be relaxed regarding her management as well as that of the twin sister who did not have diabetes. Almost always we concurred with the parents' good judgment; reassurance from us was important. By age four and one half Debbie was participating in her urine checks and knew which foods to avoid. The parents remained very open and knowledgeable about diabetes; family activities were numerous and problems anticipated, planned for, and hence avoided. When Debbie started kindergarten, the mother was able to express her anxiety as well as discuss her feelings about Debbie's first insulin reaction which occurred shortly thereafter. When Debbie was five and six years of age, the parents asked to speak with our social worker about how to help Debbie not feel different and how to discipline her when she cheated on a diet. They reported that family discussions were their usual means of discipline. The parents suggested the entire family should follow the same diet and asked help from the clinic nutritionist for suggestions. The parents had previously expressed guilt at having to enforce her diet and wanted other ways to avoid feeling bad. They were also concerned that Debbie frequently seemed preoccupied with death since the death of a young friend from leukemia. The clinic staff was able to help Debbie realize that diabetes and leukemia are not the same and that blood sampling for tests did not mean she had a blood disease like her friend.

SUMMARY. These three children have done well and seem to be developing normally both emotionally and physically. All have stable, knowledgeable parents who have dealt with their diabetes in a consistant manner. Their dietary management may best be described as regulated and anticipatory but not strict or rigid. The children are all demonstrating independence appropriate for age. Johnny's mother was undoubtedly helped by her prior experience with her own diabetic brother. The problems of three very young children, one of whom had diabetes, might have been too much for some families to cope with. Debbie's family likewise is very stable and was initially very relaxed with her diabetes. Now that Debbie is away from home and subject to peer acceptance, anxieties again arise and are dealt with openly by the parents who requested further counseling. This family always had many questions for the clinic staff and sought what they needed for themselves whether it was reassurance or advice. Not all families are able to thus seek what they need or realize that they indeed need guidance. It is the role of our multidisciplinary team to address these potential problems and feelings when the family is unaware of them.

Case 4

Bobby, presented to our clinic at age three and one half for advice regarding diabetic management. A diagnosis of JDM had been made at age two and one half years. He had been controlled very tightly by his parents, had frequent hypoglycemic reactions, and was reported to be on no dietary restrictions. His appetite was very sporadic. He participated in urine testing and diet selection and seemed not to have significant behavior problems. His parents were intelligent, knowledgeable about diabetes, and very interested in improving his control. We recommended less rigid control of his urinary glucose by less insulin, thereby decreasing his hypoglycemic reactions. At four years Bobby started attending nursery school when his mother began working. Shortly thereafter he had several severe hypoglycemic reactions. Injection time became more difficult. The parents were thought to be handling Bobby well, but it was becoming more apparent that he was becoming increasingly in control of the family. By age four and one half he was frequently refusing to eat. Over three months he had eight severe hypoglycemic reactions. The father stated that it was often difficult to tell when Bobby was having a hypoglycemic reaction. Because he did not want to discipline unjustly at those times, he no longer punished him. The parents reported that whenever Bobby refused to eat and became hypoglycemic he was allowed to have a lollipop; a jar of lollipops were kept for that occasion only. The clinic staff pointed out that Bobby was manipulating the family by his reactions. It was suggested that an alternative method of treating mild hypoglycemia due to decreased intake be adopted. The lollipops might be best given for hypoglycemia after vigorous exercise if they were to be used at all.

Case 5

David, an only child, was diagnosed to have JDM at 21 months of age. After an eight-day hospitalization he was managed by his private physician, with tight control and cooperation of both parents. He had frequent mild hypoglycemic reactions but no episodes of ketoacidosis. When David was 39 months, the family referred themselves to our clinic for advice on his management. He was reported to be combative at injection time. Urine checks showed "tight" control; excessive insulin was suspected. Observation of the injection by the parents showed it to be a long drawn out procedure. David was noted to be manipulative, uncooperative, and immature. The parents responded by infantilizing him and restricting his independence. He was dressed in plastic pants (although toilet trained) and diet consisted of bottles of pureed foods. He was not allowed to play with other children or eat at neighbors' homes. The parents appeared to have much unresolved guilt regarding both the diagnosis of diabetes and David's daily management.

It was emphasized to the parents that David's immaturity was a serious problem. Contact with other parents of children with JDM, increased exposure of David to neighborhood children and/or nursery school, and increased independence of David in daily activities were encouraged. The parents were asked to speak with the clinic social worker who reemphasized these recommendations and helped them find ways initiating these changes. Two months later the family reported that David was eating regular foods and was on a waiting list for nursery school. The parents had attended a parent group of families with diabetic children and had found this helpful. When seen in the clinic the next visit, David was no longer fighting his injections. The mother was encouraged to increase flexibility with dietary management.

Case 6

Alan was a precocious infant, achieving his milestones considerably faster than his sister, one and one half years older. At age 21 months, JDM was diagnosed shortly before his parents divorced. Early management was difficult. Hospitalization for ketoacidosis occurred at ages three, four, and five years. At age six years he was seen by a psychologist because of behavior problems that had increased over the previous year. Increasing hostility, general negativism, and both active and passive rebellion were noted. His mother complained that he became frustrated easily and disliked being touched. The psychologist found him to be sad, without spontaneity, clinging to his mother, and very distrustful. His mother related she had always treated him differently because of his diabetes, not permitting him to stay overnight with relatives or go places without her, although his sister could do these things. Because of increasing temper tantrums and rage on any attempt of control by his mother, Alan was treated unsuccessfully with medications such as Ritalin and Mellaril.

At age seven and one half years Alan was referred to our clinic for the first time for advice on his diabetic management. He denied having diabetes and appeared both anxious and depressed. He seemed obsessed with the possibility of his mother's death. His mother complained he cheated on his diet and refused to participate in his management. She was noted to have excessively high expectations of Alan in terms of his ability to understand his diabetes and felt he should be giving himself shots, checking his urine, and telling everyone he has diabetes (despite the fact that he is denied activities because he has diabetes). In spite of all the behavioral difficulties, it was felt that Alan's diabetes was in excellent control. Alan and his mother were referred for continued intensive psychotherapy, along with the recommendation for increased flexibility in management and more realistic goals appropriate for his age.

SUMMARY.   Bobby's family has been thought to be doing well; however, it is becoming increasingly evident that Bobby is quite successful at manipulating the family. Futher guidance will be necessary to help reverse this situation before it becomes worse. Both Bobby's and David's parents have great concern about keeping low urine glucose readings and the children in "tight" control. A great deal of effort on the part of parents is necessary to achieve this result, usually at too much expense to the child's psychosocial development. We therefore recommend as good control as possible, but avoidance of hypoglycemic reactions. Flexibility of dietary management is essential because of the unpredictability of outbursts of energy that children that age should have (when allowed to explore their environment in a healthy manner). David's family had a serious problem with infantilizing him; counseling them about their fears and repressed guilt helped increase their awareness that their responses were inappropriate. David seemed to eagerly respond to his new experiences at increasing independence. Although little is known about Alan's early life, it is clear that had a thorough psychosocial history been taken at the time of the diagnosis of his diabetes, it would have been evident that the family was at risk for management problems with Alan. In families where there is marital conflict at the time of diagnosis, much guilt is often repressed and/or anger displaced onto the child. Clearly, Alan and his mother are in need of more intensive counseling than can be provided by routine visits to the diabetic clinic.

Hypopituitarism

Deficiency of pituitary hormone secretion can have many varied clinical presentations because of the complex nature of hypothalamic-pituitary regulation and the numerous hormones released from the pituitary gland. The partial or complete lack of growth hormone secretion results in significant growth retardation. The child usually has an immature and pudgy appearance, and may resemble a child of a much younger chronological age. Gradual deviation of linear growth may begin in infancy or not until preschool years, depending on the degree of pituitary hypofunction. Most often, in the very young child, pituitary dysfunction results from a functional and/or anatomic abnormality in the hypothalamus, thereby resulting in deficiency of releasing hormones necessary for pituitary secretion. The more severe the hypopituitarism, the younger the child will be at clinical presentation. With combined deficiencies of growth hormone (GH), thyroid stimulating hormone (TSH), adrenocortical stimulating hormone (ACTH), and gonadotropins (LH and FSH), the symptoms are frequently manifest at birth and are associated with life-threatening illness. Increased awareness by physicians of the early clinical manifestations of hypopituitarism has led to diagnosis of these young infants who must have died undiagnosed in the past. In the short period of only three years at C. S. Mott Children's Hospital, six infants less than six months of age with multiple pituitary hormone deficiencies have been identified. Four of these infants were less than six weeks of age at the time of diagnosis. The management of their difficult medical problem is a challenge to both the physician and the family.

With deficiency of pituitary ACTH and/or GH the infant usually presents with hypoglycemia; if undetected, unresponsiveness, seizures, and death can occur. With intercurrent stress, vomiting, febrile illness, or feeding refusal, the infant does not have available energy stores to prevent hypoglycemia unless therapy with human growth hormone and hydrocortisone are given. Even with adequate replacement therapy, times of stress can still result in a crisis which requires prompt family action and immediate medical intervention. Each minor respiratory illness or feeding refusal for the hypopituitary infant may be a major emotional crisis for the family in terms of anxiety, worry, and fear of death. Prolonged or undetected hypoglycemia can ultimately be associated with permanent brain damage or the later development of a seizure disorder.

Providing the infant with medical and dietary management to withstand stress and prevent hypoglycemia are the two main aims of therapy of the hypopituitary infant in the first year of life. At the same time, if TSH deficiency also exists, thyroid replacement must be given to allow normal linear and mental development. Adequate thyroid hormone is essential in the first two years of life for normal brain growth and the prevention of mental retardation. Although enhancement of the infant's linear growth and weight gain with injections of human growth hormone are secondary in importance to the prevention of hypoglycemia and its complications, the satisfaction of watching the infant grow physically is of tremendous importance to both family and the medical team. As the child grows older and has increased body mass, he will also be better able to withstand stresses which result from intercurrent illness or fasting.

The family of the young hypopituitary child faces many problems that confront the family of a child with diabetes. Injections, while not given on a daily basis, present similar problems. The parents of the hypopituitary child frequently need to know how to give several types of injections in time of emergency. Thus the process of education of the family in the pathophysiology of the disease process becomes crucial. As with the diabetic child, dietary management for the prevention of hypoglycemia is essential. As the child grows older, he may likewise learn to manipulate the family around food by refusing to eat. Hypoglycemia and reinforcement of family anxieties may follow.

The male infant with hypopituitarism may also have small genitalia for his age. Therefore, any neonate with micropenis should be thoroughly evaluated for hypothalamic-pituitary dysfunction. Pituitary gonadotropins and perhaps growth hormone are necessary for normal phallic development during gestation. A small penile size is frequently of great concern to the family and may result in an altered acceptance of the child into the family and the bonding process. Ultimately the resulting attitudes of the family will influence the development of the child's sexual identity and self-confidence. Attitudes regarding the child's genital appearance must be thoroughly discussed and reassurance given when appropriate. In some circumstances, short courses of small doses of intramuscular testosterone will result in some penile growth and may be indicated in situations where family anxiety is of concern. The long-term outcome of these infants, with regard to future genital growth, is still largely unknown and remains the subject of considerable medical controversy. In situations where the infant has a severe micropenis, sexual reassignment should be considered and the child referred to a medical center experienced in evaluation of this difficult problem.

The case histories of Laurie and Greg illustrate the difficult medical problems which can accompany panhypopituitarism in the first few years of life.

Case 1

Laurie had severe problems with hypoglycemia, hypocalcemia, respiratory distress, and hepatitis at birth, but did well at home after two weeks of age. At age one year she was hospitalized after a febrile seizure. Developmental milestones progresssed somewhat more slowly than those of her brother, two years older, except that she was noted to be small. At age 23 months, her growth became more of a concern when she developed a "picky" appetite. At this time it was noted that her parents had been separated since she was nine months of age, and divorce was planned. Home life was very chaotic. Her mother feared Laurie had a serious illness and would die. She was anxious and depressed. At age three years, she was seen in our hospital and a diagnosis of panhypopituitarism was made. In spite of adequate medical compliance and replacement hormonal therapy, Laurie began to have episodes of severe hypoglycemia associated with acute infections and later with food refusal. Between ages three and four and one half years she was hospitalized elsewhere over 12 times. Growth was poor and weight gain absent. When managed in our hospital over a prolonged stay at age four and one half years, she exhibited extreme negativism and manipulated her mother around food. After several weeks a behavior modification program resulted in weight gain. A less rigid dietary program was established that would allow Laurie food choices. Since she often ate poorly in her mother's presence, individual support was given to her mother to help allay anxiety. At this time we learned that Laurie's father had been killed in an automobile accident the previous year. Laurie frequently said she wanted to die to be with him and would refuse to eat. Laurie's mother had unconsciously been reinforcing these wishes by telling her that if she didn't eat she would have a seizure and die. Attempts to involve Laurie and her mother in psychological counseling were unsuccessful because of poor compliance. However, at age six years Laurie no longer has hassles about food and eats willingly. For the first time she has begun to talk about growing. Her mother's new fiancé has helped to provide the consistency in management that Laurie's mother was unable to provide. Growth rate has accelerated.

Case 2

Greg, a twin, was 5 lb at birth; respiratory distress was immediate and followed by frequent episodes of apnea and hyperbilirubinemia in the first week of life. Hypopituitarism was suspected because of the presence of micropenis and profound hypoglycemia. Deficiency of all anterior pituitary hormones was documented and replacement medications begun during the first month of life. He went home for the first time at six weeks of age to join his parents, twin, and five-year-old brother. He did well until six months of age when he developed his first respiratory infection; his dietary intake was poor and was followed by a seizure. On arrival at the hospital he was unresponsive in hypoglycemic coma that responded promptly to intravenous dextrose. Over the next several months he had multiple recurrent hypoglycemic and nonhypoglycemic seizures, frequently necessitating hospitalization. Developmental milestones were reached significantly later than his twin brother but progress was steady. At 19 months, after a respiratory infection, anorexia, and high fever, he was found unresponsive. During a severe illness that followed, tracheostomy was necessary; decanulation has been a problem. At 26 months of age, he is developmentally about 18 months of age. Greg has had very supportive parents who delight in him in spite of the stresses his illness has brought to their family. Regardless of initial anxieties about whether he would live, they have been able to integrate him into the family without neglecting the other two children. Their outlook for the future is optimistic. They feel that Greg is a "special child" and his presence has strengthened their marriage.

SUMMARY.   Laurie's serious medical problems did not become apparent until the time of her life when she was expected to be showing independence. Her mother's attention to a younger sibling, a chaotic life style, and multiple family stresses made management of Laurie's hypopituitarism difficult and the source of extreme maternal anxiety. Attempts at forceful dietary control led to increasing negativism and the family manipulation by Laurie. Hopelessness, helplessness, and severe depression followed for her mother who was unable to cope with the situation. Foster placement of Laurie was strongly considered. At this time, with increased family stability, Laurie has been able to give herself permission to grow. Fortunately, not all young children with hypopituitarism have problems to the degree as in this family. Greg certainly has had similar problems, but emotionally he has had a secure home with stable, nuturing parents. Even so, Greg's family has not had an easy time. Panhypopituitarism in the very young child can quickly deplete the resources of even the most educated, stable family. These families frequently need not only medical advice and pyschological reassurance, but tremendous support from the community as well.

As the hypopituitary child grows older, it must be emphasized to the family that the child may be smaller than his or her peers for many years in spite of the degree of catch-up growth seen with human growth hormone injections. The tendency of family, community, and medical staff to treat a child according to appearance and size is tremendous. It is important for us to remind ourselves and others of the child's chronological age and set expectations of the child accordingly. Otherwise, psychological and behavioral immaturity are inevitable. Education of families, teachers, and friends is essential to promote normal emotional as well as physical growth.

CONCLUSION

The care of infants and young children with chronic illnesses such as juvenile diabetes mellitus and hypopituitarism is challenging. *Early identification* of psychological problems and altered family interrelationships are crucial in the management of these children, and essential to ensure medical compliance as well as healthy mental and physical development. *Education* and *reeducation* are necessary to provide the family with a thorough knowledge of the physiological relationships between emotions, nutrition, physical activity, and hormones that are necessary to an understanding of the daily management of the young child. The educational process is aided by input of a multidisciplinary team approach, especially in management of the young child with diabetes. The individual team members are familiar with the child and his family and can offer the important *reassurance* and consistency of approach that all of these families will need during the early years of the child's disease. Support groups such as the Juvenile Diabetes Foundation, American Diabetes Association, Human Growth Foundation, and Little People of America are valuable to the family by providing educational programs as well as decreasing the isolation that many families experience.

Since the effects of a chronic disease on children are far-reaching, optimal management must address both the physiological and emotional needs of the children *and their families.* We think that a comprehensive, consistent, and supportive approach such as we have described helps meet these needs.

REFERENCES

1. Bennett, DL, & Ward, MS: Diabetes mellitus in adolescents: A comprehensive approach to outpatient care. *So. Med. J, 70:* 705–708, 1977.

2. Drash, PW: Psychologic counseling: Dwarfism. In L.I. Gardner (Ed.), *Endocrine and genetic diseases of children.* Philadelphia: Saunders, 1969.

3. Fleegler, FM, Rogers, KD, Drash, A, Rosenbloom, AL, Travis, LB, & Court, JM: Age, sex, and season of onset of juvenile diabetes in different geographic areas. *Pediatrics, 63:* 374–379, 1979.

4. Grunt, JA, Banion, CM, Ling, L., Siegel, C, & Frost, M: Problems in the care of the infant diabetic patient. *Clin. Pediatr., 17:* 772–774, 1978.

5. Jochmus, I: The influence of maternal patterns of child rearing upon diabetic children and adolescents. *Pediatr. Adolesc. Endocrinol., 3:*52–54, 1977.

6. Klein, AH, Meltzer, S, & Kenny, FM: Improved prognosis in congenital hypothyroidism treated before age three months. *J. Pediatr., 81:* 912, 1972.

7. Koski, M-L: The coping processes in childhood diabetes. *Acta Paediatr. Scand., Suppl 198:* 1969.

8. Koski, M-L, & Kumento, A: The interrelationship between diabetic control and family life. *Pediatr. Adolesc. Endocrinol., 3:* 41–45, 1977.

9. Lovinger, RD, Kaplan, SL, & Grumbach, MM: Congenital hypopituitarism associated with neonatal hypoglycemia and microphallus: Four cases secondary to hypothalamic hormone deficiences. *J. Pediatr., 87:* 1171, 1975.

10. Ludvigsson, J: Socio-psychological factors and metabolic control in juvenile diabetes. *Acat Paediatr. Scand., 66:* 431–437, 1977.

11. Moore, TD (Ed.): Report of the Sixty-Seventh Ross Conference on Pediatric Research. *The care of children with chronic illness,* 1975.

12. Segal, J: "Psychosomatic" diabetic children and their families. DHEW Pub. No. (ADM):77–477, 1977.

13. Seidman, F, & Swift, C: Psychologic aspects of juvenile diabetes mellitus. In H.S. Traisman (Ed.), *Management of juvenile diabetes mellitus.* St. Louis: Mosby, 1971.

14. Smith, DW: Growth and its disorders. In A.J. Schaffer and M. Markowitz (Eds.), *Major problems in clinical pediatrics,* (Vol. 15). Philadelphia: Saunders, 1977.

15. Sterky, G: Family background and state of mental health in a group of diabetic schoolchildren. *Acta Paediatr., 52:* 377–390. 1963.

16. Treuting, TF: The role of emotional factors in the etiology and course of diabetes mellitus: A review of the recent literature. *Am. J. Med. Sci., 244:* 93–109, 1962.

Part III

ATTACHMENT AND SEPARATION

The problems of attachment and separation are touched upon throughout this book. Premature babies, addicted babies, babies with CNS dysfunction, etc., and their families have attachment problems. This section discusses more specifically the nature of some of these problems.

Chapter 13

THE LANGUAGE OF PARENT-INFANT INTERACTION

A Tool in the Assessment of Jeopardized Attachment in Infancy

Michael David Trout, M.A.

INTRODUCTION

In most psychiatric settings therapists are dependent on the report of a "problem" to do their jobs. We are accustomed to having patients seek *us* out, organize their behavior in order to arrive at *our* door at the appointed time, and sit in *our* room describing what is "wrong" in their lives. All of this requires not only a substantial amount of motivation, but likely indicates that the patient has given consideration to his/her discomfort, and has probably even begun the process of putting labels on the discomfort so it can be described to others. The therapist and patient usually share some common knowledge about the existence and nature of the problem, and a joint commitment to work toward a resolution.

In the relatively new field of infant mental health, however, many of the rules and assumptions of traditional outpatient psychiatric treatment are challenged by the nature of the problems encountered, as the following examples illustrate.

Case 1

Miss S., a young, unmarried mother of a nine-month-old daughter, is angry about someone turning her in to Child Protective Services for allegedly failing to feed her baby regularly and dress her warmly enough, and for yelling at and striking her in public. She assumes the infant mental health therapist, to whom a referral was made by the Protective Services worker, is part of a neighborhood and agency plot to make her look "deviant or something." She insists that her daughter is simply " . . . hard to handle—just like my little sister was—and sometimes you have to show them who's running the show." When baby falls down during the therapist's visit, mother fails to respond, and uses the opportunity to instruct the therapist that babies " . . . will run you ragged if you let them. You just can't be jumping up and down every time they want something or get hurt. Besides, they have to learn what kind of place this world is . . . it isn't cuddly and it isn't easy." With her pain so much in evidence, how can the infant mental health therapist acknowledge Miss S.'s experience that life is rotten and babies are better off learning that fact early, and still draw her into an alliance to make it different for *this* baby?

Case 2

Mr. and Mrs. J. and their 20-month-old daughter are referred by the pediatrician who was unable to find, during the baby's two-week hospitalization, an organic cause for her apparent failure to thrive. The referral notes that the child is in the second percentile for weight and head circumference, barely above that for length, and is in serious developmental jeopardy. It is also noted that parents report an earlier female child was also "small" and that their nine-month-old male child not only exceeds the weight of the 20-month-old, but is more developed motorically. The parents state emphatically that the pediatrician is crazy, and they alternate between insisting that there is no problem at all and saying that the baby has some physical ailment. Confused by their baby's affective brightening and weight gain in the hospital, angered by the accusing looks of the pediatric nurses and by the doctor's hint that there may be a family problem, the parents are less than enthusiastic when the infant mental health therapist offers to make a visit. The therapist is faced with a number of questions that have ramifications for both diagnosis and treatment: Why do girl babies do poorly in this family, while the male child thrives? Were these parents saying something important when they observed their daughter greeting the pediatric nurse with a smile and angrily reported that she never does that with them? Of what consequence is it that neither parent looks at or touches their daughter during their visits to the hospital, preferring merely to stand near the crib and speak to the charge nurse?

SUMMARY.   In the situations above, it is nearly impossible for the families to describe "the problem" in language generally understood by mental health clinicians. Denial, distancing, and projection are often the order of the day. Families may struggle to assure the therapist that his services are not needed. Often it seems clear that the family does not want help, resents the offer, and entirely devalues the therapist's suggestion that something may be amiss—or even that someone in the family may be in pain.

In many such circumstances, common sense would seem to dictate a rapid exit for the mental health clinician, whose understandable tendency toward self-preservation may inspire a wish to return to the more traditional therapist role. The patients back at the office more often know how to behave properly, speak appropriately, and appreciate the therapist's professional status and competence. All would be fine except for the annoyingly unavoidable question: What about that baby? Having just taken refuge behind the ethical stance of respecting a person's right to deny a problem and refuse treatment, the therapist is now forced to attend to an equally demanding ethical consideration: a failure to intervene may mean that an already at-risk baby's chances for optimal development may be further reduced. The therapist may feel compelled to call the family back, to see if something was missed, to ask permission to take another look.

But exactly what do we look for when we take another look? Is it possible, given what our training told us about ambivalence and the nature of resistance and denial, that the angry parent was giving us two messages at once? We understood and started to act on the overt message: "Go away, nothing is wrong here." What would it look like or sound like or feel like if the opposite message were also being given? Is there a language of interaction between baby and parent that becomes that dyad's way of speaking covertly to the therapist? How can that language be read? How can those messages be heard by the therapist who also sees clearly what an investment the family has in hiding the very same messages?

THEORETICAL ASSUMPTIONS

It shall be the thesis of this chapter that a troubled parent of an infant may attempt to speak to a helping professional (family physician, public health nurse, therapist, even an obstetric nurse during the perinatal period) about "the problem with baby" with an incredibly subtle mixture of cues and signals, all designed (perhaps unconsciously) to alert others not only to the existence of a problem, but even to its nature. Taking this particular posture toward work with families with infants at risk mandates several assumptions.

First, it is assumed that the infant is part of a family system and cannot adequately be treated apart from that system. Approaching the infant means approaching the infant-family unit (at least the infant-primary caregiver dyad), since one cannot understand the infant without also knowing the caregivers. In terms of the focus of infant mental health intervention, one can also not understand the primary caregiver without knowing the infant. From an assessment point of view, if we accept that it is in the nature of the infant mental health' work that most messages about "the problem with baby" are coded, and probably served up through interactions with baby, then it follows that we are *required* to use a family approach, with *at least* baby and primary caregiver. If we settle for anything less (or fall back on anything less because of our discomfort), we are much less likely to get the message. From a treatment point of view, it is equally bankrupt to see mother or father alone, without baby. Alone, a parent is stripped of the anguish (as well as the nurturance) of interaction with baby, stripped of the keys to the past, and deprived of a language system for describing what is wrong and how and when it gets better.

A key concept here is the role and presence of the baby as not merely another family member, but as a *transference object* for the primary caregiver. A brief look at the meaning and place of transference in psychotherapy may help in understanding the unique position baby may play in the treatment of a disturbed family: "Strictly defined, transference is powered by the repetition compulsion and refers to those feelings and attitudes which belong to past objects but which are displaced and projected upon the therapist . . . mistaking the present for the past."[1] If we substitute "baby" for "therapist" in this definition, we catch a glimpse of the power of baby's presence in the family and the critical role baby plays in treatment. In many cases that catch the attention of an infant mental health therapist, the baby's arrival into the family has stimulated repetition of grief, disappointment, terror, or other feelings associated with earlier events in the caregiver's life, perhaps even in the caregiver's infancy. It does not end here, however, as the mechanism of transference forces the caregiver not only to remember or relive (although the memory, often not yet available to conscious processes, may reveal itself only as agitation, a wish to flee, a direct or mildly distorted repetition of the earlier event), but also to make the baby part of the past, part of the self. The line between past and present becomes blurred, as does the line between baby and parent. Baby may become for parent not a pure object, but sometimes part object and part self: a more pathological and unrealistic version of "Oh, he's nasty to the new baby just like I was when my sister was born." The difference in a more pathological family situation, of course, is that baby may not be seen as *like* the parent (or some other object), but *as* the parent (or the other object), as repeating now the exact horrors of the past. Additionally, baby may be unconsciously viewed as a collection of objects. Baby may no longer be just baby, for example, but also a current representative in the series of males who have caused mother pain or as the reappearnace of the baby sister whose arrival so disturbed father in his own toddlerhood.

Just as in more traditional outpatient treatment, where transference is noted and often encouraged, so it is that intervention with a family troubled about baby must note and make use of the baby's position as a transference object for the troubled parent. While the quality of interaction with baby may be a key to parents' feelings and the depth and nature of the attachment disturbance, treatment is not directed at creating interactional change per se, but to understanding what baby means to the troubled parent. As the "ghosts"[3] are revealed, understood in their *historical* context, and banished from the present nursery, baby becomes less a symbol of conflicts from the past, less a transference object, and gradually becomes the parent's real baby. Only with self and object now more clearly distinguished is there opportunity for a healthy attachment to blossom. Just as interactional behavior formerly was the stage for playing out the pathology, so will interactions now display the growth of love bonds.

Second, the assumption is made that a parent and a baby will display both the healthy and the conflicted parts of their relationship through their behavior together. Therefore, the material for the therapeutic work often lies in what is happening between the baby and the parent at any one time. In other words, to understand best the kinds of conflicts a parent experiences, one must watch that parent be a parent. This assumption is critical to the assessment task; without it we would have to rely exclusively on parents' words and dismiss all parent and infant behavior as meaningless and unrelated to the conflicts. Given this assumption, parent and baby have available a rich and broad language to tell the story of their struggle to attach to and live with each other. Baby may be moved from close ventral-ventral contact to a distant position on the end of parent's knees, facing away, as the parent speaks of a conflict that has driven a wedge between them. Baby may be hit, teased, cuddled, fed, looked at, scowled at, smiled at, threatened, caressed, and ignored in the space of one therapy session. It all serves to tell the story that the therapist needs to hear and see in order to understand the strengths and the struggles of the family. In the same session, baby may avert his gaze, visually check for the caregiver, fall down too much, tease, refuse kisses, cry, coo, refuse food, mold comfortably, search for the caregiver, or jerk back from the caregiver's approach. Again, the interactions are played out on a stage for the therapist, so that the messages of both conflict and health are offered.

One additional note relates to the location of the assessment work. While it is not impossible to see and hear at the office, home visits offer the family vastly expanded opportunities to display how things are for them. If it is our task to be *taught* by parents how they go about their parenting jobs and why, when, and how it all goes awry for them and for their babies, then we need to go where those parenting jobs are usually done: in the family's home, probably in the kitchen or living/play room. The infant mental health therapist's words have a special significance to many families when he explains —as he sits on *their* turf, in *their* chair, drinking *their* coffee —that he wants to *learn* about the baby; he wants to see what it is like for this family. That message often rings hollow when spoken at the office, where the therapist is deprived of direct contact with the smells, sounds, sights, chaos, despair, and cramped nature of life at home.

He is also deprived of critical information not available at the office: What kinds of toys does this baby have? How are they available to him, and how does the caregiver use them with the baby? What does the baby eat? How is food prepared and presented? What are the caregiver's expectations about the baby's eating? What dangers are there in the home and how is baby protected from them? Who else (besides those who might come for an office visit) lives at the home? How do they interact with the baby and with the caregiver, and in what ways do they sabotage the work of helping this family with their baby.

In addition to serving up a far richer slice of data to aid in assessing the problem, assessment and treatment are far richer when there is the opportunity for the insight, relief, or despair to affectively discharge in a "natural" interchange with baby. It is not uncommon, for example, for a parent to strike the baby during a particularly depressed or agitated mood during the therapy time. This may be less likely to happen in the more socially restraining atmosphere of a professional office. At the same time, a parent may act on a sudden and uncharacteristic impulse to reach over and pull baby into a lovely cuddle in the caregiver's favorite chair following the joy of discovery or relief in a session. This "natural" opportunity, with its promise for healing in a reciprocal caregiver-infant relationship, might be missed in the colder, less permissive office. Certainly it would be missed entirely if the baby were left at home when the caregiver came to the office for the therapy appointment—which is a tendency when office visits are permitted.

THE LANGUAGE OF INTERACTION

The language of love is familiar to most who have been in love and who have searched for cues from the love partner (or searched for signals to give back to the love partner). We have at our disposal an amazing range of smiles, touches, words, sounds, looks, positionings, and movements to speak of our joy, despair, fear, pleasure, love, and ambivalence. Researchers at two hospitals have suggested that this langauge is used even with newborns, as mothers display a range of responses upon first seeing their babies.[4-6] T. Berry Brazelton has suggested that baby participates fully in this language, not only as a reciprocating part of communication initiated by mother (as in affective and motoric responses to mother approaching the crib), but also as an initiator of communication (as when baby tries to stimulate a response from a stone-faced mother with body movements, facial expressions, and sounds).[2]

For this language to have meaning to the therapist, however, we must accept that such language involves choice (albeit unconscious choice, in many instances) to *say* something. It used to be convenient to declare that most infant smiles before four months of age were "gas smiles." This view encouraged us to think of baby as less than a truly human, truly alive, reciprocating, and communicating (and, therefore, *choice*-making) creature. As long as smiles just erupt, or cries are chalked up vaguely to colic, then we do not view baby as speaking to us. Similarly, as long as we view as entirely accidental where mother positions her baby as she speaks of memories of her family of origin, then we are spared understanding her behavior as a choice (again, an unconscious one), as a way of *talking* to us. But if we are willing to look upon infants and their parents as complete people capable of lots of feelings and lots of ways of speaking about them, and as fundamentally striving toward health, then our eyes and ears open up suddenly. Before us is a collection of messages more varied and more complex than we dared imagine, and we are sorely challenged to take it all in.

The most oft-selected methods chosen by parents in this writer's practice to communicate to and about the baby fall into these three areas: tactile-kinesthetic interaction, visual interaction, and vocal interaction. Rarely is only one of these modes in use at a time. More often there occurs a multifaceted, multidimensional *series* of interchanges. These are in operation even when the caregiver and infant are only in remote proximity to each other. It is not necessary for parent to be *acting* in order for an interaction to be observed. Sometimes the *absence* of a response on parent's part is as significant diagnostically as a particular kind of active parental behavior.

The observing therapist may be helped to recognize the language of interaction by asking pertinent questions in the context of each interactional mode:

A.   Tactile-kinesthetic:

1.   How much *touching* does parent do?
2.   What *kind* of touching is it? (Are parents' hands open or closed? Is parent using fingertips or a full palm? What part of baby's body does parent focus touch upon? At what point in the therapy work does touching occur? In juxtaposition with what talk does the amount or quality of touching change?)
3.   How does parent *position* the baby? (Is the ventral-ventral posture allowed, or is baby turned away from parent's chest? Is baby placed at the end of parent's lap or tucked in close to parent's body? Does parent allow baby inside parent's postural circle or is baby encouraged to stay out of the circle by parent's posture?)
4.   What sort of *synchrony* is there in parent's movements and baby's movements? (Are there relaxed postural adjustments to baby's cues? Are postural changes so abrupt as to frighten baby or so out of touch with baby's cues as to stimulate a breakdown in baby's pleasant mood?)
5.   What sort of *approaches* does parent make to baby with his or her body? (Does parent move his head to an *en face* position when appropriate? Does parent move his body into baby's line of sight when baby is searching? Does parent

use his or her body to greet baby, to protect baby, to comfort baby?)

    B.   Visual:

    1.   Does parent routinely use a *visual check* on baby's whereabouts and safety?

    2.   Does parent initiate *mutual* gazing?

    3.   Does parent *respond* to baby's looking with a return gaze?

    4.   Does parent *avert* gaze?

    5.   In *juxtaposition* with what talk does parent look over at baby or avert his or her gaze?

    6.   What is the *quality* of parent's look at baby? (Is there affective brightness or blandness? Does parent seem to be "looking through" baby? Does parent's facial behavior change in response to visual cues from baby?)

    7.   Does parent look at baby "full face" or from the corner of his or her eye? (Is there *en face* positioning?)

    C.   Vocal:

    1.   What is the *content* of parent's words? (Do words include allusions to past events or other people? Are there references to giving baby away, selling baby, sending baby back where he came from? Is baby blamed for problems parent is having? Is baby credited with malicious intent? Does parent speak for baby in a manner demonstrating understanding of baby? Do parent's words show appreciation for baby's point of view? Do words include threats, even in apparent jest? Do words include planning of future activities with baby, or do they otherwise reveal parent's pleasure in baby?)

    2.   How *much* vocalizing is there?

    3.   What is the *quality* of the vocalizing? (What is the tone of voice? In juxtaposition to what talking with therapist does the tone change? Do the vocalizations succeed in their purpose: for example, in soothing baby, in comforting baby

after a fall? Is there a teasing quality to parent's words or tone? Is there cooing or gentle "nonsense" talk?)

There are, of course, two actors in this complex dance of interaction, so it is appropriate to ask questions about the baby's behavior in each of the same three modes:

A.   Tactile-kinesthetic:

1.   Does baby seem to achieve a *"fit"* during holding?
2.   Does baby *stiffen* or arch his back while being picked up or held?
3.   Does baby seek physical proximity to caregiver?* How does baby use proximity seeking (when distressed, all the time, as a temporary "stopping off place")?
4.   Is this a *cuddly* baby? Do parent and baby seem comfortable in thier physical contact, or is contact stressed, unsatisfying to one or both?

B.   Visual:

1.   Does baby engage in visual *checking*?* What is the ratio of the baby's reliance on physical proximity to baby's reliance on visual checking at stress times?*
2.   Is there *synchrony* in eye-to-eye contact with parent, or do parent and baby miss each other's looks?
3.   Does baby achieve *satisfaction* in visual checking or establishment of a mutual gaze, as evidence by smiling or stress reduction?
4.   Does baby *avert* his gaze? If so, in response to what parental behavior?

C.   Vocal:

1.   How *much* does baby cry?

*Interpretations in this area may vary, of course, as a function of baby's age and developmental level.

2. What is the *nature* of baby's crying? (What is the pitch? What is the intensity, and how does it change in response to parental inputs? How persistent is the cry?)

3. How *much* other vocalizing does baby do?*

4. What is the *quality* of baby's vocalizing? (Is there cooing, babbling at objects, squealing, screaming, change in vocalizing when parent approaches?)

5. After language acquisition what sorts of adult phrases does baby repeat? How does baby use language to state needs? How does baby talk to dolls, toys, and playmates? How does baby refer to self, parents, and others?

Perhaps the following clinical illustrations will make the task of understanding the language of interaction easier:

Case 1

Patty and her husband birthed premature twin sons and decided to place one of their newborn twins with Patty's mother, 30 miles away, for the first seven months of his life. Visits occurred rarely. While the signs of Patty's differential attachment with her sons were evident in her behavior with them, she was unable to speak of it until a home movie was made of her and the boys. Patty gasped as she and the therapist watched the film together and only then could she begin to speak of the fact that she did not feel close to the separated infant and had not since the day the twins were born. On that day she revealed for the first time that she had looked at her newborns in their incubators and saw Jimmy (the one soon to be separated) sleeping and Johnny " . . . looking up at me and smiling at me!"

On the film we see Patty display—even under the stress of a filming situation—what she cannot say with words. She repeatedly looks over Jimmy's head, as she washes his face and hands, to gaze at Johnny. When she does finally permit eye-to-eye contact with Jimmy, her face contorts into a grimace before she averts her gaze again. When Jimmy approaches her on the couch, she keeps a rigid posture that prevents him from climbing on her lap. After she seats the boys at the table for breakfast, she positions herself on a couch such that Johnny can see her and exchange gazes with her freely; Jimmy has his back to her. Later in the session in which the film was viewed, after telling a story of loss and fear in her own early years, Patty reached over to Jimmy and clumsily pulled him to her lap. (She had touched him so rarely in his lifetime that the pair had trouble knowing how to have physical contact comfortably with each other.) As she finished the story and the session ended, Patty was cuddling Jimmy for the first time since treatment began. Not only had her interactions with Jimmy given a message about her conflicts with him, but some of the conflict began to resolve upon her seeing that the message was heard. Her interactions with Jimmy then displayed the beginnings of that resolution.

Case 2

Mr. and Mrs. L. were unable to speak of their terror at caring for their premature infant, even after the baby reached 5 lb in weight (from a birthweight of 2 lb, 3 oz). As a result, they were unable to ask their therapist for help or even admit to each other how frightened and inadequate they felt. They giggled often and changed the subject when the baby was brought up and became serious only when they expressed their rage at the hospital for allegedly incompetent neonatal care. Only when arrangements were made to do a developmental exam during the baby's third month did they display in their interactions with baby the conflict they experienced in caring for her. On that day mother spoke repeatedly of how heavy Vicki was on her lap—in obvious denial of Vicki's extremely low weight. She urged the baby over and over not to cry, as if to announce to all that things would surely fall apart if Vicki needed or demanded too much. During most of that session Mrs. L. turned Vicki away from her, thus preventing any cuddling or eye-to-eye contact; and mother averted her gaze when baby was turned toward her. When Vicki spit up, mother asked, "Why do you do that to me?" Mother giggled as she watched Vicki perform on the developmental test and frequently called her daugher, a "burn out," then quickly added that she "sure is fat!" or "weighs a ton."

While Mrs. L could not ask with words for help in adjusting to her newborn—perhaps because such a request would constitute an admission of the very feelings of helplessness she was fighting against—she could speak through her interaction with, and words about, her baby. Her denial of the reality of Vicki's small stature seemed to belie a wish to make her baby normal and easy to care for like other infants. The extreme anger at the hospital may have been a displacement of her own sense of incompetence in caring for such a fragile creature. The references to "burn out" may have hooked up with vague allusions by both parents about their use of drugs and may have implied a worry that drug use during the pregnancy caused the premature delivery and the close brush with death that Vicki suffered. Finally, Mrs. L's distancing behavior (demonstrated in her posturing and touching) may have been her way of saying that her baby remained a symbol—we had not learned what kind of symbol yet—and no attachment was possible until some other conflicts were resolved.

Case 3

Miss N. reported that she could not imagine how the therapist could be of assistance to her and her baby, as all was well. She conceded that her own childhood had been rough—too many kids, an abusive and absent father, a harried and cold mother—but she insisted that her own past would not hamper her nine-month-old daughter. She did not, after all, want her baby to suffer as she had. She was even going to make sure her child had a father, and he was not going to be like her own father, who left the family. She admitted not loving the boy she was about to marry but added that she knew little about love anyway. She rarely touched Katrina, and her infrequent over-tures of physical contact were usually greeted with limp, non-cuddly behavior from her baby. At other times Katrina stiffened as she was being picked up and was not able to mold posturally into her mother for the comfort and nurturance it might have provided both of them. Mother responded with anger when Katrina hurt herself, and she offered no caressing. The pair seemed unable to look at each other, and Katrina did no visual checking. At nine months Katrina was quite uncon-cerned when her mother left the room. Mother spoke often of giving her baby away to the Indians and of stringing her up by her toes but assured the therapist that these were meaningless statements. She could admit no disappointment that her baby was unable to cuddle with her and seemed to prefer being alone to being on her mother's lap.

Case 4

Miss J. is the Caucasian mother of a black one-year-old. She seemed, in the first session, to have a warm relationship with her baby. She spoke proudly of not needing the baby's father—"or any other man, for that matter!"—and of being unconcerned about townspeople looking critically at the color of her son's skin. She said that most men were jerks anyway and that she never allowed herself to get close to any of them, "because then you just find out all their faults, what they're really like." However, with Sam, Miss J. was attentive and loving and she proudly displayed an unusually large number of pictures of him covering the wall. She did remark that things had been bad between her and her baby when he was a couple of months old and she was working. She said that her work schedule conflicted with his waking schedule such that she slept little. She characterized that time as one when she yelled at Sam often, hit him sometimes, threatened to sell him regularly, and resented his being around. She expressed relief that things were not like that any longer.

It was a surprise, then, for the therapist to observe her behavior on the second and third visits. Having just told him with words what it had looked like when things were bad with Sam, she proceeded to act out each behavior earlier described. She yelled at him, threatened to sell him, and adopted a resentful and angry stare that had a chilling effect on her therapist and an agitating effect on Sam. He changed from the normally active, responsive, and cuddly child he had been in the first session to a whining, demanding, teasing, distant, fretful baby who was difficult to satisfy. This mother went to greater extremes than most to display both sides of her ambivalence in alternate sessions. She seemed to drive the point home further with a warning about what might happen if her therapist failed to heed the message and help her. In the third session, she invited to the house a girlfriend who proceeded to act out viciously most every negative interaction imaginable, including hitting and slapping, with her own two-year-old. In the space of only three sessions this mother had denied the existence of any "problem about baby" with her words, but had also described for the therapist what behavior he should look for that would imply a problem, then acted out those behaviors. The coincidence of the presence of an overtly abusive mother in the third session must not be overlooked as an additional plea by this mother for help in protecting her baby from herself.

CONCLUSION

This chapter has attempted to describe a particular strategy sometimes unconsciously selected by a parent—often joined by the baby—to alert helping professionals to the nature and existence of a struggle about the baby. The communication is by way of the language of interaction: the subtle mix of touch, looking, and vocalizing that may display just how things are between parent and baby. While the very nature of the conflict and the defenses surrounding it may mean that the observer is pushed away vigorously by the parent, even as the observer is being invited in to hear the story, it behooves all professionals who have contact with infants and caregivers to learn to hear the unspoken messages. If there were not a part of caregiver that wanted to protect the baby, the unconscious motivation to speak about what is wrong would go away. We are clearly being invited to hear. If we do not hear the first time, the parent and baby are likely to show us again. If we do not hear at all, however, we must be aware that we have made a *choice* to be deaf. The side of parental ambivalence that is frightened of the "ghosts"[3] and wants to hide them away will applaud our deafness. The side of parental ambivalence that wants to tear at the walls that are preventing attachment with baby, the side that wants to stop generational cycles of shallowness or abuse, the side that longs to love the baby and be loved back—that side will resent our choice. Further acting out will then become necessary for the family, until someone gets the message.

REFERENCES

1. Blanck, G, & Blanck, R: *Ego psychology: Theory and practice.* New York and London: Columbia University Press, 1974.

2. Brazelton, TB: The neonate's behavior and how it shapes his environment. An address at the annual conference of the Michigan Association for Infant Mental Health, Ann Arbor, Michigan, March, 1977.

3. Fraiberg, S, Adelson, E, & Shapiro, V: Ghosts in the nursery: A psychoanalytic approach to the problems of impaired mother-infant relationships. *J. Am. Acad. Child Psychiatry, 14:*387–421, 1975.

4. Klaus, M, Kennell, J, Plumb, N, & Zuehkle, S: Human maternal behavior at the first contact with her young. *Pediatrics, 46:*187–192, 1970.

5. Klaus, M, Jerauld, R, Freger, NC, McAlpine, W, Steffa, M, & Kennell, J: Maternal attachment: Importance of the first post-partum days. *New England J. Med., 286:*460–463, 1972.

6. Newton, N, & Newton, M: Mothers' reactions to their newborn babies. *J. Am. Med. Assoc., 181:*122–126, 1962.

Chapter 14

YOUNG CHILDREN IN BRIEF SEPARATION

A Fresh Look

James Robertson
Joyce Robertson

During the last quarter of a century much has been published about the effects of separation from the mother in early childhood, mostly in the form of retrospective or follow-up studies. The few direct observational studies appear to have been done exclusively in hospitals and other residential institutions[6,7,15,18,20–22,26,41–44]. These provide a consensus that young children admitted to institutional care usually respond with acute distress followed by a slow and painful process of adaptation. James Robertson[22,26] described the phases of *protest, despair,* and *denial* (later termed *detachment*).

Protest, the first phase of response to institutional care characterized by a multiplicity of nurses, may last from a few hours to several days. The young child has a strong conscious need of his mother and the expectation, based on previous experience, that she will answer to his cries. He is confused and frightened by the unfamiliar surroundings, and seeks to regain his mother by shouting and crying. He has no understanding of his situation and is distraught with fright and urgent desire to find his mother.

Despair, which gradually succeeds protest, is character-ized by a continuing consciousness of his mother coupled with an increasing hopelessness. He is less active and may cry monotonously and intermittently. If a young child continues in a situation where he is looked after by changing nurses, with none of whom he has the possibility of having a meaningful relationship, he will enter the phase of denial/detachment.

Denial/detachment gradually succeeds despair. Because the child cannot tolerate the intensity of distress, he begins to make the best of his situation by repressing feeling for his mother. By absence which he cannot understand, she fails to meet his needs, particularly his need of her as a person to love and be loved by. No one is allocated to mother him, and he gives up trying to attach himself. He turns instead to what-ever satisfactions of food and fleeting attentions come his way.

When he sees his mother he seems hardly to know her and not to mind whether she comes or goes. This is the first form of detachment—detachment from the mother he loved but with whom he does not have enough contact to maintain their rela-tionship. If the separation becomes lengthy and if he continues to be subjected to fragmented care, he will in time seem not only not to need his mother but not to need mothering by anyone. He is superficially friendly to all. This is the final stage of detach-ment which can be seen in young children in many long-stay hospital wards and institutions.

Institution-based studies have been valuable in many ways, but have the limitation that the data they provide do not permit the responses to separation from the mother to be reliably differentiated from the influence of associated adverse factors such as illness, pain, bed confinement, multiple caretakers, and the confusion which follows transfer from home into a strange environment. Writers routinely caution the influence of asso-ciated factors, but without being able to indicate their relative importance. For lack of means of differentiation the literature on early separation therefore remains substantially a literature on an assortment of factors of unknown weight among which loss of the mother is only one.

But Bowlby[2,3], theorizing principally on institutional data collected by James Robertson, makes generalizations which can be summarized as follows: (a) that acute distress is a usual response of young children (between about six months and three to four years of age) to separation from the mother, regardless of circumstance and quality of substitute care; and, by implication, that there is no differentiation between the responses of these infants at varying levels of development; and (b) that the distress shown is the same in content and manifestation as the mourning of bereaved adults.[*]

Anna Freud[13], commenting on Bowlby's grief and mourning theories said:

> Neither the Hampstead Nurseries nor hospitals and other residential homes have offered ideal conditions for the study of separation per se ... We, as well as Dr. Bowlby, used data collected under circumstances where the children had to adapt not only to the loss of the mother but also to the change from family to group life, a transition very difficult to achieve for any young child. Whereas the mother herself had been the undisputed possession of the child, ... the nurse as substitute mother had to be shared inevitably with a number of contemporaries; also, inevitably, it is never one single nurse who substitutes for the all-day and all-night care of the mother.

[*]"In this [paper] my principal aim will be to demonstrate that the responses to be observed in young children on loss of the mother figure differ in no material respect (apart probably from certain consequences) from those observed in adults on loss of a loved object".[2]

". . . young children, even when they remain in their own homes and have familiar substitutes immediately available nonetheless respond to loss of a loved figure with despair and mourning" (1960, p. 21).

"All that has been said [about adult mourning] applies equally to infants and young children of over six months. When for any reason they lose their loved object the three phases of mourning described are experienced. At all ages, we now see, the first phase of mourning is one of Protest, the second one of Despair, and the third one of Detachment"[3].

Although Anna Freud agreed that the overt manifestations of (institutional) separated infants resemble those of bereaved adults, she doubted that from six months of age there is an identity between the underlying processes. Her view is based on the one hand upon the theoretical ground that the capacity to mourn is a function of object constancy and ego maturity: "The nearer to object constancy, the longer the duration of grief reactions with corresponding approximation to the adult internal process of mourning." On the other hand, she stresses the lack of relevant data: "We need to supplement our observations, excluding group or ward conditions . . . From direct observation we know little or nothing about the duration of grief in those instances where the mother has to leave temporarily or permanently while the child remains at home" (p. 59).

Yarrow[46] in a definitive review of research in this area showed that "Maternal separation has never been studied under pure conditions" (p. 471). Heinicke and Westheimer[15] discussing their observations on young children in residential nurseries, acknowledge that their data cannot determine the influence of institutional factors, including that of multiple caretakers. They speculate that "If it were possible to contrast a minimal care situation with one involving highly individualized care then one might get quite different results" (p. 196).

But in Bowlby's most recent book *Attachment and Loss*[4], although there is passing reference to the complexities of the institutional situation, emphasis remains on the assertion that regardless of age and conditions of care the young child's response to separation is usually the mourning sequence initiated by acute distress:

> The subjects of the various studies differ in many respects. For example, they differ in age, in the type of home from which they come, in the type of institution to which they go and the care they receive there, and in the length of time they are away. They differ, too, in whether they are healthy or sick. Despite all these variations, however, and despite the different backgrounds and expectations of the observers, there is a remarkable uniformity

in the findings. Once a child is over the age of six months he tends
to respond to the event of separation from mother in certain
typical ways. (p. 26)

Without citing the "good evidence" which he claims to exist
regarding the influence of each class of variable, Bowlby asserts
that "by far the most important variable" is absence of the
mother, and summarily dismisses other variables as relatively
unimportant. He deals thus with strange environment, previous
mother-child relationship, and the state of the mother as in
pregnancy; and omits to consider other variables such as quality of substitute care, multiple caretakers, and age and level of
maturity of the child at separation.

PURPOSE AND SPECIAL REQUIREMENTS OF THE STUDY

In the attempt to get closer to separation per se we sought
to create a separation situation from which many of the factors
that complicate institutional studies are eliminated; and in
which the emotional needs of the children would be met as far
as possible by a fully available substitute mother. This would
also give us an opportunity to observe the influence of such
variables as level of ego maturity and object constancy, previous
parent-child relationship, and length of separation.

Foster Care

An implication of this approach was that we ourselves
should undertake the total care of the children, thus insuring
consistency of handling and high coverage of observation. We
therefore combined the roles of foster parents and observers,
and ordinary family life went on during each child's stay. A
previous fostering provided a basis for realistic anticipation of
the time and effort that would be required for total care, observation, and regular writing up. It was decided that four chil-

dren, taken one at a time, were as many as could be coped with. According to studies published up to that point, a 10-day period was presumed to be long enough to allow protest and despair to show, but only the beginning of detachment, if at all.

Residential Nursery Care

In a contrast study intended to obtain comprehensive naturalistic observations within the well-established patterns of response to institutional care, one child of comparable status to those fostered was observed in extended coverage during a nine-day stay in a residential nursery.

SELECTION OF CHILDREN

Suitable subjects were defined as first and only children:

(a) of between about one and one-half years to two and one-half years of age (the age range upon which much of the separation literature is based);

(b) who lived with both parents;

(c) who had not previously been separated from the mother except for an occasional few hours in the care of a familiar person;

(d) whose mothers were going into the hospital for about 10 days to have a second baby. (Since there must always be a reason for a separation, it seemed best that this should be the same in each instance— mother going to have a second baby in a hospital which still kept mothers in for 10 days and did not allow visiting by children. Many hospitals, of course, discharge mothers after much shorter periods.)

The fostered children were found through hospital maternity units and child welfare centers and were the first four offered who met the criteria. Two of the children stayed longer than the expected 10 days, for 19 and 27 days, respectively, because of complications in the births.

FEATURES OF THE TWO FORMS OF SUBSTITUTE CARE

Foster Care

During the month or so prior to the separation, the child was introduced to the foster home and foster family so that he would transfer to a setting with which he was already familiar. This was done in a series of interchange visits between the families. Our family consisted of the foster parents, a 15-year-old schoolgirl daughter, and a 20-year-old daughter who came in occasionally from University.

The substitute mother-to-be discussed with the parents the child's characteristics, toilet habits, food fads, sleeping patterns, comfort habits and by observation and discussion gained some idea of the parents' ways of handling the child—so that many features of the home could be brought into the separation setting and by their familiarity contribute to the child's security.

On coming into foster care the child brought with him his own bed and blankets, toys, and cuddlies, and a photograph of his mother. The foster mother sought to keep alive the image of the mother by talking about her and showing the photograph. Play with a family of dolls (father, mother, boy/girl, baby) gave the children opportunity to recall family life and express feelings they could not put into words. The two and one-half-year-olds used the dolls, but the one and one-half-year-olds could not do so because of their inability to symbolize.

Fathers were free to visit as much as they wished and commonly came in the early evening after work, sometimes to share a meal with their child.

At the end of the separation each child was reunited with his mother in the presence of the foster mother. During the ensuing weeks and months the foster mother visited a number of times to help the child transfer from foster mother back to mother and, incidentally, to test the child's reactions to the foster mother as a separation-linked person.

Residential Nursery Care

Contact with this child, John, was obtained only a few days before his admission to the residential nursery and after the parents had taken him there on a visit. The parents had chosen this form of care in consultation with the family physician.

John was admitted to a toddlers' room where there were five other children of about the same age. Most of the others had been in the institution from birth. The young nurses were not assigned to individual children; they did whatever jobs came to hand and changed frequently because of time off and being posted to other duties. There was therefore no continuity of mothering care.

METHODS OF OBSERVING AND RECORDING

Foster Care

A primary consideration was the well-being of each child —to give the best possible care and, while doing so, to observe to what extent and by what means the child coped.

The foster mother, Joyce Robertson, was also the principal observer. Her observations were direct, clinical, and ongoing; a running account was kept on a freely available pad, filled out when time allowed; some use was made of a tape recorder. The full day's record was written up each evening, together with an assessment of the day, and checklists were completed.

The foster father, James Robertson, used a handheld movie camera at intervals each day to capture special events and shifts of behavior around regular happenings such as meals, bedtime, and father's visits. Principal rooms (living room, child's bedroom, bathroom, kitchen) had sufficient indirect lighting to allow high-speed film to be used. As had already been established, a small movie camera in the hands of a trusted person is quickly ignored by young children and does not appear to affect their behavior (James Robertson, 1960). Filming took no more than 20 minutes on any day.

Residential Nursery Care

On being advised of the pending admission, we paid one short visit to the family to gain an impression of the developmental status of the child and his relationship to the mother. During the separation we observed most of the child's waking hours and made written and film records comparable to those done on the fostered children.

In order not to be too conspicuous, Joyce Robertson wore a nurse's overall and, without becoming involved in the tending of children, gave some assistance to the nurses at mealtimes.

SYNOPSES OF FILMS

The full written data have yet to be published but a series of five films based on our assessments have been released.[27–31]

Case 1

Kate, age two years, five months, was in foster care for 27 days. The expected duration of her stay became extended when the mother was detained in the hospital because of complications in the birth of her second child[16,27]. Kate was the first and much-loved child of an immigrant Irish Catholic family. She had lived quietly with her parents in a small apartment on the fifth floor of a working-class tenement and was unused to spending time away from her mother. We first met Kate in her own home. She was a bright, attractive child who, after a few minute's initial shyness, made contact easily and talked well. During subsequent visits to our home Kate was increasingly relaxed and friendly. There was sometimes an overexcitedness in her manner, which perhaps denoted her awareness of the part that Joyce Robertson was to play. (Figure 14–1)

Figure 14–1   Kate, 2 years, 5 months

Kate's upbringing had been on the rigid side. Her father would smack her, but relied as much on prohibitions couched in quiet but threatening tones. Although the mother was softer and Kate had more latitude with her, the mother's demands were high.

Kate was more self-controlled than is usual for a child of her age, yet she was lively and spontaneous. The natural bond between mother and child was close and intensified because of their isolation together on the top-floor apartment. There was little body contact between them but a close relationship was maintained by looking and talking.

The parents explained to Kate why she was to stay with us, and she was included in many of the discussions of arrangements, but it is improbable that she could really anticipate what being away from parents and home would be like. The mother was at home waiting to be taken to the hospital when the foster mother collected Kate. Kate left her mother quietly with the words: "Kate come back soon." For the rest of the day she was friendly and cheerful in the foster home, ate a good supper, and slept throughout the night.

First Week.   During the first five days of the separation Kate was unusually cheerful, cooperative, and active. She laughed a great deal, talked loudly and rapidly, and moved about in an excited, exaggerated way. She showed no distress or bad humor, and was heard repeating to herself the parents' instructions and prohibitions: "Be a good girl, don't cry." "Eat up your potatoes," "Don't make a mess." She was reserved and tried to maintain herself on the basis of the remembered parental relationships and codes. The father's daily visits helped her in this. She used the dolls to show with a smile a united family from which the foster mother was excluded.

Second Week.   By the end of the first week the defensive activity lessened. She related well to all the foster family, ate and slept well, and managed her own toileting—even during the night. There was much good humor and spontaneous natural laughter. But anxiety often broke through. Kate was less independent and often turned to the foster mother. She was fearful of getting lost and began to cling to the foster mother, especially when they were out in the street. She was less able to tolerate frustrations, could not always be the "good girl" who behaved as she remembered her parents wanted her to, and she wanted more bottles and sweets.

During this second week Kate often looked pensive and drawn, her eyes dark as though she needed sleep, and she cried more easily. When her mother was mentioned, she sometimes seemed not to hear, or she would point to the foster mother and say, "That's my Mummy." She played less constructively and was aware that sometimes she managed her body less well, occasionally falling over. Sometimes she did not comprehend what was said to her and answered vaguely as though preoccupied. Or she walked about dreamily, calling for the foster mother to rescue her from her fog. "What is Kate looking for?" she pleaded. But this behavior was episodic, and most of the time Kate was alert and cheerful. Colleagues who saw her were surprised by the good impression she made more than a week after losing her mother. The dolls were used to help Kate understand that she would only be visiting her mother and would have to return to the foster home.

On the 10th day the hospital allowed Kate to visit her mother. She was at first distant and only gradually warmed up to her mother. But throughout the visit she was like a rag doll, allowing herself to be cuddled and kissed but not responding. After half an hour she left with the same bland, smiling acquiescence. But when back in the foster home, her feeling broke through: "I found my Mummy. Take me to see my Mummy. Kate get in Mummy's bed." And she threw her first temper tantrum. In doll play afterwards, she warmly recalled the hospital visit, even to the detail of the stool on which she stood and the love pat mother had given to her bottom.

For several days afterward Kate was often negative and aggressive, particularly to the foster mother, but also to the other Robertsons. She was intensely aware of everyone's movements and needed to know where members of the foster family were, where they were going, and when they would return.

Although for much of the time she was bright and cheerful, there were grizzling spells and tears were often near the surface.

THIRD WEEK. During the third week Kate often said directly and with sadness: "I want my Mummy and Daddy." But sometimes, just a few minutes later, her sadness changed to crossness and she denied that she wanted them. She said: "I don't like my Mummy. Mummy is naughty." She paid less attention to her father during his visits (to his growing discomfiture), and on the 17th day pushed him prematurely to the door, saying, "You go." The father began to visit less often, ostensibly because he had a heavy job to do and his wife to visit, and because he knew that Kate was well-settled; but undoubtedly he was saddened and hurt by Kate's growing coolness toward him.

On a second visit to the hospital on the 17th day Kate chatted nonstop with her mother but still kept a distance. She left without resistance, but in the street outside she looked tense and smacked at the foster mother's face.

Between the two hospital visits she had been affectionate and clinging, often calling the foster mother "Mummy" and showing jealousy when Jean, the 15-year-old daughter, made legitimate claims on her parents' attentions.

In the third week Kate was greatly at ease in the foster family and appeared to be finding a niche for herself. Much of her behavior was natural and spontaneous, showing the range of affect associated with a child in a secure setting. Her general competence and ability to play were returning. She no longer held on to the foster mother's hand in the street; and on an occasion when she was angry, she hung back and allowed the foster mother to get out of sight before she followed. Kate's doll play reflected conflict of feelings towards her parents. After arranging the dolls as a family back in their own home, she suddenly swept them onto the floor. "Throw them in the dust bin," she cried.

FOURTH WEEK.   During the fourth week Kate's dominant wish was still to be reunited with her parents. She was in constant danger of being overwhelmed by the feeling that they did not love her, did not want her back. The foster mother tried to keep Kate aware of reality—that her parents *did* love her and wanted her back. This seemed to help counteract the projection of her feelings.

Kate became still more demanding of the foster mother's attentions, and her friendliness to others often gave way to angry scowling when they went near the foster mother. But for long periods she was relaxed and happy with her foster mother.

Throughout the separation Kate's relationship to the foster father reflected her changing feelings toward her father. Her initial pleasure in his visits gave way during the second week to disappointment and during the third week to anger that he did not take her home. The more angry and disappointed she became with her father, the more she turned toward the foster father as a substitute.

As preparations were made to take Kate home on the 27th day there was an upsurge of anxiety. She vomited and had to be held. She resorted again to hyperactivity and mirthless laughter. All the way across London by car she denied she was going home and sang gay nonsense songs. But when she recognized her street, all pretense disappeared. In a strong voice she said, "That's my Mummy's house." Once across the threshold Kate disengaged from the foster mother's hand, which she had been gripping tightly, and for the next hour completely ignored the foster mother while she set about courting her mother with smiles and sweet talk.

AFTER REUNION.   The foster mother visited occasionally during the next month, and Kate was predominantly friendly and even affectionate—although excitement, quick speech, and heightened color sometimes betrayed unease. Six months later she was able to revisit the foster home in a relaxed and pleasurable way, with easy recall of her stay there.

During the first week at home Kate showed only slight upset. She slept restlessly, wet her bed, wanted more bottles, and cried more than she had previously. She warmed up to her father, and kept close to her mother by looking and talking as she had done before. Her frustration tolerance was lowered and her demands more urgent and frequent. She resisted her parents' wishes, and despite explanations from the foster mother, the parents could not tolerate this departure from her former good behavior. Kate was forced into submission by the father's smacks—actual and threatened—and by his firm disapproval. Her aggression became displaced onto an unoffending aunt.

Fourteen days after returning home Kate was taken by her mother to be enrolled for school two years in advance, as was necessary in a district with few Catholic schools. That night she screamed as with nightmares, and in the morning was acutely breathless. The family doctor diagnosed bronchial asthma, the first attack Kate had ever had, and inquired about stress. With hindsight the mother realized that at the school there had been talk of Kate being "taken," etc., so it seemed that the first (and only) attack of breathlessness was a reaction to the threat of another separation—and to the parents' intolerance of direct expression of feeling, particularly of aggression. Denied this outlet, Kate had no other outlet than the psychosomatic one.

Case 2

Thomas, age two years, four months, was in foster care for 10 days[30]. His parents were in their mid-20s. The family lived in a small, comfortable apartment over the family business. The father was a warm, outgoing man, a keen rugby footballer. He was family oriented, proud of his son, and very ready to consider his needs. There was boisterous affection and quiet understanding in their relationship, with an occasional tinge of irritation when their needs clashed. The mother was a gentle, affectionate person, who showed empathy and understanding for Thomas; but she was rather more controlling than at first appeared from her quiet, easy manner. She rarely compelled obedience, but instead pleaded or disapproved. Usually, if he did not comply, she withdrew interest with an "Oh, Thomas!" and this quickly brought him into line with her wishes. (Figure 14–2)

Figure 14–2   Thomas, 2 years, 4 months

Thomas was a well-developed little boy who had a friendly, confident manner and talked very well. He was not reliably toilet trained and had a strong resistance to going to bed. The relationship to his parents was secure and demonstrably affectionate. The parents had talked a lot to Thomas about the new baby and the coming separation and were fairly confident that, if cared for well and visited every day by his father, he would be all right. During several preseparation visits, mostly at our home, Thomas maintained a friendly but reserved manner. He interacted with all members of our family on the basis of his books and toys and talked of the time when he would stay with us.

FIRST WEEK.   Thomas went with his father to take the mother to the hospital and then was brought to us. He solemnly waved goodbye to his father, acknowledging with a quiet nod the promise of a visit later in the day. Like the other children in the study Thomas did not break down upon separation, but for the first two days defended against the anxiety by overactivity and pseudocheerfulness. He was never still. Then more appropriate feeling emerged—longing for his parents and home and sadness when his father left after visits. But for most of the time he was in good humor, in friendly contact with his caretakers, and able to enjoy play and activities offered. He ate well and resisted sleep as he had done before separation.

Thomas asked about his mother and talked spontaneously about her; mingled among the comments were recollections of times when his mother was angry with him, as though wondering whether her going away was related to his having been naughty. Sometimes he cuddled his mother's photograph to him and kissed it. At other times the photograph made him uneasy; he would take a quick glance and turn away with pink cheeks. He thought a lot about his parents and momentary sadness often overcame him. He would say, "Thomas is thinking."

The highlight of each day was his father's visit, and at first these visits were totally enjoyable with brief tears afterward. But soon Thomas's grasp of the situation made him unhappily aware that visits were temporary and that a goodbye was inevitable. He pleaded with his father not to go back to work but to "stay with Thomas," and after a few days visits were punctuated by tears. He cried bitterly, but briefly, when his father left. Thomas held tightly to the pen his father gave him to look after. He would not allow us to sit on the chair his father sat on and would not even sit on it himself: "No! That is my Daddy's chair. I want to sit on my Daddy's lap."

The parents had suggested that Thomas would need plenty of activity and this proved to be right. He welcomed every diversion, and unhappiness could always be averted by going shopping or playing in the garden. On one occasion when tiredness was combined with inactivity he became very unhappy, crying, "Where's my Mummy? I want my Daddy." On the fifth morning, his voice bold and his mood cheerful, he said, "My Mummy is sitting in the hospital bed. Daddy has gone to work. Daddy has big boots. Thomas has little boots. The baby has bootees." Letting his hand move over his chair from home, he said, "This is a nice chair, Mummy bought it." He stroked the foster mother's arm and face with gentleness, "Nice Mrs. Robertson." He cuddled his mother's photo under his arm and then asked to have it pinned on the wall and told us all to look at it. He had a realistic view of the total situation and, though under strain, was coping well.

Thomas fluctuated between wanting the foster mother's affection and strongly resisting it; his need of mothering and his growing attachment conflicted increasingly with his love for his mother. Late on the sixth day sitting on the foster mother's knee, tired and wanting his parents, he pushed away her encircling arms. "Don't cuddle me! My Mummy cuddles me." At other times he lay on the floor near the foster mother chatting in a relaxed friendly way about his parents, what they said, and what they did with Thomas.

SECOND WEEK.   Thomas was affectionate, but often from the sixth day onward the affectionate gestures would without warning or provocation change to aggression. This highlighted the mixed feelings that Thomas was coping with. Sometimes the foster mother could avert the aggression by accepting but not returning the affection. Sometimes, especially just after a visit by the father, it was our daughter Jean to whom Thomas turned for comforting. There was no conflict, because Jean did not perform the caretaking functions associated with his mother.

In respect to ego development and level of object constancy Thomas was the most mature child in the sample. He was able to express his anxieties verbally, and it was therefore easier to help him maintain the understanding of the situation as given him by the parents. He used the temporary foster relationship adequately, while maintaining a clear memory of his mother.

Thomas did not initiate play with the dolls and often refused to handle them. But he pressed the foster mother again and again to use them to show what was happening to the family members—mother in hospital, father visiting Thomas and mother. The doll baby was of little interest to him. It was not part of the family he knew.

The father's daily visits were very important to Thomas. He anticipated them with longing, experienced them with intense feelings of pleasure and sadness, and was openly unhappy for a brief period afterward. Toward the end of the separation it took Thomas several minutes before he warmed to the father. They then became enveloped in a quiet sadness. On the ninth day the father said, "We've both had enough," and Thomas showed more signs that he was less able to contain the strain. He was impatient, slower to respond to the foster mother's requests; he spoke in a whining voice and chewed his clothing.

In interaction with the foster mother he was generally warm, affectionate, demanding, and aggressive. Sometimes he angrily pushed off her care: "Not you do it. My Mummy do it," he shouted.

In the afternoon of the ninth day he played a new game, that of being a baby. "I a baby. Got no teeth. Can't walk. Want a rattle. I get in a pram." The game went on and on, and his usual boyish constructive games were set aside. Thomas knew he was to go home the next day. He awoke in lively good humor and announced, "I thinking about my rocking horse at home. Mummy says, 'No. Mustn't climb,' makes Mummy very cross."

When the parents arrived, Thomas looked uneasily at his mother for about 30 seconds, then went toward her with gentle affectionate gestures, stroking her hair, touching her face, and taking her in with his eyes. He dutifully greeted his father, but quickly returned to his mother. His first concern was to rediscover her by looking and touching; his next, that her "rest" in the hospital was finished. He made "pretend" tea for his mother and several times broke off the game to kiss her. His caresses were gentle and his voice soft and affectionate. Thomas's full attention had moved to his parents; after bestowing a perfunctory kiss, he left the foster mother with every sign of urgency to get home.

AFTER REUNION.   Thomas returned to his family much the same state as he had arrived in the foster home—untrained toiletwise, with a dislike of bedtime, and with easy expression of aggression and affection. He had been well-supported by the foster mother and by his father and returned home to parents who continued to handle him with empathy and understanding. During visits over the next few weeks he was friendly to the foster mother, but cautious. He stayed close to his mother.

Thomas came through the separation better than any other child in the study. But afterward he was less easy to control than before, and in his relationship with his mother there was a defiant and aggressive element that was new. This was still prominent when the observations finished two months later. He was then also very aggressive toward the new baby.

Case 3

Jane, age 17 months, was in foster care for 10 days[16,27]. She was a lively, attractive child of young parents in modest circumstances. They lived in the same block as we did, but the two families were on no more than smiling terms before we were brought together by the research project. The mother was devoted to Jane's care and provided activities in an imaginative way. Fussing and crying were discouraged, and high standards of obedience set. Jane's father gave a good deal of time to his professional studies but made his presence felt by disciplinary interventions. At 17 months Jane understood many of her parents' prohibitions. (Figure 14-3)

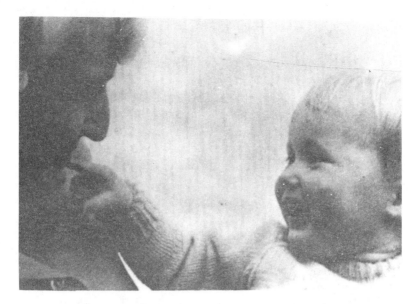

Figure 14-3   Jane, 17 months

Familiarizing Jane with the foster family was more difficult than with the older children in the study. While the mother was available, Jane had only fleeting interest in the foster mother. It was therefore several weeks before the rudiments of a relationship were established. There were unexpected difficulties in acquainting Jane with the layout of our home, mainly because she transferred her parents' prohibitions to the new setting; she would not, for instance, enter the bathroom because it contained a washing machine like her mother's, which she had been taught not to touch. However, by the time the separation began, Jane was fairly at ease and had briefly visited us without her mother.

Jane was awake when the parents went to the hospital in the middle of the night. But the foster mother, by then a familiar figure, was in the apartment before they left. After lying awake for an hour in her cot Jane fell asleep. The foster mother stayed until Jane awoke at 8:00 A.M., showed her around the empty apartment, then carried Jane to the foster home. She ran with pleasure to the box of toys.

FIRST WEEK.   Jane immediately accepted mothering care from the substitute mother and entered into a warm and pleasurable relationship. During the first few days she functioned well, feeding herself, sleeping and playing well, and did not cry. She was gay, lively, and directed intense, purposeful smiles at her caretakers. These grimaces were clearly intended to elicit answering smiles from those about her, and in this she was successful. The gay overactivity and the intense smiling were understood as defensive, a means of combating anxiety. When a smile stopped, it was replaced by a blank, tense expression.

After the first few days the smiling behavior lessened and was then seen only immediately after sleep, as though at each awakening Jane had to assure herself that this was a friendly and safe place. The mother, on seeing the film record of these first days, commented, "Jane smiles a lot like that after I have been angry with her and she's trying to placate me."

By the fourth day gaiety had given way to restlessness and lowered frustration tolerance. More appropriate cross, negative behavior appeared. Jane played less well, sucked her thumb more, and wanted to be nursed. None of these changes were very marked, but they combined to give an impression of a child who was under stress and was at times bewildered. There was no crying, but increasingly she wanted attention and company.

On the fifth day there was less smiling and some irritable crying. She wanted to be held more and resisted routine handling. For the first four days she had played in the communal garden without going to her own garden gate or even appearing to notice it, although the setting was very familiar to her. On this morning she went to the gate and tried to open it, but failed. She looked over the low wall into the empty garden where she had played with her mother, shook her head in a negative gesture, then turned away with a wide smile filling her face. She ran a few yards into the communal garden, then stood as if uncertain which way to go.

On the sixth day Jane again went to her garden gate, and this time it pushed open. She ran down the path and tried the handle of the door into the apartment. Then she turned and hurried back to the garden gate with a distorted expression on her face. She closed the gate very carefully, but for some minutes hovered nearby. She strained to look over the garden wall and peered through the bars of the garden gate at the empty house. Then for the first time she resisted going into the foster home, and for the first time during the separation she spoke the word, "Mama."

Jane's father visited for an hour each day. At first she played happily with him and cried when he left. Then as her general frustration tolerance declined, she got angry with him. Later she would pointedly ignore him throughout a visit but cling and cry when he made to leave.

SECOND WEEK. In the second week Jane continued to relate warmly to all members of our family. She had gained a new word, "Flower," associated with the flowers on her foster mother's apron. Although she was quieter and ready to cry at minor frustrations, she continued to eat and sleep well. On a visit to a weekly playgroup run by the foster mother Jane was completely at ease, interacting competently with the other children.

By the 10th day Jane was firmly attached to the foster mother and called her "Flower." That morning she was lacking in energy and became upset when the foster mother moved away from her. When her mother came to take her home, Jane recognized and responded to her with only slight hesitation. Initially there was uncertainty and shyness; but then sweet, smiling, placating behavior came to the fore—a remembered way of getting her mother's attention and approval. Mutely she invited her mother to take over; first she wanted her potty, then she fetched her hairbrush, then her dress needed attention. When the mother arrived, Jane and the foster mother had been playing a familiar game of putting pennies into a purse. Jane transferred the game to her mother, and in a teasing way, avoided the foster mother with whom she had been so intimate.

AFTER REUNION. During the first two days the placating behavior toward both parents alternated with its opposite—doing what she knew would bring their disapproval. Smacks and frustrations now led to outbursts of severe crying, which was a new feature. This was very different from the obedient Jane of preseparation days who at a clap of the hand or a sharp call would heed their prohibitions. It was several weeks before there was a lessening of the provocation toward her mother. But the easy obedience did not return, and with a second child in the family the parents no longer pressed as hard. Although Jane had responded to her mother with recognition and pleasure, she was reluctant to give up the foster mother.

In order that the child should not suffer the sudden ending of a good substitute relationship, the foster mother visited several times in the next few weeks. She was at first warmly welcomed by Jane and not willingly parted from. Then, as the relationship to her mother became more established, Jane hovered uncomfortably between the two mother figures. A week after her return home she ran toward the foster mother, but the mother put out an inviting hand and caused her to change course. Jane reached neither mother nor substitute mother but fell between and cut her mouth. Two weeks later Jane had weaned herself from the foster mother. Although the foster relationship had lost importance, it remained friendly and warm.

Case 4

Lucy, age 21 months, was in foster care for 19 days because complications in the birth detained her mother in the hospital [17,31]. Lucy's parents were graduates, intelligent, and extroverted. The father was an outgoing, optimistic young man; although he was married and his second child was nearing birth, he still managed to indulge his active bachelor hobbies. He was warm and demonstrative to Lucy, but their interactions tended to occur when it suited him and not when Lucy asked for them. The mother was cheerful and lively in the last weeks of pregnancy, but some of this liveliness revealed itself as a defense against anxiety about the birth; she responded appropriately to Lucy but did not prolong the contacts.(Figure 14–4)

Figure 14–4   Lucy, 21 months

Lucy's early developmental history was normal, reflecting the adequate mothering she had received. At 21 months her body control was excellent, and she played intelligently and constructively. But there were also less satisfactory aspects. Lucy did not talk, she slept a great deal, had an eating problem, and tended to withdraw when frustrated. Her expression was somber, and she dribbled. These features possibly related to lowered cathexis in the mother during a difficult pregnancy.

During the first few familiarizing visits Lucy was often glum, her face puckered and brows drawn together to give a disgruntled expression. Even when she had warmed up, there remained a great deal of reserve and caution. On later visits she became quietly friendly, using her toys to make contact. She showed little variation in mood.

The foster mother collected Lucy from home an hour before the mother went to the hospital. The parting of mother and child was as undemonstrative as if Lucy had been going for an outing to the park. That first evening she interacted quietly with all of us, singling out the foster mother as the most familiar. At the first attempt she objected to being put to bed, but after a period of play with the family she went peacefully and slept soundly throughout the night.

First Week.   Lucy left her mother without protest and without a change of facial expression. In common with the other children she was active and cheerful for the first few days. This gave way to turbulent behavior—anger, petulance, gaiety, and affection toward the foster mother. Her expression lost its flatness and reflected changing feelings. The father commented that Lucy's laughter had a new artificial quality about it. During the first two days Lucy cried only when put into her bed and when her father left after visits. She was affectionate to the foster mother, often running to bury her head in the foster mother's lap.

By the fifth day Lucy presented a very different picture from the preseparation one. Descriptively there was a marked improvement, contrary to what is expected of young children during separation. Lucy looked bright and happy and only occasionally withdrew. She was eating proper meals and the dribbling had stopped. Solitary play had given way to interaction with the foster mother, who was followed about or pushed and pulled into Lucy's chosen direction. The father's daily visit was pleasurable to both, and Lucy cried when he left. On the sixth day the father commented on her improved physical appearance, and the greater animation and responsiveness.

SECOND WEEK.   In the middle of the second week Lucy became cross, negativistic, and could not accept comforting. She refused food and threw everything away from her, including her own cuddly toys. The feeding disturbance, which had been observed at home prior to separation, was now transferred to the foster mother with all its anger and provocation. A few days later the mood was different again. Tears rose quickly. Sometimes Lucy sought comforting and could accept it, but at other times she isolated herself by crawling under a table or behind furniture out of reach. Then she would come to the foster mother to recover in her arms.

On the 10th day Lucy's father took her to a park where she had often been with her mother, and on return she was unsettled and aggressive toward the foster mother, screaming and scratching. As the range of feeling became more richly expressed within the foster family, Lucy was less involved with her father during visits. On the 11th day he was disturbed that she was distant and that he could not get into their former warm relationship. That night Lucy slept badly.

THIRD WEEK.   Friendly distance continued to characterize Lucy's attitude to her attentive father, but within our family she was most often relaxed and responsive. She sought more attention from the foster father. In her relationship to the foster mother she was affectionate, could tolerate prohibitions, could accept comforting, and could play quietly apart while remaining in contact. But without warning she would for a few hours be negative and defiant. Lucy was in a highly sensitive state and needed careful handling.

On the 17th day the father again took Lucy to the park near her home. She returned in a good mood and greeted us affectionately. But after the father left, she threw herself on the floor and rolled about miserably, refusing to be comforted.

After a time she allowed herself to be picked up, and at bedtime she clung tearfully to the foster mother and could not be put down.

On the 19th day Lucy's mother came to take her home. With hardly any hesitation Lucy withdrew from the foster mother and responded to her mother's overtures. She looked intently at her mother, then smiled; after piling all her toys onto mother's lap, she climbed on top with a pleased expression. Without words Lucy had shown where she and they belonged. But before leaving for home, she ran affectionately to the foster mother.

AFTER REUNION.   After two days of serene behavior the changing moods and demands which had manifested during the separation reappeared and were focused on the mother. With the pregnancy safely behind her, the mother now responded fully to Lucy's new demands. This richer interchange between them was maintained, as were many of the improvements that occurred during the fostering.

But Lucy had great difficulty in weaning herself from the foster mother. During a visit by the foster mother three days after reunion, Lucy oscillated between affection and apprehension, smiling and frowning, clinging to her mother yet crying bitterly when the foster mother left. Several visits over the next three weeks were necessary to enable Lucy gradually to reestablish the relationship to her own mother and to decathect the substitute relationship.

Case 5

John, age 17 months, was in a residential nursery for 9 days[20,14,19,40]. John and his mother had a quiet, harmonious relationship. He was an easy, undemanding child, and the mother was competent and unfussy in her handling. Toilet training had not begun. He was a sturdy, good-looking boy who ate and slept well and said few words. The father, a young professional man, was at a critical point in his training, and it was impractical for him to look after John while the mother was in the hospital. The family doctor recommended that he be put into the local residential nursery, an institution used by local authorities and approved for the training of nursery nurses. John accompanied his parents when they went to see the nursery. The parents were reassured by the liveliness of the group of five toddlers that John was to join and by the friendliness of the young nurses. They anticipated that John would show some upset after the separation but that they would be able to handle this. At 17 months John had, of course, no understanding of the preliminary visit. (Figure 14–5)

Figure 14–5   John, 17 months

FIRST WEEK. The mother's labor began in the night, and John was left at the nursery when she was en route to the maternity hospital. John cried for half an hour, then fell asleep. When he awoke he found himself in a strange setting, a room with five other cots and in each a child of his own age clamoring to be dressed. He watched as they were attended to, and when 18-year-old nurse Mary approached him with a smile, he responded in a friendly way and interacted as she dressed him.

At breakfast it was another young nurse, Christine, who fed him, and to her he was also friendly, as he was to two others who gave part of his care during the day. Any one of these could have become a substitute mother, but this the system of nursing did not allow. The young nurses were not assigned to individual children but turned to whatever duties came to hand. Although John found the nurses friendly, the contacts were fleeting and unsatisfactory to a child who tried hard to find one who would stay by him.

The other children had been in the institution from birth and were noisy, aggressive, self-assertive, and demanding; they had never known stable relationships and in many ways fended for themsleves in a violent little community. They knew from experience that they could not expect their needs to be antici-pated and met. John was bewildered by the noise, occasionally putting his hands to his ears, and as a family child was no match for the aggression of the other children. When his father walked into this strange environment, John looked blankly before wid-ening into a smile of recognition. He made no objection when his father left.

It was Mary, the nurse who had dressed him in the morn-ing, who put John to bed. He was again ready to make a relationship. But Mary had to move on to other duties, and John gave a shout of protest and disappointment.

On the second day John still coped quite well. While the institutional children rushed about, snatching and fighting, he played constructively as he had done at home—in a corner away from the commotions. Occasionally he still sought to find a nurse who would mother him. But usually his tentative ap-proaches were overlooked as the nurses responded to the more clamorous children; or if he got a nurse's attention, he was either displaced by a more assertive child or the nurse put him down to do other tasks. The young nurses were not concerned about John; he ate well, was quiet and undemanding, and cried only when he was put in his cot.

When his father made to leave after visiting, John's quiet uncomplaining manner changed to crying and struggling to go home with him. Nurse Mary comforted John, and he soon emerged smiling with expectation of play. But again the young nurse could not linger, and John shouted in tearful complaint as she walked away from his cot.

From the third day John was increasingly distressed. His overtures to the nurses did not bring him the care and affection he was used to. His needs were overlooked, and he was assailed by the noisy clamor and attacks of the other children. He still cried little, but either stood forlornly at the end of the room or played quietly in a corner with his back to the group. When his father visited, John smacked him crossly and pulled at his glasses.

On the fourth day there was marked deterioration. There were lengthy spells of sad crying which merged with the din of the other children and went unattended by the nurses. His play was listless, he sucked more, and his fingers often strayed over his face and eyes. He ate and drank hardly at all and walked with a slow, shambling gait. He still tried, though with less effort, to get close to one or another of the changing nurses, but was generally unsuccessful and several times crawled under a table to cry alone.

On the fifth day his constant misery attracted some attention from the nurses. But they could not comfort or interest him in toys and he ate nothing all day. And as no nurse had direct responsibility for him, their concern was dispersed and ineffectual. His face was drawn and his eyes swollen. He cried in quiet despair, sometimes rolling about and wringing his hands. Occasionally he shouted angrily at no one in particular and in a brief contact smacked nurse Mary's face. John now made fewer direct approaches to the nurses; and as if defeated in his attempts to get comfort from them, he turned to a teddy bear that was larger than himself. While the other children were rushing about or clambering over the young nurses, John would be sitting somewhere burrowed into the teddy bear. Sometimes he stood looking around at the adults as though searching for one who would hold him. Nurse Mary made herself more available than did the other nurses, but she came and went according to the duty rota and not according to John's need of her, and was not much help to him. John's father had been unable to visit for two days.

On the sixth day John was miserable and inactive. When nurse Mary was on duty her face registered concern for him, but the system of group care frustrated them both and her concern was lost in the babel of the other toddlers. John's mouth trembled with tears held in check. In contrast to the beginning of his stay when he stood out as the brightest and bonniest of the children, he was now unhappy and forlorn. Nurses picked him up briefly and put him down when other children needed attention. He cried a great deal. He manipulated the big teddy bear, twisting it this way and that in desperate attempts to find comfort. When his father came, John pinched and smacked. Then his face lightened, and hopefully he went to the door to show mutely his wish to go home. He fetched his outdoor shoes, and as the father humored John by putting on the shoes, the child's face broke into a little smile as if thinking this presaged going home. But when the father did not move, John's face became overcast. He went to Mary, looking back at his father with an anguished expression. Then he turned away from Mary, too, and sat apart clutching his cuddly blanket.

On the seventh day John cried weakly but continually all day long. He did not play, eat, make demands, nor respond for more than a few seconds to the fleeting attempts of the young nurses to cheer him. He stumbled as he walked, unhappy and whimpering. His expression was dull and blank, not like the lively good-looking boy who has been admitted a week earlier. John got some comfort from being held; it did not matter by whom. But always he was put down within a short time. Toward the end of the day he would walk toward an adult, then either turn away to cry in a corner, or stop short and fall on his face on the floor in a gesture of despair. He huddled up against the large teddy bear. The father came late and John was asleep.

SECOND WEEK.   On the eighth day he was even more miserable. There was an angry note to his cries when another child sought to oust him from a nurse's knee. But there was no respite to his unhappiness. For long times he lay in apathetic silence on the floor, his head on the large teddy bear, impassive when other children came to him. He still ate little. When his father came at teatime and tried to help, John was so distraught that he could neither eat nor drink. He cried convulsively over his cup. At the end of the visit John was abandoned to despair and no one could comfort him, not even his favorite nurse Mary. When she tried to take him on her knee, he squirmed down on the floor and crawled into a corner beside the teddy bear. There he lay crying, unresponsive to the troubled young nurse.

On the ninth day he cried from the moment he awoke, hanging over his cot and shaking with sobs. All but one of the nurses were new to him, and he was slumped motionless on her lap when his mother came to take him home. At the sight of his mother John was galvanized into action. He threw himself about crying loudly and after stealing a glance at his mother, looked away from her. Several times he looked, then turned away over the nurse's shoulder with loud cries and a distraught expression. After a few minutes the mother took him on her knee, but John continued to struggle and scream, arching his back away from his mother and eventually got down and ran crying desperately to Joyce Robertson. She calmed him, gave him a drink, and passed him back to his mother. He lay cuddled to her, clutching his cuddly blanket but not looking at her. A few minutes later the father entered the room and John struggled away from the mother into the father's arms. His crying stopped, and for the first time he looked at his mother directly.

It was a long, hard look. His mother said, "He has never looked at me like that before." In the discussion with nursery staff afterwards, they agreed among themselves that "We have had many children like John."

AFTER REUNION.   In the first week John had many temper tantrums. He rejected his parents at all levels—would not accept affection or comforting, would not play with them, and removed himself physically by shutting himself up in his room. He cried a great deal and could not cope with the slightest delay in having his wishes met. He was aggressive and destructive in his play. Instead of carefully manipulating his toys, he now scattered them angrily.

During the second week the tantrums stopped and he was undemanding. For much of the time he played quietly in his room. But in the third week there was a dramatic change. His behavior became more extreme than in the first week. The tantrums returned; he refused food so resolutely that he lost some pounds in weight; he slept badly at night, did not rest during the day, and became clinging. The parents were shocked by this deterioration, particularly by the gulf that had appeared between them and their son. They reorganized family life around the task of supporting John and giving him maximum attention in an attempt to help him regain whatever had been lost.

A month after returning home John had a much better relationship with his mother. But his "good" state was precariously held, and a visit by the observer (Joyce Robertson) threw him back into the original state in which he refused food and all attentions from his parents. He recovered after a few days, but three weeks later (seven weeks after returning home) another visit by the observer again elicited extreme disturbance which this time lasted for five days and included a new feature of aggression against his mother. Presumably the observer's visits reactivated anxieties and fears related to the separation experience.

Three years after his stay in the residential nursery, when

John was four and one-half years old, he was a handsome, lively boy who gave much pleasure to his parents. But there were two marked features which toubled them. He was fearful of losing his mother and got upset if she was not where he thought she would be. And every few months he had bouts of verbal aggression against her which came "out of the blue" and lasted for several days. These features seemed to be legacies of the traumatic experience of being for nine days in a residential nursery which did not meet his emotional needs. John's story is in the well-established pattern of institutional separations: "The infant is at the mercy of the compliance of its environment, and of the ability of the institution to provide an adequate object."[43].

THE INFLUENCE OF VARIABLES

The four children who were given adequate substitute mothering in a supportive setting showed with a clarity not previously reported the influence of variations in (a) level of ego maturity and object constancy; (b) previous parent-child relationship and/or defensive behavior; and (c) length of separation. The contrast study of John, who was observed in a residential nursery, brought out more clearly the importance of additional stress factors such as (a) inadequate substitute mothering, multiple caretakers; and (b) strange environment.

LEVEL OF EGO MATURITY AND OBJECT CONSTANCY

Since ego maturity and object constancy bear some relation to age, certain effects of these variables can be illustrated by comparing the over-two-year-olds (Kate and Thomas) with the under-two-year-olds (Lucy and Jane).

Over Two-Year-Olds

Thomas (2.4 years), comparatively advanced in ego maturity and object constancy, thought and talked a great deal about his mother; he pinned up her photo in a prominent place, kissed it, and got angry with it. He expressed verbally his difficulty in leaning emotionally on his foster mother while remaining true to his mother. While edging near to sit on the foster mother's knee he warned, "Don't kiss me, my Mummy kisses me." Comparing her gray hair with his recall of his mother's black hair, he said, "Your hair is the wrong color"; and later, looking at her blue eyes, he remarked that his mother had brown eyes. Thomas spent long periods expressing his thoughts and concerns about his parents. In a tearful mood he said, "I'm thinking of my rocking horse at home. My Mummy says, 'It's a nice day, Thomas.' I like my Mummy best." And after a thoughtful pause, "Mummy says, 'Thomas is a naughty boy.' Sometimes my Daddy's eyes are angry." Talking and thinking about his parents kept feelings uncomfortably at sur- face level and Thomas's behavior reflected this. His growing closeness to the foster mother and need of her attentions con- flicted with his remembered love of his mother and resulted in aggressive outbursts toward the foster mother.

Kate (2.5 years), too, could remember and talk about her own home and parents. She spoke of the preparations she and her mother had made for the new baby and how she was going to help her mother look after it. She compared her mother's domestic equipment with that of the foster mother, noting what was like and what was unlike. She asked often, "Where is my Mummy?" Kate explained that the foster mother was Jean's mummy and not Kate's mummy. But as the separation became extended into a third week, there were times when Kate said loudly and with emphasis to the foster mother, "*You* are my Mummy" and prefaced every remark with "Mummy."

During the first few days both Kate and Thomas were reserved and kept the foster mother at a distance because the relationship to their own mothers was vivid and real. Then their need of mothering and their growing attachment to the foster mother sometimes brought conflicts of loyalty and provoked negative or aggressive episodes with the foster mother. Because

Thomas and Kate had clear memories of mother and home they could be helped to maintain these memories and anticipate eventual reunion. When Kate in unhappy spells said, "My Mummy doesn't love me, she won't come to take me home," it was possible to help her separate fantasy from reality. This reduced the buildup of hostility against the mother and kept alive the memories of a mother who cared. There was no doubt that these two children missed their mothers and were under stress; but there was no desperate unhappiness. Memories of the absent mother, their understanding of the reality situation reinforced by the ability to play out their preoccupations through the doll family, the support they got from their fathers, and the emotional interaction and ego support provided by the substitute mother combined to enable them to weather the experience without being overwhelmed. Both Thomas and Kate were able to drop the foster relationship as soon as the real mother returned.

Under Two-Year-Olds

Jane (1.5 years) and Lucy (1.9 years), a year younger than Thomas and Kate did not have the sophistication in ego development of the older children; nor had they reached the older children's level of object constancy[11]. They were more dependent on the adult for physical survival, and their needs were more urgent. Jane and Lucy could therefore not be helped to the same extent as the two older children to keep the absent mother in mind. They could not talk about her, nor had they the maturity to use the doll family. Because of this and the intensity of their physical and emotional needs, these two younger children accepted the mother substitute without the loyalty conflicts of the two older children. Almost immediately they related warmly and wholeheartedly to her.

It seemed that at their level of development the two younger ones did not carry a clear image of the absent mother and did not have the older children's ability to spontaneous recall. Specific reminders were needed to bring the mother into mind and for simultaneous resistance to the foster mother to be felt. For instance, after Jane saw her own garden gate and Lucy had been taken by her father to a park near her home, both children for a brief period pulled away from the foster mother. But these explicit feelings for the mother and the related resistance to handling by the foster mother could not be sustained because Jane and Lucy had not reached the level of object constancy that Thomas and Kate had attained. At reunion Jane and Lucy greeted their mothers with spontaneous pleasure, but they had more difficulty than did the older ones in reestablishing the relationship with the mother and in disengaging from the substitute mother.

PREVIOUS PARENT-CHILD RELATIONSHIP AND DEFENSIVE BEHAVIOR

Over Two-Year-Olds

Because the children were so young, it was not always possible to differentiate between defensive behavior and the precursors to defenses which are still dependent upon remembering parental attitudes. Kate had been strickly brought up; angry feelings had to be controlled; crying was "naughty"; she had to be a "good" girl who always did as she was told. During the first week in foster care Kate was obedient, reasonable, and very easy to handle. She recalled vividly her parents' disciplines and instructions: "Kate must be a good girl, mustn't make a mess. Kate mustn't touch your books. Must eat my potatoes first," she instructed herself. She recalled that her mother smacked her when she was naughty. She was overactive and cheerful, making tremendous efforts to maintain herself without her parents: "Look, I'm a good girl. I'm laughing," she repeatedly told the foster parents, laughing artificially. She kept herself busy cleaning windows and sweeping floors, activities she had shared with her mother. For five days the defensive behavior served Kate well. But when on the sixth day she was taken for an hour into a strange setting among strange people the precarious balance was lost and she cried for the first time since leaving her mother. For most of the first week Kate behaved in line with her parents' expectations. Then she began to find it hard to maintain that standard of "good" behavior without their support and demands. The defensive behavior fell away and she became much more anxious and clinging.

Thomas's (2.4 years) parents allowed free expression of feelings and did not make excessive demands for good behavior. Initially, he coped with the stress of separation by overactivity —running, jumping, kicking balls almost nonstop. But by the third day he was expressing sadness with almost adult understanding of the situation. Thomas showed his feelings much more openly than any of the other children. He was overtly aggressive and affectionate. This was in line with his preseparation behavior and with the parents' expectations of him.

Since Thomas and Kate were the same age and at the same level of ego maturity, the differences in their behavior seemed to be attributable mainly to preseparation parental expectations.

Under-Two-Year-Olds

Jane (1.5 years) had been expected by her parents to be a smiling child. Crying was discouraged. To smile was to be "good." The mother reported that Jane always smiled more when she had been naughty and wanted to placate her mother. This behavior carried over into the foster situation. Jane smiled a great deal in obvious need to get answering smiles from her new caretakers. Her smiles gradually took on an intense grinning quality which would suddenly disappear and leave her with a confused, unhappy expression. This lessened after the first three days, but for some further days the soliciting smiles were seen when she awoke from sleep. At home Jane had been an obedient child who could be stopped from forbidden activities by a handclap and a "no" from her parents. She could even deter herself; within reach of her father's cabbage patch she would stop, clap her hands, shake her head, and refrain from pulling a plant, but this behavior was still dependent upon her parents' demands and threatened withdrawal of approval. Patterns of behavior were not yet internalized, so that in her parents' absence she could not hold on to the prohibitions for long. After the first two days of separation, cautions went unheeded; Jane was indifferent to the foster mother's disapproval.

Lucy (1.9 years) was unusually solemn and silent. Because her development was good in every other area, we thought this a response to the mother's partial withdrawal of cathexis in the latter stages of a difficult pregnancy.

Unexpectedly, during the first week of separation Lucy became active and animated. We understood this to be because she rediscovered fully responsive care in the foster mother. After a period of turbulent behavior in the second week she became relaxed and affectionate towards the foster mother, transfering to this new relationship the feeding disturbance which had been part of her relationship to her mother.

LENGTH OF SEPARATION

The influence of length of separation cannot be considered separately from the age and level of maturity of the child and the quality of substitute care. John and Jane, for instance, both 17 months old and at comparable levels of maturity, were separated for about the same length of time. The difference in outcome is primarily attributable to the extreme difference in the conditions of care during separation.

Inadequate Care

For John, in the oppressive conditions of the residential institution, the longer the separation went on the more upset he became. Loss of his mother, aggravated by the stresses of the strange environment, unfamiliar routines, and multiple care-takers, overwhelmed the immature child and swept him along the path from protest into despair. If the separation had contin-ued he would in time have moved into the two stages of detach-ment—first into detachment from the parents he had loved and second, for lack of adequate substitute care, into detachment from all relationships.

Adequate Care

For the four fostered children the situation was very differ-ent. Given good conditions of care and a substitute mother, the maturity of the child determined the effect of various lengths of separation.

UNDER TWO-YEAR-OLDS. The younger children managed the first few days of separation by mobilizing defenses against their anxiety, and when these began to fail they turned readily to the foster mother for comfort and support. This relationship then held them in a state of manageable anxiety during which they functioned well and their development continued—in contrast to John's despair and disorientation.

After 10 days Jane had some difficulty in relinquishing the foster mother, and after 19 days Lucy had infinitely more diffi-culty because in the extra days her relationship to the foster mother had deepened. Had Lucy's separation gone on for sev-eral months the substitute relationship would have superceded the mother-child relationship. (This is a problem for fostering agencies dealing with very young children.) Within a very few weeks, or months, the foster relationship becomes strong, and the child cannot then be moved back to the blood parents without risk of hurt being caused by the severance of the new relationship—hence the weaning procedure shown in our films *Jane* and *Lucy*[28,35]).

The older children also began by using defenses against anxiety. But, because of the greater maturity of their relationships to their parents, when sadness broke through they turned to the foster mother for comfort with more reserve than did the younger ones.

Thomas at the end of 10 days was still in a state of sadness and longing for his mother. He used the foster mother and was fond of her, but unlike the younger children he could give her up without difficulty. Kate at 27 days had gone beyond sadness to anger and disillusionment with her absent mother. She had moved into an affectionate and trusting relationship with the foster mother, but alternating with her anger, there remained a positive wish to return to her mother. Had Kate's separation gone on, the foster relationship would eventually have become more important than that to her mother.

None of the four fostered children reached despair/detachment. It seemed that confusion and sadness were held by the supportive care and that, with the passage of time, reaction to loss of the mother was mitigated by and merged with the developing warmth of the substitute relationship.

INADEQUATE SUBSTITUTE MOTHERING, MULTIPLE CARETAKERS

In ordinary family life there is always some awareness of the changing needs and moods of a younger member. There is a measure of certainty that unhappiness, hunger, tiredness, and playfulness will usually be answered more or less appropriately and without too much delay. For the young child in a family there are known and expected responses because the same one or two people will be tending him. Even if his first cry is not taken too seriously, a real need is unlikely to go unanswered. Not so in the majority of institutions with their changing caretakers.

These respond in varing ways to what they see, if and when they see it. They are unlikely to see or understand the subtleties of the new child's gestures, language, needs, and anxieties. Just when he most needs to be understood, protected, and reassured, he is most likely to be overlooked or handled without empathy and understanding. Several strange people will deal with him, one after another, and no one of them will share his anxieties or support him through the maze of new experiences.

John, accustomed to turning with confidence to his mother or father, found no consistency of response from his many caretakers. He tried again and again to get a response, to relate to his new caretakers, at first by asking for play, by giving gifts, then by seeking comfort by tears. But to no avail. No one was sufficiently aware of his experience; the nurses came and went according to their duties, not according to his need of them. They busied themselves with other children, with other tasks. Multiple caretaking meant for John that his previous methods of communicating his needs and of getting a response did not bring results. He tried, but eventually withdrew in the face of repeated failure. It was not only that he was cared for by many people, but that they all failed to recognize his needs. His confusion and despair were partly a result of this.

In contrast, the fostered children continued to use their usual methods of communication and demand and were answered in ways which approximated the responses they were accustomed to. There was, of course, some variation; but not more than the fostered children could cope with.

STRANGE ENVIRONMENT

"Strange environment" is a vague term which is commonly used in the literature with a facility that conceals how complex and gross the factor may be. For the young child a strange institutional environment is a multitude of harsh experiences, deprivations and demands which place a great burden on him. He will be offered strange foods and strange implements with which to eat. He may be helped too much or too little. The noise and movement during mealtimes are likely to impose strain. His toileting will be fitted into the institution's routine, not geared to his particular rhythm as at home. His special signs or calls will probably not be seen or heard. Toileting accidents will happen; recent gains will be lost. The child who is toilet trained may be put back into diapers, or the child used to diapers may find himself without them. Had we not intervened, John, an untrained child, would have been toilet trained by strangers at a time of stress. "Strange environment" may mean the sudden withdrawal of a comforting "dummy" or bottle just when the child has most need of comfort. It may mean the unavailability of his special cuddly blanket or toy, not deliberately but by the accidents of institutional life.

The child used to sleeping for several hours in the morning and having a late lunch may find himself too tired to eat, wakeful when others sleep, and ready for sleep just as the rest wake up. His sleeping rhythm will be disturbed. John was a child used to sleeping until he woke in the morning, then having a nap when he needed it. His rhythm was not that of the institution, and he was very distressed when woken up from

Figure 14–6   Jane, 17 months, given warm substitute mothering in a supportive environment, copes well and reunites warmly with her mother.

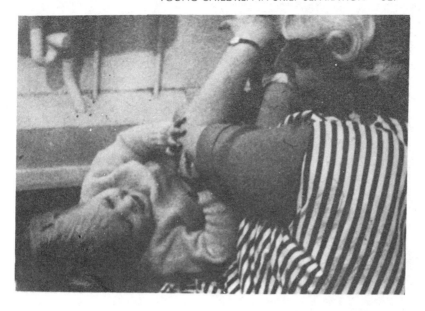

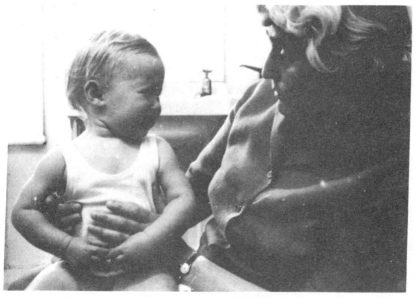

Figure 14–6   continued

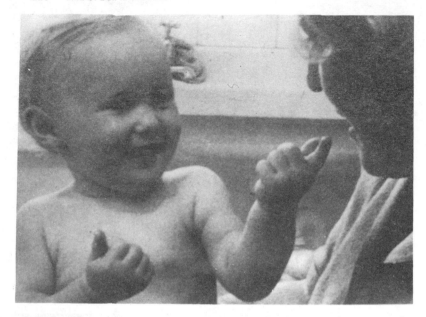

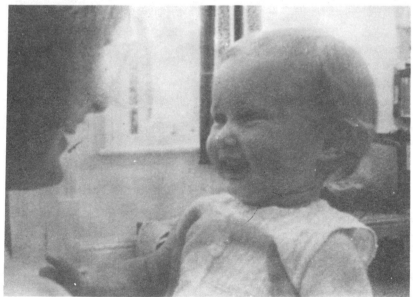

Figure 14–6   continued

Figure 14–7 John, 17 months, denied substitute mothering and subjected to the stresses of institutional life, is overwhelmed and at reunion rejects his mother.

Figure 14–7   continued

sleep because the clock had struck the hour for walks in the park.

The noise and movement of group life are strenuous for the adult not accustomed to them—much more so for the young child struggling with so many confusions.

In the literature insufficient attention has been given to "strange environment" and "inadequate substitute mothering." It has been implied, for instance, that if a young child is not upset by a strange environment while his mother is present, the strange environment can have little significance if he shows distress in her absence[4]. This overlooks the fact that even in a totally strange setting the mother remains the most essential part of a young child's environment,** whereas if she is absent

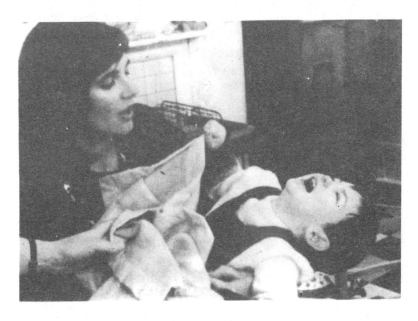

Figure 14–7   continued

**Burlingham and A. Freud[6] tell how young children buried under bomb-damaged buildings emerged emotionally unscathed because they had been close to their mothers throughout.

and there is no familiar substitute he not only loses her but is totally exposed to the impingement of the environment. The mother is the person who "helps" to mediate the environment, to keep it within his limits of tolerance"[19,23,25,36,37].

Fraiberg[12] gives a sensitive account of the early histories and parental relationships of two blind young children and the outcomes of brief separations at 14 months and 19 months. The negative responses of the younger child were much more severe than those of the older one. Fraiberg relates this to the difference in the quality of the children's relationship to their mothers and to the difference in developmental phase and abilities. Although Fraiberg mentions that during the separation the older child was cared for by familiar and well-loved grandparents, while the younger was looked after by "various relations and friends who helped out," only passing reference is made to the influence of the very different separation experiences of these two blind young children. In fact, the child who was less affected, in addition to being older, better developed, and in a better relationship with his mother, also had much better substitute care.

DISCUSSION

It has been shown that when the stress factors which complicate institutional studies have been eliminated, and adequate substitute mothering provided, four young children separated from their mothers for 10 to 27 days did not respond with the acute distress and despair described in the literature. In varying degree, reflecting their differing levels of object constancy and ego maturity, all four transferred cathexis to the substitute mother. Because they were not overwhelmed, as children admitted to institutions commonly are, their inner resources were available to cope with the loss of the mother. Individual differences in response, which are obscured by the severity of institutional separation, became apparent. None of these followed the sequence—protest, despair, and denial/detachment—described of institutionalized children.

During the first few days all four showed an increase in laughter and activity, which was understood as defensive against anxiety. The crying which occurred was mainly when the fathers left after visits and lasted no more than 1 or 2 minutes.

By the time the children might have been expected to show despair (according to earlier studies), that is, on the second, third, or fourth day, there was sadness, a lowered frustration tolerance, and aggression. But this did not have the quality of despair. By that point each child had developed a relationship to the foster mother sufficient to sustain him and had begun to cling to her. The relationship to the foster mother then held them in a state of manageable anxiety. They used her increasingly and with growing intimacy. Although under considerable strain throughout, all four children cared for in our supportive foster situation functioned and related well, learned new skills and words, and at reunion greeted their mothers warmly. The separations had not been traumatic. The children had not been overwhelmed.†

†In a complementary study our social colleague, Katrin Stroh, investigated the behavior of nine small children who, while the mothers were in the hospital to have a second baby, remained in their own homes in the care of a familiar relative such as father, aunt, or grandmother. This study was intended primarily to check in a general way the findings of the small foster sample being studied more intensively, including the extent to which we had succeeded in eliminating the factors of strange environment and multiple caretakers. At least three home visits were made before the separation—two each week during separation and two after separation—to make observations on the children and to interview parents and caretakers. The behavior of these nine children who stayed in their own homes was similar to that of the four who were fostered. There was no immediate distress. After delays of two to four days they became clinging to the substitute caretakers and more irritable, but all continued to eat as before and learned new words. Reunion with the mothers was smooth and pleasant, with only short delay. This complementary study therefore supports in broad terms the findings of the more intensive foster care study.

This was in contrast to John, the 17-month-old child observed in the residential nursery. Denied responsive substitute mothering, and exposed to the multiple stresses of the institutional environment, John protested and moved into despair. He deteriorated in all areas, and at reunion rejected his mother with struggles and desperate crying. At the beginning of the separation John had shown himself ready to accept substitute mothering. It was stress factors additional to the loss of the mother which converted separation anxiety into trauma. In our view, the difference between the responses of the fostered children and those of John was qualitative, not merely of degree.

That our foster children came through so well does not mean that the hazards attached to early separation can be eliminated entirely. At that early and vulnerable phase of development even the best of substitute care is not a certain prescription for neutralizing the risks. It will be recalled that after return home there was in all four children an increase of hostility against the mother which, although infinitely less than with John, carried some potential for disharmony in the mother-child relationship. Kate's initial aggression, for instance, was mishandled by her parents and but for our intervention could have developed into a buildup of recriminatory interaction. Although Jane had had good substitute care, the discontinuity or relationship with her mother appeared to have resulted in a subtle disturbance of her superego development; it cannot be ruled out that other unobservable processes had been interfered with. The two younger children, Jane and Lucy, had a second experience of loss of a loved person; in their immaturity they had related wholeheartedly to the substitute mother.

These risks to well-being arose despite the children having been highly protected by good conditions of care which are not always available to separated children. They were healthy, had never been separated from their mothers, had plenty of time for familiarization with the foster family, and were put into the care of a fully available substitute mother who by reason of training and experience was specially competent to understand and meet their needs.

In everyday life young children face separations in emergencies, in illness and pain, often having previous histories of separation and family upset, and with still more factors complicating their situation even if stable substitute mothering is provided. It is not a simple opposition between foster care and institutional care. In addition to the loss of the mother, foster care can include many stresses due either to mishap or bad planning. Even in an ostensibly appropriate foster situation there may be a balance of adverse factors which can produce acute distress and despair[8,9]. The complexities which commonly affect substitute care are such as to reinforce the view that separation is dangerous and should wherever possible be avoided.

There is an occasional child to whom a well-managed supportive separation appears to bring some benefits, as happened to Lucy, who was afterward able to initiate a richer interaction with her mother. In that instance the improvement resulted from a positive balance of the factors listed on Table 14–1, and from there having been a recent and remediable detriment to an essentially good mother-child relationship.

It will be clear that we do not subscribe to a simple view of responses to separation from the mother. There are individual differences resulting from a balance of factors: some working in the child's favor; some working against him; some making the actual separation easier, but the return home more difficult; and some doing the reverse, making the separation more difficult, but the return home easier. How a particular young child reacts to separation can be understood as a product of the interplay of these factors. Table 14–1 suggests how some of these factors influence the separation experience of a child.

The differences in response by John and Thomas, for instance, can be understood with reference to the table. John suffered many stresses in addition to the loss of his mother:

Table 14–1 Factors Which Combine to Determine Individual Differences in Young Children's Responses to Separation from the Mother

A	B	C
Factors in addition to loss of the mother which are likely to cause stress.	Factors likely to reduce stress.	Child's psychological status which may increase or reduce overt distress during separation, may increase or decrease the overt upset after separation; may increase or decrease the long-term effects.
(1) Strange environment	(1) Familiar substitute caretaker	(1) Level of ego maturity
(2) Inadequate substitute caretaker	(2) Known foods and routines	(2) Level of object constancy
(3) Strange caretaker	(3) Toilet demands unaltered	(3) Facets of quality of mother-child relationship
(4) Multiple caretakers	(4) Own belongings	(4) Defense organization
(5) Cues/language not understood and responded to	(5) Unrestricted body movement	(5) Fantasies about illness, pain, physical interference, disappearance of mother, etc.
(6) Unfamiliar food and routines	(6) Familiar environment	(6) Preseparation experience of illness/separation
(7) Unusual demands and disciplines	(7) Reassurance of eventual reunion	
(8) Illness, pain, bodily interference	(8) Keeping apart fantasy and fact ("My Mummy doesn't love me")	
(9) Bodily restriction	(9) Reminding child of parental disciplines	
	(10) Support from father	
	(11) Willingness of caretakers to talk about parents and previous life	

abrupt transfer to a strange environment; strange, inadequate, and multiple caretaking; strange food and routines; unusual demands and disciplines (see column A). There were few factors that might have reduced stress (see columns B and C). The balance between stress and support operated against John. His immature ego was overwhelmed and trauma resulted. Thomas, on the other hand, had much in his favor. He lost his mother, but suffered only minimally from other stresses; he benefited by factors (in columns B and C) that reduce stress. His relative ego maturity aided understanding of the reality situation, and his level of object constancy made it possible to help him keep alive the image of a caring mother who would return.

Table 14–1 has particular reference to the age group of 18 months to two and one-half years upon which much of the separation literature is based, but with modifications it is applicable to younger children down to the first months of life. For older children of about three to five years it would be necessary to incorporate additional factors associated with more advanced development.

This study has thrown no light on reasons for separation as variables influencing behavior during separation, since all the children were separated for the same reason—the birth of a second child. It is sometimes said that the prospect of a new and rivalrous sibling must be an additional stress. We had no access to fantasies, but the manifest behavior of the four fostered children suggested that the expected babies impinged hardly at all until they were physically present and taking their share of the parents' attention.

Kate, for instance, knew there was to be a new baby; but, as with the other children, did not appear to have the capacity to anticipate this as a threat. She took a little girl's pleasure in seeing babies in their prams in the street and talked freely of the coming baby who would cry and sleep in a cradle. However, when given a family of dolls as an aid to expressing her feelings, she did not use the baby doll. It did not appear to us that she avoided the baby. Rather, with the mother, father, and little girl dolls, she played out her past experience and immediate concerns about herself and her parents.

As always happens in research, questions answered present still more questions to be asked. Kate, Thomas, Lucy, and Jane did not show acute distress and despair, and in their longer separations Kate and Lucy even appeared to be adapting and finding secure niches in the foster family. But what would have happened had the separations gone on indefinitely? Would the two younger children, Jane and Lucy, with their slender object constancy and ego immaturity, have merged the memory traces of the mother with the image of the foster mother and achieved a complete transfer of cathexis? If so, would this have been a progressively smooth transition with no more manifest upset than had been shown during the duration of this study? Our data suggest that Jane and Lucy, two children of 21 months and under, would have transferred cathexis from mother to substitute mother without a phase of grief and mourning. This would be consistent with Anna Freud's view that the capacity to mourn is a function of the level of object constancy and ego maturity[13].

Even had Jane and Lucy changed mothers without extreme upset, what might have been the consequences for their subsequent development—bearing in mind the indications of disturbance to superego development in Jane? From birth, internal structures, including precursors to object relationships, are in the process of increasingly refined development, and these are endangered by interference with, or interruptions of, the affective interactions unique to the particular mother-infant couple[38]. Infants from birth to approximately two years may show less upset than those over two, but the level of overt upset is not a true indicator of the damage that may be occurring[42].

In a longer or permanent separation would the two older children have reached a point at which the acute distress and despair that are characteristic of mourning would have broken through? Or would they, too, as hypothesized for Jane and Lucy, have shed their mothers, more slowly but with no more distress than they had shown during the project? In the third and fourth week of her separation Kate was becoming more and more attached to the foster mother and at ease within the foster family, but was still directing positive and negative affect toward the absent mother.

These are questions for another study.[‡]

SUMMARY

The work reported in this chapter extends and refines the observations by James Robertson[22] on which his concepts of protest, despair, and denial were based. These phases were explicitly attached to separation from the mother when aggravated by strange environment, confinement to cot, multiple caretakers, and other stress factors associated with institutional care.

This chapter describes how a total sample of 13 young children (17 months to two years, five months) coped with separation from the mother when cared for in conditions from which the adverse factors that complicate institutional studies were absent. Four were fostered by the Robertsons and 9 were looked after in their own homes by a familiar relative. Separations ranged from 10 to 26 days. None of the 13 children responded with protest and despair. In the authors' view, the difference between their responses and those of children observed in institutional settings was qualitative and not merely of degree. All were able to use the substitute for the absent mother.

[‡]Wolfenstein[45], studying the reactions of school-age children to the death of a parent, found that mourning did not take place. An adaptive substitute for mourning was possible when there was an available and acceptable parent substitute to whom the child could transfer piecemeal the libido he gradually detached from the lost parent (p. 458).

The four fostered children, observed in special detail in the Robertson family, showed variations in response related to age, levels of ego maturity and object constancy, previous mother-child relationship, length of separation, and defense organization. Their behavior conformed to the psychoanalytic view that the capacity to mourn is a function of ego maturity and object constancy.

In a single contrast study, John, who in addition to loss of his mother was subjected to the inadequacies of residential nursery care, displayed the acute distress and despair commonly described of institutionalized children.

In 1960 *The Psychoanalytic Study of the Child*[13] included a paper by Bowlby, "Grief and Mourning in Infancy and Early Childhood," together with critical essays on it by Anna Freud and others. In that paper and in subsequent work, Bowlby acknowledges that he draws mainly upon James Robertson's institutional data. But in developing his grief and mourning theory, Bowlby, without adducing noninstitutional data, has generalized Robertson's concept of protest, despair, and denial beyond the context from which it was derived. He asserts that these are the usual responses of young children to separation from the mother—regardless of circumstance—and on this basis equates the separation responses of young children with the bereavement responses of adults in both form and content[2-5].

Our findings do not support Bowlby's generalizations about the responses of young children to separation from the mother per se; nor do they support his theory on grief and mourning in infancy and early childhood. Although we have shown that variables have much greater importance than Bowlby has attached to them, and that adverse factors may cumulatively overwhelm and traumatize the separated young child, this does not imply that separation per se does not threaten development. Our approach is now substantially different from that of Bowlby, but we continue to share his concern about the potential harm associated with early separation from the mother.

ACKNOWLEDGMENTS

This study was supported by the British National Health Service, The Tavistock Institute of Human Relations, and The Grant Foundation, Inc., of New York. To all of these our thanks are due.

REFERENCES

1. Beardsworth, T., & Stevenson, D: The effect on a young child of brief separation. Five films by the Robertsons. *Brit. J. Social Work,* 6(3): 393–401, 1976.

2. Bowlby, J: Grief and mourning in infancy and early childhood. *Psychoanal. Study Child,* 15:9–52, 1960.

3. Bowlby, J: Processes of mourning. *Int. J. Psycho-Anal,* 42:317–340, 1961.

4. Bowlby, J: *Attachment and loss.* (Vol. 1: *Attachment*). London: Hogarth, 1969.

5. Bowlby, J, & Parkes, CM: Separation and loss. In *International yearbook for child psychiatry and allied disciplines.* In E. J. Anthony & C. Koupernik (eds.), Vol. 1: *The child and his family.* New York: Wiley, 1970.

6. Burlingham, D, & Freud, A: *Young children in wartime.* London: Allen & Unwin, 1942.

7. Burlingham, D, & Freud, A: *Infants without families.* London: Allen & Unwin, 1944.

8. Cook, PS: A two-year-old's mother goes to a maternity hospital. *New Zealand Med. J., 61:* 605–608, 1962.

9. Deutsch, H: A two year old boy's first love comes to grief. In L. Jessner & E. Pavenstedt (Eds.), *Dynamic psychopathology in childhood.* New York: Grune & Stratton, 1959.

10. Elkan, I: Film Review: John, seventeen months: For nine days in a residential nursery. *J. Child Psychother.*, *2*:82–84, 1969.

11. Fraiberg, S: Libidinal object constancy and mental representation. *Psychoanal. Study Child, 24:*9–47, 1969.

12. Fraiberg, S: Separation crisis in two blind children. *Psychoanal. Study Child, 26:*355–371, 1971.

13. Freud, A: Discussion of Dr. John Bowlby's paper [1960]. *Psychoanal. Study Child, 15:*53–62. 1960.

14. Freud, A: Film review: John, seventeen months: Nine days in a residential nursery. *Psychoanal. Study Child, 24:*138–143, 1969.

15. Heinicke, CM, & Westheimer, IJ: *Brief separations.* New York: International Universities Press. 1965.

16. Kennedy, H: Film Review: 1. Kate, 2 years 5 months: In foster care for 27 days. 2. Jane, 17 months: In foster care for 10 days. *Brit. J. Med. Psychol., 42:*191–193, 1969.

17. Kennedy, H: Young children in brief separation. A critical review of five films by James and Joyce Robertson. *Int. J. Psychoanal., 57:*483–486, 1976.

18. Micic, Z: Psychological stress in children in hospital. *Int. Nursing Rev., 9:* 23–31, 1962.

19. Murphy, LB: Some aspects of the first relationship. *Int. J. Psycho-Anal., 45:* 32–46, 1964.

20. Prugh, D, et al.: Study of emotional reactions of children and families to hospitalization and illness. *Am. J. Orthopsychiat., 23:*70–106, 1953.

21. Robertson, J: Film: A two-year-old goes to hospital [16mm, b & w, sound, 45 and 30 minute versions; English/French]. London: Tavistock Institute of Human Relations, 1952. New York: New York University Film Library, 1952.

22. Robertson, J: Some responses of young children to loss of maternal care. *Nursing Times, 49:*382–386, 1953.

23. Robertson, J: Film: Going to hospital with mother [16mm, b & w, sound, 40 minutes; English/French; guide booklet]. London: Tavistock Institute of Human Relations. New York: New York University Film Library, 1958.

24. Robertson, J: On the making of two mental health films. *International catalogue of mental health films.* London: World Federation for Mental Health, 1960. And as: Nothing but the truth. *Film User,* 1960.

25. Robertson, J: *Hospitals and children: A parent's-eye view.* London: Gollancz, 1962.

26. Robertson, J: *Young children in hospital.* Second edition, with a postscript. London: Tavistock Publications. New York: Methven, 1970. (Also in Danish, Dutch, French, German, Italian, Japanese, Norwegian, and Swedish.)

27. Robertson J, & Robertson, J: *Young children in brief separation,* Film No. 1: *Kate, 2 Years 5 Months: In Foster Care for 27 Days* [16mm, b & w, sound, 33 minutes; guide booklet]. London: Tavistock Institute of Human Relations. New York: New York University Film Library, 1967.

28. Robertson, J, & Robertson, J: Film No. 2: *Jane, 17 Months: In Foster Care for 10 Days* [16mm, b & w, sound, 37 minutes; guide booklet]. London: Tavistock Institute of Human Relations. New York: New York University Film Library, 1968.

29. Robertson, J, & Robertson, J: Film No. 3: *John, 17 Months: For 9 Days in a Residential Nursery* [16mm, b & w, sound, 45 minutes; guide booklet]. London: Tavistock Institute of Human Relations. New York: New York University Film Library, 1969.

30. Robertson, J, & Robertson, J: Film No. 4: *Thomas, 2 Years 4 Months: In Foster Care for 10 Days* [16mm, b & w, sound 38 minutes; guide booklet]. London: Tavistock Institute of Human Relations. New York: New York University Film Library, 1971.

31. Robertson, J, & Robertson, J: Film No. 5: *Lucy, 21 Months: In Foster Care for 19 Days* [16mm, b & w, sound, 30 minutes, English/French, guide booklet]. London: Tavistock Institute of Human Relations. New York: New York University Film Library, 1976.

32. Robertson, J, & Robertson, J: Quality of substitute care as an influence on separation responses. *J. Psychomatic Res., 16:*261–265, 1972.

33. Robertson, J, & Robertson, J: Substitute mothering for the unaccompanied child in hospital. *Nursing Times:* November 29, 1972.

34. Robertson, J, & Robertson, J: *Young children in brief separation: Illustrated guide to the film series.* Robertson Centre, 1976.

35. Robertson, J, & Robertson, J: The psychological parent. *Adoption and Fostering, 37:*19–22, 1977.

36. Robertson, J: A mother's observations on the tonsillectomy of her four-year-old daughter. With comments by Anna Freud. *Psychoanal. Study Child, 11:*410–433, 1956.

37. Robertson, J: Mothering as an influence on early development: A study of well-baby clinic records. *Psychoanal. Study Child, 17:*245–264, 1962.

38. Robertson, J: Mother-infant interaction from birth to twelve months: Two case Studies. In B. M. Foss (Ed.) *Determinants of infant behavior.* London: Methuen, 1965.

39. Robertson, J: *What is bonding?* Robertson Centre, 1977.

40. Rosenfeld, S: Film Review: John, 17 months: For 9 days in a residential nursery. *Brit. J. Med. Psychol., 18:*105–108, 1970.

41. Schaffer, HR, & Callender, WM: Psychological effects of hospitalization in infancy. *Pediatrics, 24:*528–539, 1959.

42. Spitz, RA; Hospitalism. *Psychoanal. Study Child, 1:*53–74, 1945.

43. Spitz, RA, & Wolf, KM: Anaclitic depression. *Psychoanal. Study Child, 2;*313–342, 1946.

44. Vaughan, GF: Children in hospital. *Lancet* (June 1):1117–1120, 1957.

45. Wolfenstein, M: Loss, rage, and repetition. *Psychoanal. Study Child, 24:* 432–460, 1969.

46. Yarrow, L: Maternal deprivation: Toward an empirical and conceptual re-evaluation. *Psychol. Bull., 58:*459–490, 1961.

47. Yarrow, L: Separation from parents during early childhood. *Rev. Child Dev. Res., 1:*89–136, 1964.

INDEX

Abuse, 237
Accommodate, 188, 191
Addicted infants, 63, 64
Adrenarche, precocious, 17, 19
Adrenocortical stimulating hormone (ACTH), 254
AIDS Scale, 169, 170, 176, 177, 178, 179, 180
Affect, 51, 170, 178, 180
Ambivalence, 281, 282
Apgar score, 96, 101
Apnea, 257
Asphyxia, 96
Assessment, 272
  process, 235, 238
  and intervention, 226
Assimilation, 188
Asymmetrical tonic neck reflex, 118, 203
Attachment, 48, 51, 52, 191, 199, 220, 232, 270, 277
  failures, 164
Attractiveness, Infant, 76, 79, 80
Autistic, 163, 167
  autism, 167, 185, 186
  children, 187

Bayley Scales, 47, 48, 49, 50, 62, 65, 73, 83, 98, 102, 108
Basic Trust, 233, 234, 235
Behavioral strategy change, 124
Blind Baby, 221
  children, 226, 227

Blindness
  emotional impact, 228
Bowlby, J., 285, 340
Bradley, R. H. (*see* HOME Inventory)
Brazelton Neonatal Assessment Scale, 62, 63, 97, 273
BSID Motor Scale, 115, 119, 122

Caldwell, B. M. (*see* HOME Inventory)
Cerebral palsy, 90, 112, 121, 200
Collateral sprouting, 124, 126
Communication
  Verbal, 161, 162
  Nonverbal, 162
Compensation, 124, 126

Denver Developmental Screening Test, 100, 111
Denervation supersensitivity, 124, 126
Denial, 283, 284, 333, 340
Despair, 283, 284, 323, 324, 333, 340
Detachment, 283, 284, 323, 324, 333
Developmental assessments, 97
Diabetes
  mellitus, 242
  juvenile, 243